Louis S. Sorana

# MAIN STREET BEAT

HENRY W. CLUNE

# MAIN
# STREET
# BEAT

W · W · NORTON & COMPANY · INC · New York

TO
GEORGE L. EATON

# Contents

CONTENTS

# CHAPTER I

# THE MURMUR OF THE WORLD

THERE IS a peculiar charm about the city of Rochester that is rarely noticed by casual visitors and that the native residents themselves are unable very specifically to define.

It is an insinuating thing and, until he is exposed to it for a reasonable period of time, the newcomer may feel rather out of things, scold about his indifferent neighbors, inveigh bitterly against the abominable Rochester winters, and regret the day he first set foot inside the city's borders.

Yet if circumstances require the most recalcitrant outlander to remain for two, three, or four years, he will find that he has been insensibly acclimatized and that a strange sort of contentment has come over him. He may still openly protest against his continued residence in the city. But in his heart he will be reluctant to wrench up his ever deepening roots to press on to some new community where the climate may be more salubrious and the opportunities for worldly success more alluring. For by then the charm of the city will have laid its mesmeric spell upon him. He will have found new and good friends, a new and satisfying way of life, and upon him the cachet of the thorough-going Rochesterian will be deeply impressed.

Native resident though I am, and thoroughly devoted to the city, in my younger and more adventurous years I often desired to migrate to the greener pastures far away; and twice I attempted to live beyond the city's borders. Each time I aban-

doned the trial after a few months. I longed for Main Street
and the friendly nod, the warm greeting, the buttonholing by
this, that, and the other passer-by. I wanted to be where I knew
the folks.

This attitude is typical both of the native Rochesterian and
the completely indoctrinated adopted son. Secure in his own
bailiwick, confident of his position, and sure of his friends, he
succumbs to a provincialism that is peculiar to the town. Rochester becomes, not the small center around which the world
revolves, but almost the world itself, and its people and the
things that happen there assume for him momentous importance. Perhaps Tennyson described the attitude of the dyed-in-
the-wool Rochesterian in two lines in *Geraint and Enid:*

> *Ye think the rustic cackle of your bourg*
> *The murmur of the World!*

He leaves the city for even so short a journey as to New York,
and once there immediately gravitates to some Rochester friend
or friends who have preceded him to the metropolis. And I have
known Rochesterians with money and time to travel anywhere
they desired who refused to make a world cruise until they
were assured that they might do so as members of a "Rochester
party" consisting entirely of Rochester friends. I suffer myself
from a curious sense of inadequacy once I find myself in a
strange city and am always cheered and consoled by coming
unexpectedly upon a branch store of the Eastman Kodak
Company.

Removed temporarily from the city, the good Rochesterian
will eulogize the town to all who will listen and to many who
won't. He will tell about its grandeurs and its heroes; the
beauty of its women and its parks; the superior quality of its

industries and the comforts of its life. In his enthusiasm he may
even recall that its hospital for the insane, which already occu-
pies an enormous tract in the southern section of the city, is
growing prodigiously.

These boasts are not all vain, extravagant though the language used in expressing them may become. Actually Rochester
has a great deal to justify the pride and loyalty of its citizenry.
The slogan created, I believe, by an inspired secretary of the
Chamber of Commerce, "Rochester Made Means Quality,"
truthfully describes the products of a number of its leading
industries. Rochester is the home of many specialized industries
which, for the most part, require skilled labor. Because of the
character of the workmen employed in these industries and the
conscientious effort made to keep them satisfied and happy,
serious labor difficulties are uncommon and most civic enterprises are marked by an enviable spirit of fellowship and co-
operation upon the part of both management and labor.

Rochester is the twenty-third largest city in America. It is on
the main line of the New York Central Railroad approximately
halfway between its smaller neighbor Syracuse and the much
larger city of Buffalo. Its northern boundary extends to the
shore of Lake Ontario. It is bisected by the Genesee River, the
upper valley of which rolls away in farm and pasture lands
celebrated for their fertility and beauty. The city was largely
founded by settlers who moved west from the New England
states and whose early and greatest industry was the production
of wheat flour. The fame of the old-time millers for many years
caused Rochester to be known as the *Flour City*. When the
city fathers became sensible of the natural beauties of the town
and made its park system one of the finest in the land, and its
commercial nurseries achieved an international reputation, the
original appellation was changed to *Flower City*.

The city prides itself upon its culture; and its university, though not large in student enrollment, is one of the most richly endowed in America. Its school of music is widely known and its medical school encourages a varied program of research that already has brought the Nobel Prize to two members of its staff.

There is some grumbling because of the fact that not all trains on the main line of the New York Central stop there, and there is a feeling that if the great plant of the Eastman Kodak Company were removed from the city's environs a sign might be erected on the station platform, "This *was* Rochester." But the remote possibility of this tragic circumstance is rarely openly expressed.

Years ago a group of prominent citizens organized what is known as the Society of the Genesee, a sort of Mutual Boosters' League in the grand manner. The Society met once a year for an enormous dinner in the ballroom of New York's Waldorf-Astoria for the avowed purpose of paying tribute to Rochesterians who had achieved notable successes, usually in the field of industry.

On this annual occasion hordes of the city's leading people flocked to New York, the soup spots carefully removed from their evening finery, to indulge in a round-robin of preprandial cocktail parties before assembling at the decorated tables to gorge themselves on a seven-course dinner and listen attentively to stiff-shirted orators declaim on the Horatio Alger theme of rags to riches in a single generation.

In recent years the Society has nearly exhausted its quota of local celebrities worthy of its accolade and in desperation has reached out to bring as honored guests to its dinner distinguished industrialists from other parts who once, as one irreverent cynic remarked, had passed through Rochester on the Twentieth Century Limited.

The implications of this remark are neither sound nor worthy. No man has been honored by the Society who has not resided at least a fortnight in Rochester before leaving town to make his mark. The annual meetings of the Society have not been resumed since being interrupted by the war. When they are it is presumed that they will continue as in the past as fine, brilliant, and lively barn-raisings, the guests carefully selected for their ability to handle three dinner forks.

During one of these occasions a friend of George S. Kaufman, whose late wife was a native Rochesterian, encountered the playwright in front of the Waldorf-Astoria.

"George," said he, "this is the night of the dinner of the Society of the Genesee. It looks as though everyone from Rochester was down here to attend."

Startled by this information, Mr. Kaufman bolted forward. As he fled, he called over his shoulder, "What a wonderful time to be in Rochester!"

~~~~~~~~~~~~~~~~~~~~~~~~~~~~~~~~~~~~~~~~~~~~~~~~~~~~~~~~~~~~~~~~~~

# CHAPTER II

# THIS REPORTER STAYED HOME

D URING most of my adult life I have worked as a newspaper writer in Rochester, and the public's familiarity with my name at the top of a column on the first local page of the *Democrat and Chronicle* has given me something of the character of a local institution. I am as familiar to many people as the curbstone poles that hold the Main Street lamps and enjoy in my home town a reputation of being Locally, Internationally Famous.

My younger professional associates address me as *Mister* Clune. Intended as a mark of respect, this formality sometimes too pertinently reminds me of the fact that I have lingered overlong in a business that at its very best requires the keenness, the enthusiasm, and the unflagging energy of youth. If a prominent octogenarian dies, the City Desk turns to me for biographical data, on the theory that the ancient burgher must have been one of my contemporaries. And often I have been asked to describe in print the character of our downtown district in the Mesozoic Era when horse cars required an extra quadruped for the haul up Main Street hill.

I am supposed to be a storehouse of local lore and even the public, in the naïve belief that all newspaper columnists are as omniscient as John Kieran or F.P.A., constantly request of me such varied information as the name of the last husband of the late Miss Lillian Russell, the time of the fastest mile ever ridden on a safety bicycle, the first line of William Blake's

14

"The Tiger," or the date of the great conflagration that once razed Rochester's largest department store.

As an example of the public's confidence in the occult and encyclopedic knowledge of a newspaper writer of as long a tenure as my own, only recently my slumbers were rudely disturbed at the illicit hour of 2 A.M. by the persistent ringing of the telephone in my home.

Stumbling and groping through the dark I raised the receiver, called a sleepy "Hello," and had this inquiry flung over the wire into my ear.

"Mr. Clune," a feminine voice demanded, "is it true that Betty Grable is going to have another baby?"

I was sorry to disappoint a reader. But how should I have known?

The legend that newspaper men "meet such interesting people," the stock joke in newspaper city rooms, actually has some merit. Though I cannot say that I am fascinated by people who awaken me in the middle of the night to make the sort of question related above, during my long career as a newspaper worker I have met a great number of interesting people. I like people and they are an inexhaustible source of copy. It is my interest in and my liking for people that are mostly responsible for what modest success I have enjoyed in this business.

I like policemen and politicians, bankers and horse players, grande dames from the Avenue, pitchmen on street corners, and the tinseled little ladies from the cheaper cabarets. I like industrialists, cab drivers, college profs, the boys in the back alley saloons and the debutantes in the Country Club. Even stuffed shirts fail to bore me; for I am always curious to know what fears or inhibitions cause them to pad themselves with fustian and eager to ascertain if behind their false façades they are not very much like the rest of us. Mostly I have found that they are.

During my tenure as a newspaper reporter I have written numerous stories about men and women of national and international reputation, but these stories have largely been done to pattern. It is not the so-called celebrity (a word considerably discredited in my mind because of the free and easy and meaningless use of it by Broadway columnists), but ordinary men and women who have given me the best copy. Lincoln said that God must have loved the common people, he made so many of them; and since most of us fall into this category, stories about our own kind seem to me to have the most universal appeal.

I do not hold with the opinion that New York, New Orleans, and San Francisco are the "story" cities of America. For stories are primarily made by people, and the story material that could be supplied by the people in my own home town, if searched out and put into print, would make volumes of fascinating reading. From the most obscure quarters sometimes come the best stories; and finding them is comparable to the thrill experienced by a prospector who turns up a golden nugget under a most unpromising mound of soil.

Poking around my home city I have discovered a back-street barber who, in the days of the Boer War, was an intimate of Winston Churchill; a great lady of the movies masquerading as a bourgeoise housewife; a hardware clerk who formerly made a dangerous living by three times daily thrusting his head into the mouth of a lion; a nurse for an aged woman who was once the leading aviatrix in America; a man who fulfilled, at the advanced age of seventy-two, a lifelong ambition to enter the ministry; a meat cutter, once the partner of a celebrated dancing lady who subsequently gave command performances before the royal heads of Europe.

When someone tells me that Rochester is a dull city, I answer that he has failed to look around, to know its people, to inquire into their stories, to learn that there are notable adventurers, men of genius, poets, murderers, great lovers, scientists of international distinction, living—often obscurely—among us. For years it has been my job to dig out stories of people. I am still working at it. I still like it. To me it is an interesting and satisfying way of life.

I was an only son in a family that included three daughters, and my father was determined that I enjoy the educational advantages he himself had been denied. One of his business associates was a Yale graduate. This man talked often of the advantages of a Yale education, and my father decided that one day I should be enrolled in the great university at New Haven. But I applied myself poorly in high school, failed miserably, and presently my father sent me to Phillips Academy in Andover, Mass. There again I was an academic failure, and left at the close of the school year in 1910 to return to Rochester with advice from the headmaster that my presence in the school was no longer desired.

My father was baffled, disappointed, and angry. He could not understand why I had almost deliberately renounced the educational advantages he was able to offer me, and since I could not return to school he suggested that I hire out to a successful fruit farmer of his acquaintance.

This was not to my fancy. I had worked one summer vacation on a farm, and had decided at that time that there were easier and more interesting ways of obtaining a livelihood. Though I had failed in numerous subjects, my English grades had usually been passing, and occasionally I had been complimented by my instructor for my work in English composition. I had a vague

notion that I should like to write, and made this known to a
distant cousin of my father's, a middle-aged spinster who had
recently made a substantial sum of money through the sale to
the *Ladies' Home Journal* of an anonymous autobiography,
which later appeared in book form.

For many years my cousin had taught the classical languages
at Miss Spence's School for Girls in New York City. But always
in the back of her mind was a desire for self-expression that was
denied her in the cloistered halls of a fashionable finishing
school, and one day she had the courage to resign and take a
job as reporter for the *Springfield Union*, in Springfield, Mass.
She held it two or three years, then left to write her book. The
stories she told me about her experiences as a reporter fired me
with an ambition to follow in her footsteps, and footloose and
jobless—at the close of my last semester at Andover—I applied
for and was given work as a "sub"—not a cub—reporter for
the *Rochester Democrat and Chronicle*.

There was a distinction between these terms. A cub was a
young reporter who was paid for his apprenticeship. A "sub"
wasn't. He was the humblest figure in the city room, a cut below
the copy boy, who was usually a high-school student earning a
small stipend in his spare hours. The "sub" was a probationer
with no previous experience who, if he displayed sufficient
aptitude for newspaper work after a few weeks' trial, would be
added to the payroll and automatically advanced to the status
of cub.

To my knowledge there are no "subs" in the newspaper business today. Publishers, either at the prompting of their
conscience, or under the pressure of the Newspaper Guild, have
abandoned the practice of putting young people to work for
periods of unpaid apprenticeship and if a young man or woman
is considered worthy to be entrusted with the handling of even

the smallest news items he or she is paid for this work. In its earlier days, and under the old regime, the *Democrat and Chronicle* got a great deal of leg work and picture chasing done by youthful enthusiasts who were willing to perform these services for nothing more substantial than the vague promise that at some future day they might become bona fide members of the newspaper's staff.

~~~~~~~~~~~~~~~~~~~~~~~~~~~~~~~~~~~~~~~~~~~~~~~~~~~~~~~~~~~~~~~~~~~~~~~~~

# CHAPTER III

# THE SIXTY-FOUR HOUR WEEK

CONFUSION has often been caused by the use of the word *Democrat* in the title of a newspaper that has been staunchly Republican in its politics since the beginning of the Republican Party in 1855, and the reason for this is hidden in the obscurities of the past. *The Democrat and Chronicle* has been definitely anti-Democrat since its earliest history and in 1836 announced its firm devotion to the Whig Party in an editorial that in part read:

". . . The principles maintained by the Whig Party at the present day we believe to be those which nerved the arm of Washington and his compatriots, and the establishment of which was secured by the successful termination of the Revolutionary War. They admit of no compromise with despotic, aristocratic, monarchial customs, and frown upon every unholy attempt to control the will of the people."

When I began my career on the paper its stock was controlled by two middle-aged spinsters who, to my knowledge, never appeared in the plant, and consigned the operation of the newspaper to W. Henry Matthews and Colonel Nathan G. Pond, as president, and vice-president and secretary, respectively.

They were a fine team of hobble-pacers who had been traveling the golden circuit for many years. Their advertising columns, together with legitimate displays inserted by department, feed, hardware, and shoe stores, promoted a bizarre assortment of "safe" cures for tuberculosis, knifeless remedies for physical disorders that medical men knew might be cured only by surgery, herb medicines, pink pills for pale people, and numerous other quackeries that any decent modern newspaper would categorically reject.

Mr. Matthews and the Colonel carried no torch for reform. They crusaded only in the interest of the Republican Party. They were businessmen first, last, and for an unusually high return on capital investment. Colonel Pond was a tall, lank, bony man with something of the look of a hungry mastiff. A veteran of the Civil War, he was reputed in his younger days to have been a roistering rake-hell, but when I first knew him he had slowed down to the dignity his high position in the community demanded.

He rarely left his street-floor office to ascend to the city room, five stories above, and these visits were mostly made during the fall political campaign. It was then his habit to stomp his Congress gaiters sharply on the floor and shoutingly adjure the editor to "Riddle the damn *Democrats*—riddle 'em, I say," after which he would return to his sanctum presumably confident that he had given the editorial workers an excellent legend to follow and a wide open target to shoot at.

Mr. Matthews indulged in no such outbursts. He was a prim, prissy, bewhiskered little man, whose single known act of violence was squeezing the eagle on the coins of the realm. He was remote and retiring. He had nothing to do with the common run of his employees, and I recall only once having spoken to him.

At that time I had been sent by the city editor to question Mr. Matthews for facts concerning the career of one of his friends and contemporaries who had just died. He was sitting at his desk perusing a column of figures. Hat in hand I stood at

least five minutes at the threshold of his office before he raised
his head.

"Oh," he said, "you're the man sent to repair the steam
pipes?"

"No," I replied. "I work here."

"What department?"

"Editorial."

His attitude was instantly hostile. Editorial workers, and
reporters in particular, Mr. Matthews seemed to believe were
necessary evils, scarcely to be tolerated.

"Well," he said defensively, "if it's about salary adjustment,
you'll have to take it up with the editor. I know nothing about
the merit of you fellows upstairs."

I told him that that wasn't the reason for my visit, quickly
explained its purpose, obtained the necessary facts, and departed.

The next day I came face to face with him in a lower corridor
of the building and he passed me without a nod or a word of
recognition. He had forgotten me as quickly as though I actually had been the man sent to repair the steam pipes.

Faithful to the high trust imposed upon them, Mr. Matthews and Colonel Pond made the *Democrat and Chronicle*
the second best paying enterprise, per dollar invested, in the
entire city, and working for them was a joy if one was only
mildly interested in wages and considered a sixty-four hour
week a privilege. A reporter's job, however, did have the virtue
of permanency if a man once was fully established in it, for
only high crime was considered a reason for dismissal.

The city room was located on the fifth floor of the Main
Street building that housed the entire plant, and it was typical
of many city rooms of that period. It was a long, narrow, dingy,
almost windowless alleyway divided longitudinally by two fac-

ing rows of desks at which the reporters worked. There was a
square slot in each desk for a typewriter and raised on metal
brackets behind this a fat spool of copy paper.

The city editor sat at his desk in a windowless alcove at one
end of the room, and just beyond him, separated by a flimsy
wooden partition, was the sports department, which consisted
only of the desk and typewriter of its lone incumbent. The
office of the editor-in-chief, and the cubicles occupied by the
editorial writers and the vicinity editor, gave directly off one
side of the city room, and opposite these was a jerry-built com-
partment in which the AP and special wire operators worked
under the eye of the telegraph editor. Large brass spittoons,
always half filled with water, were constantly being stumbled
over; no sunlight ever seeped into the room, and the air after a
smoke-filled night's work was as foul as that from a burning
dump. It was a place of no sanitation, little comfort, crowded,
noisy, and during the night hours, bustling with activity.

My first service for the *Democrat and Chronicle* was general
assignments, and since I knew little more about the newspaper
business than my grandfather knew about penicillin, it was
months before I was entrusted with anything except the most
unimportant matters.

News at that time was a quantitative rather than a qualita-
tive product, and the capable reporter each day turned in an
astonishing amount of copy. Finishing one story he would jag-
gedly rip the typed paragraphs from the spool of copy paper
behind his typewriter, hurriedly edit them, mark "30" at the
bottom of the paper, and begin another.

Reporters began their working day at 2 P.M., for ours was a
morning newspaper. While the city editor made up the assignment book it was the duty of all of us to give a hand with the
social notices, for in those days the paper had no society editor,

and ran only a handful of Sunday "Personals" and a couple of columns devoted to indoor recreational activities under the standard heading, "Entertainment in Many Forms."

Authentic members of what was understood as "Society" as willingly would have had their names entered on a police docket as to have them printed in our Sunday "Personals" or mentioned under "Entertainment in Many Forms." The first department mostly concerned the goings and comings of the families of grocery clerks, plumbers' helpers, streetcar conductors, and other worthy people of undistinguished social status. The second related the activities of card clubs, the Ladies' Auxiliaries of Chowder and Marching Clubs, sorority pig roasts, and such. These notices began to seep into the office as early as Tuesday of each week and we were busy in our spare time until Saturday night typing them out.

But the work of deciphering the poorly written notices and checking names and initials in the city directory (our city editor was a stickler for this, properly insisting that if a person's name was printed in the paper it should be correctly spelled and initialed) made an irksome task that the older members of the staff hated. At first I did not share this feeling. For the manual act of transcribing on a typewriter the hand-written social notices afforded me much-needed practice in the use of the battered Underwood that had become the essential instrument of my trade.

Pedro, a card game that is a variety of pitch, seemed to be one of the most popular forms of indoor entertainment among the rank and file of Rochester women. We were all familiar with the ladies of the Chattering Clams, the Bashful Six, the Daffy-Dills, the Buzzards, the Jolly Eight, and the What's It To You Pedro Clubs, and the weekly activities of these assiduous card fiends inspired considerable office humor.

# THE SIXTY-FOUR HOUR WEEK 27

To our great amusement one Sunday we found this paragraph inserted under "Entertainment in Many Forms": "The Ladies of the Lonely Hearts Saturday night entertained at a mixed party at the home of Miss Hazel Vaughan. Dancing, dart-throwing, and other forms of recreation were enjoyed. A pleasant time was had by all."

Miss Vaughan was the proprietress of a notorious establishment in the red light district, and how the notice escaped censorship was a wonder to all of us. But it had, and created a great guffaw all over town, and no little embarrassment to the newspaper. After diligent inquiry it was found that it had been written out of hand by a brash young reporter, who previously had been guilty of numerous minor derelictions. This time, however, he was considered the perpetrator of a high crime, and was summarily sent on his way—presumably to rejoin his family in Kokomo, Ind.

Our city editor was Morris Adams and almost from my first association with him he was one of my idols. He was a tall, well-built, handsome man with neatly laid-down black hair. His flat-topped desk was placed in the darkest corner of the city room. There was no window near him and from the time he took his post at 1:30 o'clock each afternoon until he quit it twelve hours later he worked constantly under a green-shaded lamp and sat as erect on his armless chair as a grenadier.

He was a gentleman, a man of few and simple words, who never bellowed, used profanity, or indulged in any of the picturesque nonsense that the lay public, through its devotion to newspaper fiction and movies, invariably associates with the city desk. He was a bachelor, wedded only to the *Democrat and Chronicle*, and in the first year that I worked for him he read and edited every stick of local copy. For the wage he received,

which could not have been high under the niggardly policy of
publishers—and ours in particular—of that era, his devotion to
his paper and his employers was something of a minor phenomenon.

I admired Mr. Adams for his ability, his fairness, his sound
good sense, his seeming omniscience, and the Spartan routine
of his life. Friday was his day off. In summer he passed this on a
public golf course and in winter playing three-cushion billiards
in Johnson's Billiard Academy. He played both games in the
same steady, methodical manner in which he performed his
duties of city editor, achieving no sensational scores, but making an earnest competitive try right up until the final shot.

Beyond these two recreational interests, Mr. Adams' life was
restricted to his office routine, and he was rarely seen in places
of public gathering. Yet he knew the city like the palm of his
hand and without having direct contact with its better-known
citizens he was more familiar with them than the best-informed
members of his staff. My admiration for Mr. Adams has never
wavered. He is an unusual character and one of the most
thoroughgoing newspapermen I have known.

Mr. Adams was not encouraged by my early efforts as a
reporter. But I was, enormously. When I saw the first fullface
I had written in print, I was immeasurably thrilled. I felt that
I "belonged"; that I was one of the elect—a member of a great
and honorable profession, though the monetary reward for what
I was doing was precisely nothing. It was eight months before
I received my first envelope, which contained the princely sum
of $8.

I had a world of energy, some enterprise, and something of
Mr. Adams' own devotion to the newspaper, but my talents in
no wise matched my enthusiasm. One day after I had been
"subbing" without recompense for two or three months Mr.

Adams called me to his desk, said kindly, with a sad shake of his head, "Son, you're not cut out for this business. I'd advise you to quit and try something else."

I asked him if it was an order that I should leave the office. He replied that I might remain if I desired and continue to perform the small tasks that could be entrusted to me, but he frankly explained that he was certain I would never be made a member of the staff.

It was a bludgeon-like blow. Knowing that my father was entirely out of sympathy with my long and unrewarding apprenticeship and that he had, besides, a businessman's disdain for what he spoke of as "writing people," I dared not report to him what Mr. Adams had told me. But there was little else in the world I wanted to do and I stayed on. I have rarely regretted this decision.

In time Mr. Adams confessed that his first judgment of me was in error. It was approbation from Sir Hubert. And soon after this he assigned me to write the first newspaper column the *Democrat and Chronicle* had ever printed. I took this on as an extra chore in addition to my regular duties as a reporter. Mr. Adams entitled it *Seen and Heard*, and I am still writing it, now to the exclusion of all other work.

# CHAPTER IV

# KINNEY OF THE DEMOCRAT

C HARLIE KINNEY, the sports editor, was my second
newspaper hero. He was a caricature of a man with a
hogshead torso and legs as spindly as an anemic woman's. He was a prodigious eater, drinker, and worker. From long
slouching over typewriters in numerous newspaper shops he
had developed a shoulder-hump like a knapsack. His skin had
a pasty, midnight pallor and his large, pale eyes bulged out like
the cheeks of a pocket gopher. His hair was sparse and un-
healthy-looking as though the night lamps under which he had
worked so long had robbed it of all vitality. His feet troubled
him, for his single vanity in dress was shoes with toes like tooth-
picks, and once settled for the night he discarded these in favor
of well-worn carpet slippers.

As he sat at his battered roll-top desk, his thunderous voice
rose constantly through the night to shout, "Copy—copy boy!"
or to answer irritably telephone requests for race results, baseball scores, and other similar information. His knowledge of
sports was encyclopedic. Offhand he could name the date, place,
and winning round of the championship prize fights, the Ken-
tucky Derby winner for almost any given year, or give the lifetime batting average of most notable baseball players.

Kinney's intimacy with the greats and near-greats of the
sporting world, his crude imperiousness, his capacities as a
trencherman, and the swift precision with which he wrote,
made him a heroic and awesome figure to me. I was extremely

diffident in his presence and felt honored to have him cry out, "Kid, moisten this pastepot with water," a command which I was not required to obey, but to which I responded with alacrity. Later, as the result of a favor I did for him, we became good friends.

The favor that won his friendship was performed after I had become a full-fledged member of the staff and a reasonably capable reporter.

The Eggleston Hotel, which was razed several years ago, was then the heart of the city's sporting life. Because of the constant presence in its lobby and bar of sleek, shifty-eyed men who operated handbooks on horse races, it was often spoken of as the "paddock" or "stables," and it was reported that each morning porters swept oats and feed from the floor of its public rooms. It stood in upper Main Street, three blocks from the *Democrat and Chronicle* building, and its long bar was managed by Harry (Spike) Wilson, now a prominent local restaurateur, who had been brought from a celebrated New York café to give the place a metropolitan air.

Boxers and their managers, trotting-horse men, wrestlers, male vaudeville performers, and professional gamblers made the Eggleston their headquarters. From late afternoon until the early morning closing hour its bar was a spirited and lively place, populated by a variety of characters who would have delighted the fancy of Damon Runyon.

During the winter months professional boxing matches were held each Monday night in Convention Hall, and on his way to these assignments it was Kinney's habit to stop for a few short ones at the Eggleston bar to fortify himself against an evening of mayhem and bloodshed. The short ones sometimes became long ones and he frequently reached the auditorium in a state of considerable befuddlement.

On fight nights I often managed my own assignments so that I might sneak into the hall long enough to witness the main go, and I had done this one night when two local heavyweights staged a sensational "grudge" fight.

Leaving the elevator, the opening of which was only two or three strides from Kinney's desk, I stopped a moment politely to inquire my hero's opinion of the fight.

Kinney was slouched heavily over his typewriter, groping for the keys with both forefingers. From the fatuous grin he turned up at me I knew that he had been over-served at the Eggleston.

"Why, s'was all right, kid. Good. Fine s-scrap."

He had been at work half an hour and the first edition deadline was imminent. But when I glanced at the paper in the carriage of his typewriter I saw that nothing he had written was fit to print. He had hit the keys all right, and the carriage had moved from left to right. But each time the little bell rang, indicating that the carriage had reached the limit of its left-to-right progress, instead of manipulating the space lever which would have advanced the paper upward, and left the line below clear for a new sentence, Kinney had pushed it back without touching the lever, with the result that the hundreds of words he had written made a single and undecipherable line of smudged type.

When I called his attention to this error his head wagged loosely on his hunched shoulders. "Can't do it, kid," he mumbled resignedly. "Can't sheem to do it. How 'bout you?"

Though I had seen only the principal event, and had taken no notes, I hurried to my own machine and wrote as thrilling an account of the battle as I could conjure up out of fact and fancy and sent it to the composing room under Kinney's name. Kinney slammed down the roll-top of his desk and shambled out of the office.

For years Kinney's eating and drinking habits were legend in local newspaper circles. Each night he dined at John Callahan's North Water Street café, a three-minute walk from the office, sometimes described as the Eggleston Annex. It was a reasonably small place, with tables set in a gloomy barroom, and three or four rooms upstairs, usually reserved for mixed parties who desired that their convivial entertainments be hidden from public view.

Callahan himself was a taciturn, hard-bitten, old-fashioned saloon keeper, who served excellent food and bottle goods and was notably as close as a dead heat. The consort of card cheats and counterfeit men, he was supposed to know all the angles of these nefarious practices. Yet shortly before his death he "invested" nearly $100,000 with a mob of crooked gamblers who had promised a great cleanup on a fixed horse race—a "boat ride," as it was called—and both his money and his confederates promptly disappeared.

Kinney was one of Callahan's favored patrons, and half an hour before his dinner hour the city room workers would pause with watering mouths and listen to the order he telephoned to the café. He did this in his customary thundering voice, and the menu was of Gargantuan proportions.

"Hey, John," he'd shout to Callahan. "I want a tureen of creamed soup, a large porterhouse steak—and see that this one's thicker than tissue paper—double order of hashed brown potatoes, cauliflower with cheese sauce, salad with French dressing, a side order of fried onions, and if you've got a decent slab of apple pie, I'll have that. And coffee! Be over in thirty minutes," and the receiver would crash down on the hook.

Steak was always his *pièce de résistance*, and he regularly ate it twice a day. When his sports pages were put to bed sometime around one o'clock he would kick his carpet slippers under the desk, painfully crowd his feet into his toothpick-toed shoes, and return to Callahan's, which, behind locked doors, catered to a select after-closing-hours clientele.

There he would talk, drink, nibble at "snacks" often until the restaurant in the Eggleston opened for the day's business. Then he would engage a cab for the short haul to the hotel—usually at this point having pretty well lost his powers of self-locomotion—and sit down to a breakfast that customarily consisted of a huge pot of coffee, steak, and a whole broiled lobster. And so home and to bed.

Kinney's love of good food temporarily took him out of the newspaper business, and his devotion to the bottle once almost ended his life. In the first instance he fell in love with a stout lady who conducted a fine restaurant in the rear of Reynolds Arcade. At least he said it was love. In the city room the suspicion persisted that Kinney was more devoted to the proprietress' cuisine than to her personal charms.

In any event they were married after a brief courtship, and Charlie promptly turned in his resignation with the announcement that he was through with the "lousy newspaper business" and from then on was going to live a decent, normal life.

The normal life was of brief duration. Appointing himself cashier, one night he swept the restaurant register clean of silver and folding money and went off on a three-day toot. His return was not in the way of a triumph. The stout lady decided that her restaurant was more desirable than a husband and Kinney found himself without a job, free food, or a wife. Soon he was re-established at his old post of sports editor, disillusioned in love, and convinced that married life was a much less blissful state than he had anticipated.

His near demise resulted from a jag he brought back to the office after his dinner hour one evening and nurtured through the night with nips from a bottle he had cached in a pigeon-hole of his desk. By quitting time it had reduced him to a state of near-paralysis.

Staggering from his desk to the near-by elevator shaft, he stepped through the open door. But the elevator had been lowered to the basement, where some repairs were being made to its mechanism, and the fifth-floor door had been carelessly left open.

Kinney weighed well over two hundred pounds, and how he made that airy descent without suffering mortal injury is a mystery that has never been satisfactorily explained. Perhaps Bacchus that night had given him divine favor. For as he floundered grotesquely in space, his widely flung hands grasped the steel cable and he slid five floors to the roof of the elevator with only a pair of burned palms and a slight Charley horse as evidence of his harrowing experience.

Countless stories might be told about Kinney's escapades. There was the incident one Monday morning when, long after the final editions of the morning papers were off the press, police discovered two night watchmen gagged and bound in the basement of the Chamber of Commerce building. Several stories above, cracksmen had cut through the large safe of a wholesale jewelry company like a ripe cheese and removed thousands of dollars worth of gems.

It was the most sensational burglary the city had known in years, and the story of it would plump directly into the laps of the three afternoon papers, each of which would race to have a mid-morning extra on the street. Kinney stole their thunder.

As usual he had repaired immediately to Callahan's at the conclusion of his night's work. What was called the "late watch" (which meant that a reporter remained in the city room of the *Democrat and Chronicle* and one in that of its morn-

ing rival, the *Herald*, each morning until four o'clock to handle
late stories worthy of an extra) had ended more than two hours
before.

However, a compositor with some after-hour task to perform
was still in the composing room of the *Democrat and Chronicle*.
He was an old-timer, of a genus not too common in this day and
age. Not only a co-worker but a friend of the men in the city
room, his pride in the prestige of his newspaper was fully as
great as theirs. Excited by the magnitude of the burglary story,
he decided to "scoop" the town.

Familiar with Kinney's habits, he raced from the newspaper
building, gained admittance to Callahan's with importunate
knocks on the locked door, and found the sports editor crumpled in a chair in a rear room. Shaking him vigorously, he explained what had happened.

Like an old fire horse responding to the clang of the gong,
Kinney staggered to his feet, thrust his hat on his head, and
under the manual assistance of the printer made his way into
Main Street. A cordon of the curious had already formed
around the entrance to the Chamber of Commerce building.
Shrugging off the aiding hand of his collaborator, Kinney
shouldered through this with the imperious announcement,
"Kinney of the *Democrat*," passed the police guard, and as-
cending to the jewelry store, quickly gathered the necessary
facts.

In a few minutes he was back at his desk. The alcohol that
had addled his brain seemed to evaporate the instant his fingers
began their swift movement over the keyboard of his typewriter,
and without an instant's pause he turned out a two-column
story into which every known detail of the burglary was skill-
fully integrated. In the meantime the printer had flushed up
from all-night lunchrooms two or three of his confreres, who set

Kinney's copy as it slipped from the carriage of his typewriter, and the *Democrat and Chronicle* was on the street with the burglary story blazoned across its front page more than an hour before its nearest afternoon rival.

One other story about Kinney that I like involved an up-and-coming local lightweight boxer, Joe Goldberg, who had been matched with a young man from the Middle West who ultimately proved much more than his master.

Kinney owned what today would be called a "piece" of the local pugilist, who was proving a profitable property for his managerial staff. He was considered a promising aspirant for the lightweight championship, and though he never achieved that lofty pinnacle, his impending match with the Westerner excited wide interest.

New York had a state law prohibiting prize fights, although ten-round no-decision "boxing exhibitions" were permitted. The no-decision clause in the law made some inconvenience for persons who wagered on the outcome of these "exhibitions." But there was nothing to prevent sports writers from naming in their newspaper reports the boxers whom they considered the winners, and in time it became the practice of sporting men to settle wagers on what were called "newspaper decisions."

The night of this particular fight Kinney again had lingered over-long at the hospitable Eggleston bar, and reaching the hall shortly after the first bout had started, he promptly fell asleep in his chair at the press table.

He slept soundly through every one of the ten rounds of the main affair, during each of which the capable young Westerner figuratively hit Goldberg with everything except the ring posts and the buckets of the seconds. It was the worst lacing the local boy had ever received, and no one was in the slightest doubt as to the winner.

But the gamblers crowded down upon Kinney, aroused him from his peaceful slumbers and demanded, "How'd it go, Charlie? How'd it go?"

Like a man rising to the surface after a plunge into the chilling waters of a mountain lake, Kinney shook his head vigorously and rubbed his rummy eyes. He had not seen a blow struck but his answer was sharp and unequivocal.

"Goldberg on points," he announced imperiously. And that was the way the fight was reported in the *Democrat and Chronicle*, although all four of the other sports writers conceded that Goldberg's opponent had beaten him by the distance of a country mile.

Kinney reformed in time. He stopped drinking and went on a diet. The rigorous ordeal was apparently too much for his system, for he died shortly after he left the *Democrat and Chronicle* to write sports for a newspaper in another city. He still remains in my mind one of the fabulous figures in a sometimes fabulous business. While making no defense of his personal or professional practices, I still prefer him to some of the pundits and political economists who come fresh out of college, with lofty motives and little native newspaper skill, into city rooms the country over.

# CHAPTER V

# TWO REPORTERS

D URING my first week in newspaper work I formed a warm attachment for Will C. Richards, a young man a few years my senior, who substituted on the sports desk on Kinney's day off, and who was an extremely able reporter on the city side.

Richards was the gay blade of our newspaper staff. He was an inveterate and gifted poker player, an admirer of, and admired by, many young women. In person he was balding even as a young man, chunky and unsymmetrical of stature, a careless dresser, except on special occasions. He had a ready wit, considerable aplomb, and an air of worldliness that I envied and admired. It was he who introduced me to the first chorus girl I ever knew, and even now I recall that meeting as a rather epochal occasion.

She was a member of the cast of a musical comedy playing the Lyceum Theater, and during the week's run of the piece Richards had become enamored of her. Her first name was Maxime. I do not remember her last name or the title of the musical to which she was currently devoting her talents.

One night Richards asked me to join him and Maxime at a supper party in the rathskeller of Powers Hotel, a favorite spot of night hawks and rake-hells. I was young, naïve, and green as new-grown grass, and the notion of being in the company of a gay lady from a Broadway show inspired in me a delicious sense of adventure and wickedness.

37

Richards told me that he had become so devoted to Maxime that he had arranged with Mr. Adams to take a few days off the following week to accompany the show to Buffalo, its next stand. He had done this sort of thing in the past. Invariably when he started out on one of these brief tours he wrapped a malacca walking stick in old newspapers and carried it so disguised to the train. Unsheathing it when he reached his destination he felt that the stick dangling from the crook of his arm gave him the status of an authentic boulevardier.

It had not yet become my occasional duty to interview stage stars and I had no acquaintance even among the lesser fry of the profession. But I was fascinated by the theater's world of make-believe and had often stood in proximity to the Lyceum's stage door and observed my buskined idols hurrying through the alley after a night's performance.

Now I was to know and sup with a tender and beautiful votaress at the Thespian shrine whom my fervid fancy envisioned as the epitome of all that was desirable in young womanhood.

And when Maxime arrived on Richards' arm she seemed to fulfill my most zestful anticipations. She was a dark and sultry beauty and in dress and carriage she bore the unmistakable stamp of Broadway. I was all but speechless with admiration as she gave me a cool hand and a slurred, "How're you?"

Immediately we repaired to the rathskeller, where Richards, who drank only on such occasions, and then with little enthusiasm, and Maxime ordered libations of a pinkish, poisonous-looking compound that curiously appeared to dispirit rather than enliven the honored guest.

She was cold, bored, and as unanimated as a figure in a waxworks. An excellent raconteur, Richards conjured up a whole repertoire of amusing anecdote. Maxime heard it all with a dead-pan expression and no more than a monosyllabic response, and Will's most ardent attentions and solicitudes were similarly received.

At that time newspapers had reported the theft from the Louvre of da Vinci's "Mona Lisa." Reproductions of the famous painting had appeared in the press, and even persons previously unfamiliar with matters of art spiritedly discussed this bold depredation. With this in mind Richards attempted a last desperate bid to regain the lost favor of the fair charmer.

"Maxime, do you know what?" he said, staring intently into the lady's eyes, while his voice quivered with the anxiety of his feeling, "you remind me of the Mona Lisa."

The lovely face screwed into an unlovely grimace and the red bow of Maxime's lips parted to emit a snarled retort.

"Well," she said, "you fat bastard, you're not so much to look at yourself."

Richards tried to explain that what he had said was intended as the deepest compliment. But no reconciliation between them was possible. Scarcely touching her food, Maxime flounced out of the rathskeller and summarily left her two admirers at the hotel entrance.

Richards was only briefly disconsolate. Of course, he abandoned his plan to accompany Maxime to Buffalo. But next week the Rogers Brothers were opening in a brand-new musical, and Will knew not one, but two girls in its chorus line.

Some of the best reporters in the early days of my newspaper career were former printers who had come to the editorial department by way of the composing room. They were men whose formal education may have been limited to a year or two of high school, but whose instinctive skill in the use of the language had been quickened and enhanced by setting into type

thousands of words that other men had written. Several of
them developed into excellent newsmen and made the change
from the composing to the city room at considerable loss, for
the good compositor was often paid more than the good reporter.

Gardner B. Ellis, for many years police reporter for the
*Democrat and Chronicle*, was one of these. He was a fine reporter, if no embroidery worker in prose, and a character long
remembered by everyone who worked with him.

He was a red-faced, twitchy, nail-chewing, explosive little
man, who for years batted out all of the police news printed in
the local pages of our newspaper. He chronically complained of
his hard lot and the excessive burdens that were laid upon him,
but it was the only job he wanted and I am sure the only one in
which he would have been happy. He was nearly as devoted to
the newspaper as the city editor, Mr. Adams; and every day,
days off and summer vacations included, he regularly put in an
appearance in the city room.

Besides his multitudinous duties on our paper, which necessi-
tated his keeping in telephonic communication with all outlying police stations, the morgue, the hospitals, fire headquarters,
and the sheriff's office, he was local correspondent for half a
dozen New York dailies, parceling out part of this work to
other reporters until it became a small business, and was known
in our office as *Hides & Skins, Inc., Gardner B. Ellis, Prop.*

The *Democrat and Chronicle* building was then and still is
located in Main Street East, a short distance from the Four
Corners, once the heart of the city's business section. The Four
Corners marks the dividing line between East and West Main
Streets, and Exchange Street begins at the south and State
Street at the north side of this intersection.

Police Headquarters stands in Exchange Street, a five-minute walk from the Four Corners, and this was as far south as Ellis ordinarily proceeded. He went north in State Street a lesser distance to a favorite eating place, and his east and west operations extended no more than a couple of hundred yards in Main Street.

Except when his routine was disturbed by a murder, a large fire, or a train wreck, Ellis' movements closely revolved around the Four Corners. In this limited area were half a dozen saloons, the barber shop of a jovial ex-pug, Billy Tweedle, Johnson's Billiard Academy, and the two telegraph offices—from which Ellis filed his dispatches to the New York papers—and these "stations," as the rest of us called them, he visited each day.

Ellis was a drinking man, but one of such disciplined habits that drink was never permitted to interfere with his work, and he reserved his ceremonial drunks for Tuesday, his one day off each week. On Tuesday, as on every other working day, he would appear at the office promptly at 2 P.M., look over his mail, sort out telegraph queries for news stories from New York papers, assign various members of his "staff" to cover these, borrow a dollar here and there against Saturday's pay envelope, and from then until two o'clock next morning he was in constant circulation on his "beat."

It became customary in time for me to substitute on the police run on Ellis' day off. This responsibility I gravely accepted and fulfilled with the utmost care, knowing that if I missed even the smallest item Ellis would take me to task the next day, for he was extremely jealous of the prestige of his department.

Returning late at night from my last visit to Police Headquarters, I would frequently see him teetering on the Main Street curb, carefree, happy, and mellow after a pleasant afternoon and evening tour of the Four Corners pubs. He would grin genially, flutter his short arms in awkward imitation of the wings of a bird, and invariably announce, "I'm a Wyandotte. I'm a *white* Wyandotte," and he'd crow in poor imitation of a rooster.

He had an apartment, in which he slept, ate his midday breakfast, and to which he sometimes returned for dinner; and a wife, somewhere in the offing, to whom he occasionally referred as "Mrs. Bear." But the police run and the conviviality of the downtown resorts made the essence of his life, and domesticity was little more than a convenience.

As the vacation season approached, Ellis' associates would indulge in a good deal of mock speculation as to where he would pass his two weeks' holiday. He had come from a village south of the city, where he had learned the printer's trade, and each year he invariably announced that he intended to "get away from it all," return to the countryside of his youth and live in simple rusticity with a revered uncle who had, he said, a wonderful Seckel pear orchard.

Until the day before his vacation Ellis would staunchly insist that he was going back to his uncle's farm. And on the first afternoon of his two weeks' holiday he would appear as usual in the office, sheepishly explain that some unanticipated obligation had forced him to cancel his visit, and after attending to his correspondence he would go out on his "beat," stopping at all of his customary stations, and even examining the docket at Police Headquarters. This would be his fixed routine for his entire vacation period, and not once—except when he went home to sleep—would he get as far away as a quarter of a mile from the Four Corners.

Ellis' vacation habits once inspired a fellow reporter to hand in to a new society editor this item: "Mr. Gardner B. Ellis, of

Werner Park, is passing his two weeks' vacation at Point Aspenleiter."

The item was not seen by the editor until it had run through
all editions. Then he smilingly advised the new society editor
that Mr. Ellis was the police reporter for the paper and that to
his knowledge there was no such place as "Point" Aspenleiter.
However, the society notice was not fully in error, for most of
Ellis' vacation was passed at Aspenleiter's, not a summer resort,
but a saloon a step from the Four Corners, which that year he
favored above all similar retreats in the section.

Ellis was considerably older than myself. He had been a
member of the *Democrat and Chronicle* staff for some time
before I started in as a reporter, and he continued on the police
run for many years. When his legs failed and his usefulness on
the street ended he was relegated to the financial desk. His
habits by then had changed. He had married a second time, and
he passed many of his off hours at home with the new Mrs.
Ellis, who understood his whims and eccentricities and had
taken in from the street a stray cat to which her husband was
peculiarly devoted.

He was a tamed spirit during his latter days, and his old
haunts and associates had lost savor and interest for him. We
missed him in the city room. The rickety, old-fashioned typewriter he used, the carriage of which needed to be raised before
the lettering on the copy paper was visible, went with him; but
by then the city room had been moved forward in the building,
enlarged and modernized, and Ellis would have been an anach-
ronism in the new quarters.

He had a way of tugging at his shirt sleeves when anyone
asked a question of him while he was busy at his stint, and
shouting out "I should s-a-y yes"; and the picturesque blasphe-

mies he delivered over his battered mill, his impatience with
telephone operators, of whom he would irritably demand, "For
Gawd's sake, Mamie, you been out to lunch?" his fits of violent
coughing, provoked by an acute catarrhal trouble, that seemed
literally to rattle the loose windows of the old office, were part
of a scene that gave way to a new order when the management
of the paper ultimately changed.

When he transferred from the police run to the financial
desk Ellis regretfully bequeathed to his successor the unofficial
franchise he had held for many years as Rochester correspondent for the New York papers, but not before he had written a
final piece for the *New York Times* which, slight though its
financial reward, gave him considerable satisfaction.

It seems that Ellis was working as a compositor for a local
newspaper when a Mr. Smith from his home town arrived in
Rochester on a little roundelay which, at its close, saw him
clean out of money. He needed both the price of a meal and the
price of a rail ticket back home, and after a hasty inventory of
his Rochester friends he called upon Ellis and borrowed $1.10,
faithfully promising to discharge the debt the next day.

But neither the money nor any word from Smith concerning
it was received. By mail Ellis requested the prompt discharge of
the debt. No response. He tried again, and still again, and each
plea was met with silence deep as death. Realizing that if he
continued to pay out postage in an attempt to collect a $1.10
loan, he would soon expend more money than the debt was
worth, he presently wrote it off, but never quite forgot.

Now in time Mr. Smith moved to a larger village, established
a business of his own, grew as fat in this world's goods as a
Christmas goose, and became the sound, substantial, Number
One citizen of his adopted community. Hearing about this,
Ellis occasionally reflected on Smith's unpaid debt of $1.10,

which amount, since Ellis was a newspaper man, many times would have come in exceedingly handy. But he never saw or heard from Mr. Smith again.

Presently, however, Mr. Smith was gathered to his fathers. And the front-page story in the village press, profoundly lamenting the death of its first citizen, remarked, as obituaries concerning top-ranking citizens frequently do, that the place in the community's life made vacant by his passing would never be adequately filled.

When Ellis read this he felt that a report of the sad demise of the honored Mr. Smith was worthy of the *New York Times,* promptly put the piece on the wire, and in due course was paid by the *Times* the exact amount—$1.10—that the late Mr. Smith had owed him for a period of more than forty years.

# CHAPTER VI

# THE ADVENTURES OF
# RATTLESNAKE PETE

A N ULTRA-CONSERVATIVE city, Rochester has always been excessively proud of its sons who have achieved success in industry, the professions, and science. It likes its prominent citizens to be sound and substantial and orthodox and makes little effort to display its colorful eccentrics—its "characters"—who, lacking the virtues that win kudos from the Chamber of Commerce, nevertheless add spice and flavor to the town, besides sometimes bringing it a certain fame. One of the most colorful of the latter was a saloonkeeper, christened Peter Gruber, but known far beyond the local precincts as Rattlesnake Pete.

His sobriquet alone was something to quicken the imagination. His museum café was the resort to which all visiting firemen first repaired to revel in its variety of wonders, to drink Pete's good grog, to enjoy his fellowship, and to come away with stories that became increasingly remarkable in the retelling. He was constant "copy" for all newspaper men. He was our friend and often our companion. His rackety place stood in Mill Street, kitty-corner from the Corinthian Burlesque Theater, and only a few steps from Main Street.

Where and how he had accumulated the miscellany of strange objects that adorned the walls and the back rooms of the resort I never knew. There was no period quality to his exhibition, and many of its items were little more than junk that added by weight of numbers to the over-all display. On the shelves you could find a jar of pickled human brains, a three-legged chicken, a dwarf two-legged calf, and the well-stained Meerschaum pipe smoked by John Wilkes Booth, Lincoln's assassin. In one corner stood what was represented to be the first electric chair ever used in the State of New York, and on the walls hung the battle flag of Custer's Last Stand and the skull of the horse that carried Phil Sheridan "up from Windsor."

In the barroom proper were various mechanical contraptions that were set into motion by the insertion of a five-cent piece into their coin slots. One represented the operation of a coal mine; another an oil well. A third lured the eye to a peep hole on the promise of the sight of "nakked" women, and instead shot a padded fist into the face of the over-eager spectator. There was a strength-testing machine which, with the first try at the handles, spouted a stream of water up the pant-leg of the boasting athlete.

But the chief delight of the visitors was the rattlesnakes that Pete kept in two large glass cases in immediate view of all visitors.

Pete was a kindly man whose huge gnarled hands and powerful forearms bore numerous scars inflicted by the toad-stabber he used as a surgical instrument when bitten by a snake. It was said of him that he was fearful of no animal that walked on legs or reptile that crawled on the ground and there is some evidence to support this claim.

I remember one day being frantically called on the telephone by Pete's bartender, who said that his employer had just been summoned to a railroad express office where a "hell of a monkey is on the loose and they want Pete to catch him."

Though I acted promptly on the tip, I reached the express office too late to witness the capture. It wasn't a monkey but a half-grown orangutan Pete had been asked to cool down and put in its place.

The orangutan was being shipped to a carnival in Ohio and in transit had been laid over in the Rochester station. Somehow it had loosened the door of its cage and escaped. Once the ugly-looking brute was on the loose the shaking and white-faced clerks abandoned their work room in disorder. There was no policeman in the station at the moment; so one of the frightened clerks phoned Pete, who sped to the scene in an automobile.

Pete had had no experience with orangutans or any other members of the ape family. But it was his unalterable conviction that all of the lesser animals were afraid of man and that direct and forthright action was sufficient to subdue any of them. Without an instant's hesitation he entered the express office and started straight for the orangutan with a cry, "Raus mit you, you sonofabitch!"

Lacking a weapon of attack, he snatched up a broom and flourished it wildly over his head, and the orangutan retreated. The cage was backed against a wall in the center of the room and Pete's strategy was to maneuver the animal in front of the open door and chase him through it.

There was no compromise in his attitude; no cajolery or plea in the language he directed at the short brown ears of the anthropoid. When the ape refused to obey his commands he let fly with the broom and struck the latter sharply in the rump. The orangutan leaped on top of a packing case and for the first time showed defiance. Pete looked around for some missile to hurl. None was at hand. Bending quickly he unlaced first one and then the other shoe and with these in hand again started forward.

Conscious perhaps of the menace and determination in Pete's eye, the animal leaped from the case to the floor. Pete flung one shoe. Missed. The ape was now in front of the cage door. Taking aim Pete threw a fireball with the other shoe, and it struck the orangutan in its stubby snoot. With a grunt of astonishment and pain the orangutan leaped backward through the open door of the cage, which Pete slammed to and locked.

"There, you big yellow monk," he said, brushing off his hands. "I oughta go in there and knock your God damn block off."

The chastened orangutan was shipped out of town on the next westbound train, but by then Pete was back in his café regaling the gape-mouthed barflies with the story of his most recent exploit.

Pete was credited with the performance of numerous healing miracles, in which poultices made of rattlesnake skins were sometimes employed, two of which I know were authentic. The first saved the good right arm, and perhaps the life, of Mike Donovan, a professional boxer, and an old friend of mine.

Donovan was a tough, bruising welterweight, as durable as boiler iron. His face was pockmarked, blunt, fierce, scarred by fist blows. The nose was flat, the ears trimmed down by repeated hammerings to tiny convolutions. Mike's record in the *Police Gazette* boxing almanac was the longest of those in his class, and no opponent ever defeated him by a knockout.

In some pirate battle in a secret ring, for the Horton Law then prohibited prize fighting in New York State, Mike had used a previously worn pair of boxing gloves, and the soiled lining of one of these had infected an open sore on his right hand. In two days the hand had blown up to the size of a prize-winning rutabaga at a country fair. The third day the infection ascended up his forearm to his elbow.

The doctors Mike consulted had made no progress in their treatment. Before a week was up the arm was a swollen, gangrenous mass of flesh almost to the shoulder. The doctors made a dire pronouncement.

"If that arm's not amputated to the shoulder you'll be in your grave in a week."

"If I'm in it," Donovan replied, thinking of a match his manager had made for him, with the appearance money already posted, "that arm'll be with me."

Mike was a friend of Rattlesnake Pete's and of course knew of his reputation as a healer. So weak he had to be carried to Pete's resort, he told the snake man of the doctors' ultimatum. Pete took the big horn-cased pocket knife, his trusty toad-stabber, from a pocket, opened the largest blade and wiped it on his trouser leg. "This is going to hurt," he warned, as he thrust the blade through the puffed and purplish flesh at the original point of infection. A nauseous pus geysered from the wound. Pete wrapped the hand in a poultice of rattlesnake skins, and Donovan was taken home to bed.

The next day the infection showed signs of recession. Confident of the ultimate results of his treatment, Pete insisted that its progressive stages be photographed. The second day the infection had been pulled down to the boxer's elbow. Daily photographs of the hand and arm were made and daily poultices applied. In ten days the infection was completely healed and the photographic record of the cure was bound into a small volume to add to the other wonders of Pete's museum.

Rattlesnake Pete's second most notable cure brought him considerable newspaper fame and a gold charm which he proudly wore until his death, the gift of the famous animal trainer, Bostock. It was inscribed by its doner, "From the Animal King to the Snake King."

One summer when Bostock's show was at Coney Island, the man in charge of the snake house was bitten in the hand by a rattler. This happened early in the evening, and inside of an hour Bostock had Pete on the long-distance telephone. He said that his man was dying, but if Pete would consent to attempt to save his life Bostock would engage a special train on the New York Central for this emergency mission.

This, however, was unnecessary, for an express train was leaving shortly for New York. Pete caught this and was met by Bostock at the New York station in the morning. Though the journey to Coney Island probably could have been made more quickly by ordinary means of transportation, Bostock, with his flair for showmanship, had hired a relay of cabs to rush Pete across Manhattan and out to the amusement resort.

Pete's first act when he reached the bedside of the patient was to open the wound with his toad-stabber. With his lips he then sucked as much of the poison as possible from the wound. Then the patient was given, not whiskey, the supposed orthodox cure for snakebite, but great quantities of milk.

The milk was virtually forced down the man's throat. When his stomach was over-burdened with the fluid he regurgitated, Pete's theory being that the milk absorbed the venom in the patient's system, and that this would be cast off with the vomited milk. The milk treatment was continued all day, and by nightfall the sufferer showed marked signs of improvement. Pete remained with the patient for several days and saw his complete recovery.

Persons who came across snakes of unusual size in the fields and woods adjacent to the city, their imaginations stimulated by their fears, frequently telephoned to Pete that they had seen a rattler. When such a message was received, Pete, who fully understood the value of publicity, would telephone the newspaper office; and because I was known to be a friend of his, I was usually assigned to accompany him on these extempore snake hunts.

Pete's saloon would be in a bustle of preparation when I joined him there. Smitty, his faithful bartender and general factotum, would be commanded to fetch his forked stick and snake box, whose cover was slammed shut by a strong spring. The stick was Pete's chief instrument of attack. He would thrust the prongs on either side of a snake's head and grasp the reptile from behind and whip it into the box. With his meager equipment at hand he would call his two St. Bernards, which dozed all day on the barroom floor, as much a part of its decorations as the brass cuspidors.

Outside, his Rambler touring car would be waiting at the curb. This was adorned on one side by an enormous brass figure of a snake, on the other by a serpent-head klaxon. The two dogs would lumber into the tonneau and Pete and I would mount to the front seat. With the klaxon sounding its raucous warnings, we would depart from Mill Street like Roman potentates on an expedition of conquest.

Although I made many such sorties with Pete, we never so much as saw a snake, to say nothing of capturing one. But merely traveling with Pete was an exciting adventure. He seemed to know everyone, and everyone knew him, and since he was a gusty, hail-fellow-well-met sort of man, a mere nod or a simple word of salutation to a passing acquaintance never sufficed for him.

As we sped over the country roads he would see some acquaintance in a field or on the road, and raise not one but both hands from the steering wheel in a flamboyant gesture of greeting.

"Hi there, Fred (or Jack, or Charlie, or Jim), you damn old horse thief," Pete would cry jovially, "how's the oat crop?" Unguided by his hand, the car would careen crazily from side to side of the road, and I was in constant dread of accident. But we never so much as brushed a fender against a passing hay rig, for like so many gay and reckless cavaliers Pete was endowed with enormous luck, and defying all dangers suffered none of them.

When we arrived at our destination there would be a futile hour or two of beating the woods or poking through a hay or wheat field, the person who had summoned Pete directing these operations from a discreet vantage point. Usually when the vain search was concluded he would be invited to some near-by farmhouse for cider and country-made cookies, and Pete, his jacket loosened to display his ornate snakeskin waistcoat, would thrillingly describe more successful snake hunts he had prosecuted in the hills around Oil City, Pa., the place of his birth and boyhood.

He delighted in these expeditions, profitless though they were; and some of the stories I wrote about these unsuccessful hunts conveyed the impression that Pete had encountered the largest rattler ever seen by man and missed capturing it only by an error in tactics.

One snake hunt we made was partially recorded in photographic detail for posterity.

One of the habitués of Pete's resort was a fellow who was experimenting with a moving-picture camera, and at his suggestion Pete planned the next Sunday to dramatize a snake hunt on the bottoms of the river gorge.

Since a supporting cast was needed, Pete issued a blanket

invitation one night to all persons standing at his bar to appear at 2 P.M. the following Sunday to participate in a
motion picture that would be entitled "The Great Snake
Hunt—Starring the World-famous Rattlesnake Pete." Lunch
and several kegs of beer were promised, and none asked declined.

Indeed, not only did all who heard Pete's invitation appear
the following Sunday afteroon, but the company was considerably augmented by many of Pete's regular patrons who for
some reason or other had not been present the night it was
given. It was a formidable company of blowzy down-and-outers,
some with penitentiary records, and hard-hatted barflies with
the skirts of their turtle-necked sweaters tucked into their pants,
coatless, suspenders patent.

Pete took a loose count of the assembly and ordered another
flat wagon from the livery to carry the added starters. The
provender and iced beer kegs were packed on one rig, two others
were needed to carry the "cast," and with Pete leading the procession in his red Rambler we started for the scene of the drama.
Besides his large collection of rattlers Pete kept on display in his
resort a case of black snakes, large and vicious in aspect, but
non-poisonous and harmless to humans. It was intended that
these also should have a part in the picture, and they were
carried in a separate case in the Rambler.

Hand-carrying the photographic equipment, the beer kegs,
the lunch hampers, and the snake boxes, the company descended a steep path that wound down the cliffs of the river
gorge to the flat bottoms below. Immediately there was a
clamor on the part of the supers to tap the kegs. Pete at first
attempted to resist with the argument that business should
precede pleasure. When the company insisted they needed
food and drink to fortify them against the exertions and dangers

of even so seemingly innocuous an enterprise as a staged snake hunt, Pete presently relented.

The concession was unfortunate. For long before the lunch disappeared and the kegs were emptied, many of the super-numeraries were in an advanced state of liquor, and Pete's care-fully laid plans were threatened with complete disorganization. However, the snakes were there, the cameraman had set his equipment, and stripping off his coat, Pete grasped two forked sticks, and addressed the cast.

"I'm going to let the snakes out on these flat stones," he ex-plained. "When you hear 'em rattle, you fellows pretend you're scared and run this way and that, but not too far. Always keep in range of the camera."

Then, without further preliminaries, and before the addle-brained actors fully comprehended his meaning, he opened one of the snake boxes and poked out three or four rattlers.

The effect was galvanic. Many of the company, far gone in their cups, were recumbent on the ground. With the first sharp rattle of the liberated snakes they leaped to their feet, bug-eyed with fright, some in the confusion of their fears stumbling into the shallow water at the river's edge, others plunging along the shore, and still others attempting to ascend the sheer cliffs of the gorge.

The snakes seemed to sense that full freedom might be gained if they escaped from the rocks upon which they had been released, and Pete had the devil's own time preventing them from doing so. No sooner would he pin the head of one reptile with one of his forked sticks, than another would wriggle off the rocks. He would grab this one far down its body and yank it back and the snake would coil and strike out at him wickedly. Fully engaged with the snakes, he had no time to observe the desertion of his craven company.

I was not unalarmed myself by the sinister rattle of the snakes and the constant threat that at any moment one or two of them might escape, but despite my apprehensions the panic of the supers doubled me with laughter. It was like a Hal Roach comedy. Those who attempted to escape up the cliffs would ascend a few feet, their derby hats would tumble off, and the owners of the hats would come rolling down after them, feet often in the air, arms flung wildly about, screaming like Cherokees for Pete to lock up his God damn snakes and save them from horrid death. Then they would clamber to their feet and again desperately storm the cliffs.

The cameraman's shouts joined the vocal cacophony of the supers as he commanded them to display their unsimulated fears in closer proximity to the snakes, for all had run clean out of the focus of his lens. His commands went unheeded. The members of the company were widely separated, and those who had attempted to ascend the cliffs now abandoned this purpose and ran along the shore, some of them disappearing entirely from sight.

Pete finally got the snakes back in the box. Greatly spent by his exertions, he flopped down on the rocks and sucked deeply on a flask he had carried in one of his pockets.

"Jesus," he said, with a wry shake of his head, as he observed the members of his widely dispersed cast, "what a Roman army them guys are. They eat, drink, and run away."

Since it was now impossible to reorganize the troupe for a second act of the performance, the snake boxes, the beer kegs, the lunch hampers, and the photographer's gear were carried to the top of the gorge and packed on the waiting wagons. The procession back to Pete's place had the slow pace and gloomy aspect of a funeral. Once there Pete's bountiful nature reasserted itself, and all who had accompanied him were offered drinks on the house.

During his struggle with the snakes Pete had slipped into the river and was wet to his knees. He was changing his shoes and socks in his small office when a piercing wail ascended from the barroom and a moment later a white-faced, crazed-eyed, shaking figure appeared at the office door shouting, "Save me! Save me! There's a snake loose!"

"You're drunk again Mahoney," Pete said placidly, and resumed the lacing of his shoe. "You're on the fringe of the D.T.s'. You're seeing snakes."

This last statement was correct on both counts, as was soon evident. Hearing a wild commotion in the front of the resort, Pete, one foot bare, rushed into the barroom to come upon a scene of panic. Some of the supers had clambered up on the bar and were standing above a wash of beer foam like shipwrecked mariners on a raft. Others had leaped to chair and table tops, and their shouts of fear and cries for help were even greater than their similar manifestations at the river gorge. Pete instantly comprehended their cause of alarm. In a drunken scuffle someone had tipped over one of the snake boxes, the door had sprung open, and the floor seemed flooded with reptiles.

Pete rushed at one long dark body that was serpentining along the wainscoting, arrested its course with his bare foot, snatched it up with his hand, and twirling it like a lasso around his head, while fearful screams rose from the spectators, flung it back into the snake box. He caught another snake by this same method, and still another, until all that had escaped were returned to the box.

They were not rattlers. The box contained the harmless black snakes, which Pete had intended to employ in the cinema drama, but the use of which had been canceled when the human actors ran off the set. Pete attempted to explain this fact to all within hearing of his voice. But none of his guests was in a mood to hear or heed his words and a minute after the last snake was returned to captivity all but one had rushed into the street.

The lone survivor was Mahoney. Pete found him when he returned to the office. He was lying on the floor, foaming at the mouth, writhing fearfully, in an advanced stage of tremors. When ordinary ministrations failed to quiet him Pete was forced to send for the police, who insisted on an explanation as to how one of his regular patrons had suffered so violently from drink on a day when saloons were legally closed.

"We had a snake hunt," Pete replied simply. "Poor Mahoney got scared. I think that's the main trouble with him."

"It don't smell like snake fright—or even snake bite," one of the coppers remarked. But he had no genuine disposition to incommode a friend, and he added quickly, "We'll take him to the hospital and let the doctors decide."

The doctors decided that Mahoney indeed was suffering from the tremors, and all that night, and part of the next day, he was lashed to a bed and hypodermically treated with sedatives.

Pete later announced that he was discouraged with the whole business of a staged snake hunt, and never attempted another. When the pictures were presently shown, with the exception of Pete all the actors had their backs to the camera, and even the sight of their backs was brief.

"But what could you expect of bums and stewpots like them?" Pete remarked sorrowfully. "Drunk or sober, a *real* Barrymore would show his face to the audience."

~~~~~~~~~~~~~~~~~~~~~~~~~~~~~~~~~~~~~~~~~~~~~~~~~~~~~~~~~~~~~~~~~~~~~~~~~~~~

# CHAPTER VII

# A RETURN ENGAGEMENT OF GETTYSBURG

---

JACK TURNER was the proprietor of the Rock Cottage, a resort in the Northern outskirts of the city. It was a roadhouse that encouraged a variety of iniquities. It had a bar and a restaurant of sorts. It had rooms upstairs. The upstairs rooms were spoken of as "hideouts," and the description was correct.

Turner was not so well known nor in appearance so picturesque as Rattlesnake Pete. But he and his wife Sarah were both colorful characters. Jack and Sarah were cockney English. Turner had once been a good journeyman lightweight boxer, and in his early marital career he had instructed his wife in the "sweet science," the "manly art of self-defense." She was an apt pupil, and she became an earnest and competent performer.

I was fairly new in the newspaper business when I first visited this place in company with a friendly police officer who had a night off. We went specifically to see a pit bull terrier in a rat-baiting contest held in a cockpit in the basement of the resort.

Turner's tastes in fights were catholic, and his cellar pit had been the scene of many curious battles. Game chickens, pit dogs, and professional boxers had fought there, and now and then he staged a Battle Royal, with eight or ten Negroes clouting one another mercilessly, until all but one was rendered into bloody and battered insensibility. The late Jack McDonald, captain of the Detective Bureau, once said to me; "Turner put on every kind of a fight in that pit of his. If there'd been room he'd have played a return engagement of the Battle of Gettysburg."

I have seen cock fights, but never a formal dog fight, arranged for the edification of the spectators. I never want to see one. I am an admirer of and at times a breeder of bull terriers. Only a sadist would pit two of these courageous animals against one another, knowing death to be the probable fate of one of them. Yet the "sport" is still widely, if secretly, practiced, to bring unjust discredit to one of the most affectionate breeds of dogs.

The rat-baiting contest at least had the merit of eliminating two dozen of the destructive rodents that have been a pest to man since time immemorial. The pit was banked up like a great wooden bowl, and so sheer that even a rat would have a difficult time climbing out of it. Into this were dumped from canvas bags two dozen full-grown and ugly-looking river rats. Squealing and snapping at one another, they milled around the pit until a handler appeared with the dog, a pure white bull terrier, with teeth-torn, close-cropped ears, and the long, punishing jaw of the real fighter, Jumbo Jo by name.

Jumbo Jo was widely famed, not only as a killer of rats, but as a killer of other pit dogs. He weighed a full fifty pounds, not an ounce of which could have been torn from him with a cotton hook. Holding him by the tail and collar, the handler leaned far over the edge of the pit and dropped the dog into the vortex of rats.

The action after that was kaleidoscopic. No bark escaped the dog once the handler released him. He was too busy for that. It seemed that even before his paws touched the bottom of the pit one of the ugly rodents had been tossed into the air, to fall dead with a broken back. Jumbo Jo was as precise and deadly as a steel trap. There was no pause in his routine. His jaws would snap with bone-breaking power on a rat's back, his head would jerk backward, and another rat was dead. It was all one swift, rhythmic movement, and in less than two minutes by the stop watches of the clockers (for a pool had been made on the time it would take the terrier to dispose of the rats), only the white dog, virtually unharmed, remained alive in the pit.

"That Jumbo Jo," one sport remarked, "could clean the town of rats like the Pied Piper, if they could get 'em all together in the ball park."

Later I learned that Jumbo Jo, in a match with a great bruiser of a dog from Montreal, suffered a throat gash and died from hemorrhage, and his angry, drunken owner, who had won innumerable fights with him, kicked his dead body into the street.

I returned to Turner's several times after my first visit, but only one other experience remains vividly in mind. Saturday night was the big night at the Rock Cottage, and the feature of the entertainment was often supplied by Turner and his wife. Their repertoire usually opened with a three-round boxing exhibition, continued with Indian-club swinging and other feats of athletic dexterity, and closed with what was known as the William Tell number.

Sarah wore long black tights for these exhibitions. She was not a handsome woman, but her figure was robust, curved, and exciting by the standards of the day. The boxing was spirited, whether rehearsed or not, and both contestants indulged in fierce scowls and grimaces, and in the heat of the set-to passed remarks that would have provoked even a less belligerent married couple to combat. They gave a good show, and the crowd howled its delight and in the end showered the contestants with coins.

The William Tell number ordinarily was performed in the barroom, the black-tighted Sarah standing rigid as a statue against a steel backboard, while Turner shot an apple from her head with a .22 calibre rifle. I never saw this feat performed, for an untoward incident interrupted it the night I expected to witness it.

Among the spectators was one young blade with more money than brains, who was notorious as a disturber both in and out of his cups. His father was a staid and substantial citizen of considerable wealth who had ruined the lad by over indulgence. The young man seemed to believe that his father's wealth and position immunized him from all legal and extra-legal redress, and this night he was excessively abusive and raucous.

During the boxing his strident, drunken voice repeatedly appealed to Turner to "soak her in the watermelons, Jack. That'll get her," and he had loudly disparaged Sarah's general physical construction, which most of the audience considered admirable. Sarah heard, but made no retort. The young fellow was a heavy spender, particularly when drunk, and Mrs. Turner could stand a great deal of abuse for the solatium of a fair amount of money, loving a dollar more than anything on earth.

When the spectators ascended from the basement, where the earlier entertainment had been given, to forgather in the barroom for the William Tell number, the offensive young man continued his heckling and Sarah continued to accept it with tightly compressed lips. Resolutely she took her place in front of the steel backboard. Turner placed a large red apple on the top of her head and stepped back the length of the room to take aim.

But before he raised the gun to his shoulder, a heavy beer mug sailed across the room and crashed against the steel, showering the statuesque figure of Sarah with glass. She turned swiftly, and no grimace she had made in the boxing ring was as sinister as the one that now twisted her face into a mask as terrifying as Medusa. With a bound she reached the bar, against which her heckler, satisfied with the success of his last outrage, slouched in drunken insouciance.

"You stinking no good—!" Sarah screamed, and fetching her right fist up from the tip of her white, calf-high boxing shoes, she landed with such force on her tormentor's jaw that he sprawled to the floor, his head striking a brass spittoon. But Sarah was not through. Familiar with the rules of the Marquis of Queensbury, she also knew the technic of the barroom and alley fighter. Before the fallen young man could wrap his head in his folded arms she gave him the "leather," and a bruise like a Bartlett pear swelled on his forehead. Then she kicked him viciously in the ribs with both feet.

Fully in sympathy with Sarah's attack, the crowd nevertheless closed in upon her. Scratching, striking out, and screeching like a banshee, she was led to a remote corner. Her victim got to his feet, nursing his sore jaw and forehead. Invective spewed from his lips, and in a shrill, hysterical voice he threatened to have the law on Turner, threatened civil action, threatened to close the place up like pimpernel in a thunderstorm. But under the hilarious taunts of his fellow spectators, he departed and never returned.

I never saw Sarah Turner in another performance, rehearsed or otherwise. But the reputation she gained that night served her well, and I was told that in the future the spectators at all of her exhibitions were respectful in their attitude and discreet in their comments.

# CHAPTER VIII

# DAYS OF INNOCENCE

SOME of the happiest days of my adult life were passed during those brief years that intervened between my start in the newspaper business and the outbreak of World War I. We worked long hours in our newspaper shop. We checked in at two o'clock sharp each afternoon but had no regular hour for quitting. After our last news story was written, we had the Sunday social notes and pedro notices to do, and we kept at these until Mr. Adams gave us the good-night nod, which was often after 1 A.M.

Once a week each of the younger members of the staff was required to stand the "long" or "dog watch," which kept him in the office until four in the morning. The watch man's job was to handle any news that broke after the home edition had been put to bed and merited making over the front page for an extra. The occasions for this were rare, and the last two hours of the watch man's vigil made a heavy drag, for he was entirely alone in the city room except for the rats.

The newspaper building was built above the river bank, and the rats that invaded it were river rats, bold, obstreperous, and formidable in size. A bindery, which was part of a job printing plant operated by the newspaper, adjoined the city room, and the theory was that the rats ascended to the fifth floor to eat the bindery glue. Whatever their purpose, they were abundant in the early hours of the morning. Frolicking, quarrelling, and making love, they raced from one end of the long narrow city

64

room to the other with uncanny squeals and shrieks. There was one of such unusual size that we called him Old King Cole, and legend had it that a drunk who had come into the office one early morning had whistled to him and attempted to collar him, thinking King Cole was a Mexican hairless he had lost sometime before.

The city room was crowded with workers until midnight, and the rats were not conspicuous until after most of the human inhabitants had departed, when they came out for a field day. Alone on the "long watch" I would sit with my feet cocked on the top of a desk, having heard that rats sometimes ran up a man's trouser leg.

Working nights as a police reporter I soon acquired a fair knowledge of the city's underworld, and many of the dens and haunts of nocturnal iniquity were familiar to me.

Rochester was not a particularly scarlet city. But it had its secret gambling hells, numerous roadhouses of varying degrees of disrepute, and of course, as all cities had in that era, a restricted district, commonly referred to as the "line." The "line" in Rochester was not long. But at times, when large fraternal organizations held their annual conventions in the city and the number of inmates of its brothels was augmented for these celebrations, it was, as one delegate, stumbling drunkenly down the red-lighted steps of one of these resorts, remarked, "very intense."

The "boarding girls" occupied a half dozen houses on a short, bumpy cobblestone street paralleling the railroad yards and a minute's walk from the west end of Main Street. It was identified on city maps as Hill Street. Its main approach was made a bit sinister by the presence, just beyond the Hill Street corner, of the County Morgue, a grim, geometric building of red brick that had the aspect of death even on its façade and the obvious purpose of which must have slacked the spirits of many a libertine rollicking in a sea-going hack to a night's debauch.

One of the best-known and most popular of the Hill Street resorts was operated by Lib Goodrich, around whose colorful career many fables have been fashioned. She was a handsome woman in a bold, large-bosomed, Rubenesque manner, who had come originally from Lyons, forty miles east of Rochester, already well practiced in her profession.

In Lyons la Goodrich had been a local institution of considerable conspicuousness and tolerated disrepute. Her establishment housed half a dozen charmers and was accepted as a sort of safety valve for the sensualities of the burghers; and Lib's smart, red-wheeled gig, with her good mare Susie Q between the shafts, was a familiar sight in the village streets on pleasant summer days when its owner desired a breath of fresh air and the caress of the benevolent sun.

The Goodrich house in Lyons was well known far beyond the local precincts and enjoyed considerable out-of-town trade. It reposed on a side street, the house itself separated from the Erie Canal by a small back yard. One night in mid-November, an out-of-town visitor, in the company of several local voluptuaries, repaired to Lib's resort for an evening of wassail and song. During the early part of the festivities the guest from out-of-town was advised by one of his Lyons friends that Lib's place was occasionally raided and as a precaution against such an eventuality he was carefully instructed in the method of escape.

"The Sheriff's fellows always come to the front door," he was told. "So we always run out the rear door. It's a sure and safe dodge. Just remember, in case . . ."

Shortly after this gratuitous advice had been given a loud

hammering was heard at the front door and a basso voice authoritatively demanded, "Open in the name of the law!"

The visitor heard. He was a man of considerable repute in a near-by community, a banker, and a deacon of his church. In ankle-length underwear he sprinted behind a covey of local sports through the short lower corridor, plunged into the unlighted back yard, plunged on and into the icy waters of the canal, which had not yet been drained for the winter.

In his precipitant flight he had not noticed that the other fugitives had turned sharply to either the left or the right after they had passed through the rear door. For their part they did not realize the seriousness of their joke—for the "raid" had been arranged for the benefit of the visitor—until they heard his frantic screams.

They rushed to the bank of the canal and in the faint rays of the partly clouded moon saw their friend the banker. Unable to swim a stroke, he was disappearing for the second time. Two heroes dived to his rescue. Waterlogged and nearly frozen he was lugged to the cellar of Lib's hospitable domicile and vigorously resuscitated over a cider barrel.

It was not this incident, but a more outrageous, though unintentioned, jape, that ultimately brought an end to Lib Goodrich's career in Lyons and saw the doors of her house of pleasure permanently closed.

One night an inebriated lodge member, who was enjoying Lib's bounteous hospitality, extended to all of the young ladies, and the proprietress herself, embossed invitations to a memorial service for a departed brother on the following Sunday afternoon. The order was exclusively male. But so close was the relationship between many of the lodge members and the residents of the Goodrich house that the latter were frequently referred

to as the Ladies' Auxiliary, and Lib and her satellites were complimented to think that they had been invited to share the sad
fellowship of the memorial service.

Promptly at the appointed hour on Sunday afternoon, just
as the chaplain of the order took his place before the bier, the
assembled mourners were thrown into consternation by the
arrival of Madam Goodrich and her girls. Attired in black
broadcloth, they found chairs in the rear of the lodge hall,
primly folded their black-gloved hands in their laps, and bent
their heads in the proper attitude of the bereaved.

The commiseration the mourners were feeling for their departed brother was all but lost in a torrential surge of indignation. It was too late for protest or eviction. The chaplain spoke,
pronouncing a noble panegyric; the fraternal choir sang *The
Rock of Ages*; prayers were intoned. And the ladies knelt and
wept.

This was too much for even a liberal-minded community to
endure, and Lib Goodrich was swept permanently out of town
on a high wave of moral righteousness. She took with her both
her human and household chattels. Soon she settled in Hill
Street. And there she plied a profitable trade and enjoyed the
high regard of many satisfied patrons until the city fathers ultimately withdrew the unofficial sanction that long had permitted her resort and others of similar character to operate.

Committed though we were to a ten- and eleven-hour working day, at least the younger reporters on our paper had a rather
good time of it. There was some drudgery to what we did. But
the drudgery was compensated for by much that was exciting
and interesting. Most of us looked upon our jobs as something
above the mere contrivance of livelihood; and though we often
complained among ourselves at our hard lot, let anyone outside

of our city-room family attempt to discredit our calling or de-
fame our newspaper and we rose up in wrathful defense.

Rochester was a middle-class city, compact, self-sufficient,
prosperous, and lively. Only people of considerable means
owned motor cars, and the movement of Rochester residents
into the suburbs and adjacent rural areas ultimately inspired
and made possible by the common use of the automobile had
not yet begun. Our summers were usually fine, the winters
severe. Yet the average person living in our difficult lake climate
did not anticipate the approach of the cold months with the
shuddering apprehension so many Rochesterians manifest today.

When summer ended and the first brilliant colors were observed on the foliage of the trees that lined most of our streets,
we were all conscious of a sort of divine unrest. We were filled
with an eagerness of spirit and inspired by the promise of thrilling things impending. We knew that a small company of the
very rich migrated each January to a fabulous resort known as
Palm Beach, and the scandals and didos and galas of some of
these chosen folk were reported in the magazine sections of
what was called the "yellow press." But Miami was little more
than a name in the travel agency pamphlets, and St. Peters-
burg, later to become a well-known Florida colony of Rochester
expatriates, at that time was known mostly as the name of the
capital of the Russians.

Autumn was a time of lively stir in the city. A re-awakening
after the torpor and somnolency of summer; a period of contentment and well-being—if the harvest had been good—in
the country. The frost got on the pumpkin. There was a
champagne-like piquancy in the air. The leaves fell and the
smudge of their burning was clean and out-doorish and one of
the pleasures of the season.

With little dread of the coming winter city folks aired the mothball odors from their heavy underthings, looked to their stock of blankets, replaced screens with storm windows, saw to their coal bins. There was good philosophy about the change of seasons, and the transition was accepted merely as one of nature's immutable laws. Autumn was not a period of gloom, gray, bedraggled, a time to lament the parting of summer's brilliant glories. Eagerly city dwellers made plans for evenings of whist; for dances, lodge meetings, Hallowe'en parties, football on Thanksgiving Day, and the fine gay doings of the Christmas holidays.

The first hint of the approaching "season" was given when Dockstader's Minstrels opened in the Lyceum in late August. After Labor Day, lobster palaces put oysters back on their menus; after-midnight "owl" cars were filled to the vestibules. Flat wagons trundled loads of scenery through stage door alleys, and chorus girls bustled in and out of hotels. You might find Nat Goodwin swapping stories with Lafe Heidell, whose ornate barroom was the rendezvous of leading actors, or see the feature player on the Temple bill shooting Kelly pool in the Whitcomb billiard room.

Rochester had several "flesh shows," as they are now called, sometimes with a hint of disparagement. "Flesh shows" then meant the performances of living actors on the stage, and our town had several theaters in which living actors of varying degrees of talent were constantly exhibited during the fall, winter and early spring. There was, first of all, the now razed Lyceum, a playhouse rich in tradition, upon whose commodious stage the famous men and women of the international theater had played their many parts. Bernhardt, in the wistful, tragic role of *L'Aiglon*, aspiring in puerile fancy for the powers of the first Napoleon; the great Sir Henry Irving, crouching

with drawn sword before the witches' stew while the first ambitions that led to Macbeth's perfidy and ruin insinuated themselves into his soul; Miss Maude Adams in *Peter Pan*, in which,
the critics confidently asserted, she could draw an audience to
a desert isle; and the elegant John Drew, whose playing of
drawing-room comedies made even Berry Wall look like a
hooligan. The Barrymores, and Mantell with King Richard's
cloak majestically flung across his breast, orating to his Army:
"Draw, archers, draw your arrows to the head! Spur your proud
horses hard, and ride in blood; amaze the welkin with your
broken staves!"

And all the gay and pretty ladies of light opera. The lovely
Julia Sanderson, thrice loved by me. And Elsie Janis. And the
naughty Anna Held. The thrush-throated Louise Gunning and
exotic Fritzi Scheff; Chrystie MacDonald in *The Belle of May-
fair*, and Frenchy Adele Ritchie, and the feather-footed Bessie
McCoy. I loved them all, in those days, and once wished I might
lie down and die for Miss Lulu Glaser.

But the Lyceum was only one of several theaters. Far down
Main Street, Sam S. Shubert had opened the Shubert Theater
(now the Capitol) and was making a fight for patronage against
the Klaw & Erlanger interests. It was a spirited rivalry and
theatergoers profited because of it. The Temple was a comparatively new vaudeville house, definitely "big time," showing
seven acts twice daily from Labor Day until late spring. These
three were the "class" houses of the town.

For cheaper money and performers of lesser merit the Baker
Theater in Fitzhugh Street all fall and winter presented one
melodrama after another. Here sentimental ladies cried their
eyes out each matinee day over the sad plight of *Nellie, the
Beautiful Cloak Model*, or *Edna, the Pretty Typewriter* and
remained to exult in the final triumph of virtue and roundly hiss

the villain when he appeared, still wearing a sinister smirk, in the line of players at the final curtain call.

The Corinthian showed all of the attractions of the Columbia Burlesque Wheel. And while I recall no such alluring ladies as Miss Ann Corio and Miss Hinda Wassau, stars of later-day burlesque, the ragtag comics of these productions employed some originality and wit instead of the sewage humor contemporary burlesque comedians pass out as funny business, and not a few of them rose from their original medium to star in the $2 musicals.

The Cook Opera House, once the home of better vaudeville, its franchise lost to the Temple, settled for a medley of burlesque and vaudeville known as "tab shows"—neither very good nor very wicked—and the smaller Victoria and Gordon Theaters supplemented five or six acts of second-rate vaudeville with the vision-destroying motion pictures of the day, and both were as busy as steers in flytime.

Morning newspaper workers were part of Rochester's downtown life. We co-mingled with visiting celebrities. We toured the leading hotels and pubs, acquiring copy in the former, free lunch in the latter. We knew the scandals and the angles; all the gaudy goings-on. Our reporters' cards gave us admission to many places in which even angels might fear to tread.

The cold blasts of winter and the drifting snows meant little to us, and few desired to run away from town and miss the fun.

# CHAPTER IX

# VAUDEVILLE AT THE TEMPLE

D
URING the first year of the first World War, while I
was working for the *Democrat and Chronicle*, the
drama critic was taken from his regular job and given
charge of the telegraph desk upon which the cabled news of
the war was being handled. Five theaters were operating in
Rochester, and Mr. Adams, my city editor, decided to make me
part-time dramatic critic.

I spent every Monday afternoon reviewing the vaudeville bill
at the Temple Theater, and at night had "two on the aisle" in
the Lyceum.

The Temple was the first line, the big-time vaudeville house.
Its shows came intact from the Temple in Detroit, for both
houses were controlled by the well-known mid-West impresario,
J. M. Moore. John M. (Mickey) Finn was house manager of the
Rochester Temple. He was a tiny man, slower in speech and
movement than any well man I had ever known. He operated
the Temple like a little Czar and made it a splendid success. He
had small regard for newspapermen, and slight respect for
actors as people. He consorted mostly with downtown merchants and was a prominent figure in the Rochester Club,
where all the busy boys of business daily forgathered for three-
hour luncheons. He was tight with "paper," had strong connections with the business heads of the newspapers, and probably
was the top showman in town. Mickey Finn was never a close
friend of mine. His stage manager, Bert Caley, was.

73

I was young in those days and susceptible to the charms of more than one lady who achieved the empyrean blue of the Temple's headline spot. One of these was Miss Joan Sawyer. She had her first chance at fame at the time Irene and Vernon Castle started a ballroom dance craze that swept the country. The Castles were great troupers and the most successful of all dance teams of that period. But Miss Sawyer was my personal favorite.

Her pale gold hair, her beautiful figure, and her queenly grace made her a person who seemed too lovely for this mundane sphere. I first saw her in New York and was sure that I was madly in love with her. The announcement that she would play a full week at the Temple aroused in me all of the sweet agonies of the lovesick. It seemed incredible that so sublime a votary of Terpsichore should favor our unromantic city. Yet the three-sheets and the street car posters said that this was true.

It was never possible for me to meet Miss Sawyer, though I did cover her show. After that I made a daily practice for the remainder of the week of stopping at the Temple each evening long enough to catch her act from a stage box, and walked out into the brash, harsh lights of the downtown streets feeling exalted and remote from the jostling sidewalk throng, my heart pounding.

Her dancing partner—his name was George Harcourt, as I recall—appeared to my fevered fancy to have the most enviable job in the whole category of human work, and it was incomprehensible that he should accept money for the privilege of holding this goddesslike vision in his arms. He was a handsome young man, long, lean, beautifully gotten up in tails and white tie; a gold chain—which for some singular reason fascinated me—looped widely from the band of his trousers to a side pocket.

Harcourt did not fling his partner into the air, or twirl her like a pinwheel from his shoulder, or indulge in any of the muscular antics of modern dance teams. He and Miss Sawyer danced on the floor, where ballroom dancing should be done, their joint movements flowing together in a pattern of exquisite beauty. There was something chaste and sacrosanct about Miss Sawyer's appearance; and in one number in which her tiny rouged toes were exposed in Grecian sandals they seemed like precious jewels in a case in Tiffany's window. The gal rather interested me.

Later Caley told me a story about her which, though it failed to dampen my ardour, slightly encouraged the notion that she might be human after all. Caley said that Miss Sawyer was a holy terror—hell on wheels, he called her. Disbelieving this damning charge, I pressed him for further enlightenment. "I fixed her," Bert said, and told me this story:

In every theater in which she had played, Miss Sawyer had proved as incorrigible as a tantrum child, and word had come from Detroit to Mickey Finn that she would be a headache every one of the six days she would be with him. Twice in Detroit she had threatened to walk off the stage—or refuse to walk on it. She had inveighed against the undersized letters in her name in the marquee lights, the arrangement of her pictures in the lobby frames, the orchestra, the drafty stage, the smallness and lack of comfort of the star's dressing room. She was bitter in her denunciation of audiences who she believed had failed to show proper appreciation of her art.

Finn went to Caley with a full dossier of complaints.

"Bert," said he ominously, "You're going to have the devil's own time with this Sawyer woman. Nothing you will do for her will be right. She's got a temper like a volcanic eruption. She's likely to kick you in the teeth or chew off your fingers. Do the best you can with her. I don't envy you. I'm going to keep strictly out of her sight except to pay her off Saturday night. Wish I could go fishing for a week."

Caley witnessed the arrival of Miss Sawyer's trunks and props with brooding apprehension. She followed in a swirl of upper Fifth Avenue finery and the imperious air of an empress. Foxhall Keene, international polo player, gentleman auto racer, and noted cosmopolite, was one of her admirers, and this fact had tended to lift her even higher into the rare air of her already stratospheric self-esteem.

Caley kept away from her until after the Monday afternoon performance, which came off surprisingly well. The orchestra, carefully coached, had been splendidly co-operative; the audience so enthusiastic that Miss Sawyer had been required to take half a dozen bows. There had been no complaint yet about her dressing room, which had been especially prepared for her reception, with a vase of American Beauty roses Mickey Finn grudgingly offered as a token of conciliation. Thinking this the moment to play his card, Caley rapped diffidently on the dressing room door. Not her Negro maid, but the queen herself responded.

"Miss Sawyer," he said, removing the tattered cap he always wore backstage, "you'll excuse me for bothering you. I'm Caley, the stage manager. I just saw your act. I've been a long time in this business, and seen most of 'em. I couldn't resist telling you that yours is the finest dancing act I have ever seen."

Miss Sawyer was silent for a moment, while her eyes held those of the stage manager, who was trying to make his look worshipful. Then she spoke. "Mr. Caley," she said earnestly, "coming from a man of your professional experience, what you have said is a very great compliment. You, much more than those people out front, know good dancing when you see it. I'll cherish what you have told me. I thank you for telling me."

For the remainder of the week Miss Sawyer was as gentle as a little lamb, as docile as the good little girl who each day brings teacher an apple.

Joan Sawyer continued for two or three years as Irene Castle's closest rival as a ballroom dancer. Her popularity fell away as the result of a lot of unsavory publicity she later received. Her professional engagements from then on were mostly confined to second-class cafés, and I saw her last dancing on a dais in the inclosure of the six-day bicycle race at Madison Square Garden. It was an exhibition little appreciated by the bike fans; and the tawdry setting of the smoke-filling auditorium, with raucous shouts of peanut, program, and soft drink venders overtoning the strains of a Strauss waltz, dreadfully lessened its effectiveness. I felt sad to see my old idol come to such a pass, and never saw her more. That was a long time ago. Recently I read a single line in a Broadway gossip column saying that she was living in retirement in Canada. She was a great beauty, an exquisite dancer, and a lady of enormous allure.

Under the Finn management, the Temple booked in many men and women who later attained wide fame in the movies, a field of entertainment that virtually sounded the death knell of big-time vaudeville, sending its performers either to Hollywood or into the cabarets and night clubs that mushroomed during the fabulous, free-spending days of the early and middle twenties. The late Will Rogers and W. C. Fields were two of these.

Rogers was a friend of Caley's. He had a rope act that was interspersed with a gum-chewing patter of wisecracks. The first time he was featured on the Temple bill, he went upstage. Elevated to top billing, he parked his wad of gum on a proscenium arch, polished up his talk, and on opening day fell as flat as the proverbial pancake. He was worried and distraught. By Thursday, with scarcely an honest belly laugh to his credit, he sought out Caley.

"Bert, what's the trouble with my new line? I can't get their hands off their laps. They don't laugh. I almost hear 'em snoring."

Caley nodded. "It's not the audience, it's you, Will," he answered frankly. "I been wanting to tell you ever since the Monday opening, and didn't have the heart. You've gone highbrow. Put that gum back in your puss, and go out there and talk and act like Will Rogers. Not like John Drew. You'll get 'em back."

That night Rogers reverted to his old line and won the house from the first time he opened his mouth.

Rogers had worried Caley. W. C. Fields, Bert often said, took a couple of years off his life.

I was backstage with Caley the first night of Fields' first week's engagement as a Temple headliner. He was a tramp juggler, and the best in the business. He was cold sober when he went through his act at the matinee. Half an hour before he was to go on Monday night he had not returned to the theater, and Caley was tearing his hair and gnawing on his nails like a teething puppy on a bone. Desperately he appealed to a man who I believe was Fields' brother, and who served the juggler as dresser and handy man.

"My God," Caley cried. "Look at the time. Where's Fields? We put him in the feature spot, and he does this to me."

Brother Fields was as unruffled as a clam. "Don't worry," he assured placidly. "Bill'll be around. He's a trouper."

"But he's only got thirty minutes. Go look him up. I'll bet he's drunk."

"That's a damn good bet," the dresser said. "I'll take a piece of it myself. I'm telling you, you needn't worry."

But Caley already had worried himself into an extreme state of jitters. He paced the back stage muttering a gibberish of invective, sweat oozing through his shoes. Ten minutes passed, and no Fields. Caley was on the point of calling the police, calling the fire department, asking that the state militia be ordered out to round up his derelict headliner, when a crash sounded in the vicinity of the stage entrance. Bert leaped and flung back the creaking door.

There was a stepwell at the entrance flanked by iron hand-rails. In this slight depression lay an object that vaguely resembled a human form. Caley stooped and his hand grasped a coat collar. "It's Fields," he cried." The no-good so-and-so of a drunken lush. Oh, my God!"

Fields' brother strolled to the door.

"Yeah, it's Bill, all right," he agreed. "Just give me a hand and we'll get him up. He'll be all right."

Together they raised the boozy, sacklike figure, which emitted low groans of protest, and practically carried it to the star's dressing room. The dresser dismissed Caley with a careless toss of a hand. "I'll prepare the body for public view," he promised.

When Caley returned, Fields was propped up in a dressing-room chair. His legs were loosely stretched out in front of him and his eyes had the fixed, glassy stare of the hopelessly inebriated. The rich burgundy red of his cheeks had been heightened by rouge and his bulbous nose had been spread even wider by some artifice of make-up. "Come on, Bill," the dresser said, shaking him vigorously. "You gotta go on."

Fields' head wagged like the head of a broken rag doll. "Can't make it," he insisted. "Juss can't make it t'night. N'sur night— when the moon's full."

Caley, himself almost on the verge of collapse, agreed that Fields couldn't go on. "The man's stiff as a hinge," he said. "He can't even walk, much less juggle."

"He can juggle," the dresser said. "Let's get him started."

They practically carried him from the dressing room to the wings. Holding him between them, for his legs were too jelly-like to support his body, they waited until the number that preceded the headline act closed out. Fields' music struck. With a tremendous effort he shook himself free of the two men who were supporting him and weaved heavily out on the stage. The instant the spotlight picked him up he miraculously regained possession of his faculties. For fifteen minutes he juggled balls, knives, plates, and other objects, seemingly a dozen at a time, without a miss. He edged over toward the wings, took a bow, stepped out of sight of the audience, and fell flat on his face. "Gimme a suck a sum'pum, quick," he pleaded. "I'm dying."

He was carried back to the dressing room and ministered to as requested. He was drunk all week and never made a miscue. Bill's brother was right. Bill was a trouper.

# CHAPTER X

# THE BOSS: GEORGE W. ALDRIDGE

FOR YEARS Rochester was dominated by the two Georges, not simultaneously, but in dovetailed succession. They were, first, George W. Aldridge, one of the most notable —or notorious—Republican bosses in the country; and, secondly, George Eastman, the Kodak tycoon, whose influence in the latter years of his career was so far-reaching that it touched virtually every phase of the city's life, and the imprint of whose hand is still deeply marked upon the community's features.

They were both men with whom newspapers (with the exception, in the case of Aldridge, of the *Herald*, which fought the Republican leader with inspired Democratic fervor) and newspaper men took few liberties. Among themselves reporters might speak cynically and with disrespect of Mr. Aldridge and Mr. Eastman, but confronted by either they were at once painfully conscious of being in the presence of the mighty.

In appearance Aldridge was much the more prepossessing of this pair. He was an enormous man with great bulky shoulders and a large head and a large, well-formed nose, and in his early manhood he affected thick sideburns that reached down to the lobes of his ears. He was smooth-faced and his lips when angry or determined curved downward like the inverted blade of a scimitar. His eyes were steely blue, and I have heard men say that they could look through a stone wall. His hands and feet were large and his legs were like concrete snubbing posts. He was called "Boss" and the appellation fitted him like a pinch-backed coat.

Years before the end of the last century he was elected to the city's three-man executive board. Through the force of his personality he quickly gained control of this agency, and from then on made it the hand tool for his political machinations.

The executive board administered the fire, police, and public works departments, and authorized appointment to every non-elective position on the city payroll. These three departments were rich mines of political patronage, and virtually gave the Aldridge-dominated executive board control of the city.

He had been mayor once, in the earlier days of his forty-year reign, and once had run as Republican candidate for the House of Representatives. He was defeated for the latter when it was shown that he had accepted a check for $1,000 from a fire insurance broker after Republican legislators had passed a bill favorable to fire insurance underwriters.

While the disclosure of the fact that he had taken this tribute largely contributed to his defeat for the last elective office he ever sought, his prestige as a leader suffered only temporary discredit. As time went on his strength grew, the scope of his operations expanded, and for many years, like a master of marionettes, who sits unseen behind the curtain, he pulled the strings that made his political puppets dance as he desired.

In the end he was vastly more than a local political figure. And because of his unwavering support of Warren Gamaliel Harding at the 1920 Republican convention, he was rewarded with the lucrative post of Collector of the Port of New York, and died in this incumbency. He had the respect of Democratic as well as Republican leaders, and in my only meeting with the late Charles Murphy, I was surprised to hear from the Tammany leader this tribute to Aldridge: "If George Aldridge lived in New York five years, we'd all be Republicans down there."

Aldridge was a man of moods, of animal appetites, of certain staunch virtues, with a genuine pride in the city he ruled that his more violent detractors never recognized. He was taciturn and considered in judgment, and once he acquired the full power that he wielded with the sweeping hand of a field marshal, he withdrew from the common throng, whose reverence and respect were perhaps enhanced by a sense of mystery inspired by this seclusion.

I saw Aldridge for the first time under curious circumstances. A periodic drinker, he would go for weeks and sometimes months as abstemious as a preacher. Then he would break out in a drunk of heroic proportions, his acts of violence sometimes leaving a trail of devastation that often ended in a special cell in the County Jail, or a hotel room guarded by a pair of favorite detectives. In neither instance, of course, would he be in legal custody, but held incarcerate merely to protect his own person and the saloons and brothels into which his wild career might lead him.

One night after work when I was still a novice in the newspaper business, I left the office with a reporter who knew the ways of the city much better than I did. He invited me into a byway saloon where, when we passed through the door, it was at once apparent that something unusual was happening.

The resort was crowded and a din like the bleacher noises at a ball game filled the place. As my eyes became accustomed to the thick smoke that lay like a cloud bank under the low ceiling I saw the cause of the demonstration.

A cleared space had been formed in the center of the bar by a semicircle of patrons. In this stood a large man whose back

was to us. He had taken the pose of a boxer and with crude,
jerky blows of his fists he was menacing a bottle that stood on
the bar. The crowd around him was hooting encouragement.

Cautiously Aldridge moved toward the bottle. His chin was
tucked under his shoulder and his fists rotated in front of him.
"God damn you, I can lick any whiskey bottle ever made,"
he cried. "I can lick it to death!" He leaped awkwardly from
the floor and lunged forward. His fist missed the bottle by
inches. The spectators bellowed their delight.

Aldridge roared like a lion. He grimaced and spat upon the
floor. He jabbed and swung and pantomimed a clinch. His chest
heaved like a bellows and his face glistened with sweat as a
result of the unaccustomed exertion.

Suddenly he dropped his hands and straightened his shoulders and stomped up and down in front of the bar. "I can suck
on the God damn bottle and lick it," he announced in a great
booming voice. "I can lick any man in this room who says I
can't."

Someone in the rear of the crowd called, "That's right, Boss.
Give it a suck and lick it."

"Yes, by God I will," he answered. He snatched the bottle
from the bar and flung back his head and guzzled deeply.

As the stinging liquor poured into his throat a crazed look
came into his bulging eyes. He brought the bottle from his lips,
then raised it high above his head and crashed it to the floor.

This violent act seemed to exhaust his energy and anger. He
gazed with idiotic bewilderment at the dark pool of liquid at
his feet and his legs buckled under him. He seemed ready to
collapse. He grasped the bar for support, and his large head
wobbled from side to side as though he had lost all muscular
control. The blood drained out of his face and left it with a
livid sickly pallor.

At that moment Bill Whaley, a detective who had rescued Aldridge from these debauches in the past, entered the resort with two patrolmen in uniform.

The uniformed men remained near the door while the detective pressed through the crowd.

"Come on, Boss, that's a good fellow," Whaley said, gently but firmly propelling Aldridge from the bar.

"I'll break you, Whaley," Aldridge roared. "I'll have your badge, you Irish bastard, sure as you're alive. Take your hands off me."

But he had no strength to resist.

"Take it easy, Boss," Whaley said. "You're all right, Boss. Take it easy."

With Whaley's entrance the barroom quieted and even the men who had given the loudest encouragement to Aldridge's performance seemed suddenly ashamed and embarrassed.

We heard later that Whaley had locked Aldridge in a room in the Powers Hotel and stood guard over him all night. He left town next day and remained away more than a week. He was always ashamed and contrite when he came out of one of his worst jags, and often made a resolution—which he never kept—to renounce liquor for life.

Whaley, an excellent police officer, who philosophically tolerated Aldridge's abuse when the latter was in his cups, apparently profited by his good offices, for in time he was advanced to the position of Captain of Detectives.

Subsequently I heard numerous stories about Aldridge's drinking escapades. But they were told mostly in whispers, for the man inspired a sort of reverence even among the "better" people of the city, who, staunchly supporting his Republican rule, easily condoned his indiscretions.

The Rochester water supply is derived from Hemlock Lake,

some distance south of the city. The lake, which is owned by the city, lies like a beautiful blue gem in the soft green cushions of gently rounded hills.

Upon one of these hills, and in such position as to afford a splendid view of the lake, Aldridge caused to be erected a delightful rustic lodge, to which he often repaired on week-ends in company with visiting political dignitaries.

On one such occasion his guest was one of the top executives of the State of New York, and a man whose drinking habits were as notorious as Aldridge's. Though the country theoretically was desiccated by Prohibition, Aldridge and his guest were well supplied with illicit beverages, which had been conveyed to their sylvan retreat by a city-owned vehicle, and for two days the pair enjoyed a thoroughgoing, old-style katzenjammer.

At that time the Collector of the Lake Port of Rochester was the late John Palace, from the near-by village of Brockport, and a former friend of Aldridge's. The men had broken over a personal, not a political issue, and the quarrel had grown into a bitter feud which each was determined to prosecute relentlessly and without quarter.

When Palace learned in some roundabout way that Aldridge and the executive were sousing it up at the lake lodge he sent snoopers from his office to attempt to obtain evidence against them for transportation of illegal beverages. If brought off his scheme would have been a notable political coup. It was defeated when a farmer in the neighborhood learned of the presence of Federal investigators and promptly reported this information to Aldridge.

With the farmer's assistance the liquor was cached in some secret recess and Aldridge and the august executive, the purple habiliments of his noble office sullied by his two-day debauch, fled ignominiously into the woods, where, darting from tree to tree like fugitives, they remained for several hours.

Some of Aldridge's mightiest carousals were staged in a well-known New York hotel in which he made his headquarters during his frequent visits to the metropolis, and more than once he converted the barroom of this hostelry into a shambles before his mad career was arrested.

The bills for these depredations were forwarded to Rochester friends, who paid them without demur, and who often commissioned one of their number, a state senator who enjoyed Aldridge's full confidence, to fetch him home or escort him to some resort for a thorough boiling out.

After one New York spree marked by unusual acts of violence, with considerable difficulty the senator managed to get Aldridge on the westbound Twentieth Century Limited, their destination French Lick Springs, Indiana. The liquor had not yet been purged from Aldridge's system and he was still moody and recalcitrant. But his faithful guardian, thinking that food would give him strength and improve his disposition, ordered a large beefsteak for him.

As the waiter laid the steak on Aldridge's plate, he deposited next to it a bottle of ketchup. Aldridge glanced up with flaming eyes.

"What's the idea of that ketchup?" he shouted angrily. "If the steak's worth a damn it don't need any of that slop," and before the senator could stay his hand he snatched up the ketchup bottle and flung it through the plate glass window of the diner, chucking the steak after it.

Before the excitement and alarm this act had created among the other diners quieted, the embarrassed senator led Aldridge from the car and locked him in his stateroom.

"But what did they do?" I asked the senator, when he told me of this incident. "The railroad people, I mean. Didn't they threaten arrest?"

The Senator smiled. "The New York Central runs through Rochester," he replied. "Would it have been politic for the New York Central to arrest Mr. Aldridge?"

Newspapermen had long anticipated an open quarrel between Aldridge and Eastman because of the latter's determination to institute a city manager form of government for Rochester. The purpose of this was to remove partisan politics from the city government and thus, it was hoped, erase the political preferment lists upon which the Aldridge machine had long subsisted.

The quarrel never materialized, perhaps because Aldridge died before the new city charter was written. Eastman believed that Aldridge would not have opposed the plan, and in fact—if not in spirit—this might have been true; for Aldridge was astute enough to know, as he once was credited with saying, that "you can't fight one hundred million dollars."

But I do know that he sent a friend of mine, a former newspaper reporter, to make a secret study of several cities in which this form of government was in force, and that the report this emissary brought back was not favorable. But after Aldridge's death Eastman's plan did go through in spite of the bitter opposition of two politicians who had attempted to share the leadership dropped from the dead hands of the old boss.

I do not believe Aldridge would have made the error committed by his successors. If the city manager plan had been adopted during his lifetime he would, I feel sure, have managed still to be the master behind the puppets on the stage, and would have accomplished this with such skill that even so dis-

celling a man as George Eastman would have been unaware of
the political wool being pulled over his eyes.

In passing it might be remarked that the ideal of a nonparti-
san city government was only briefly attained with the adoption
of Eastman's cherished plan. Today politics are rampant in the
affairs of the City Hall and the municipality is much less effi-
ciently administered than it was under Aldridge's despotic rule.

# CHAPTER XI

# THE TYCOON: GEORGE EASTMAN

ALDRIDGE'S rule of the city had continued for many years before Eastman appeared to realize that the gigantic industry he had created had become so vital a part of the community that it behooved him to give some attention to the manner in which the community was being administered.

But before this belated awakening of what might be called his civic consciousness, and before he began to interest himself in both the social and the political life of Rochester, he had passed through the first of the three stages into which his career appears to have been divided.

The first of these was the least attractive and may in part have been represented by his maxim for worldly success, later expounded to a close friend. "To get on in this world you have to be *hard, hard, hard,*" he said; adding with a faint, half-apologetic smile. "But always reserve a small corner in your heart for tenderness."

During those early years when he pursued the golden gods with the ferocious tenacity of a pit bull terrier, tenderness seemed almost excluded from his nature. Labor he exploited to the hilt. Competitors were his enemies and he fought them as such, pressing out the life of some, absorbing, rather than destroying in a finish fight, others whose properties and inventions promised to enhance the growth and productiveness of his own organization.

With wealth that would have permitted indulgence in Sybaritic luxury and license, Eastman was a bachelor whose life was neither softened by romance nor sullied by personal scandal. He was fiercely intense and at times cruelly exacting and so completely in sympathy with the doctrine of the survival of the fittest that more than once he privately advocated the use of the lethal chamber for the disposal of persons hopelessly ill, crippled, or insane. When his own life shambled down the last narrowing stretch to earthly oblivion, and senility threatened to devitalize both his physical and mental faculties, it was probably this doctrine that prompted him to end it with a self-inflicted bullet, leaving, together with a $20,000,000 residue of his fortune, the motto, "My work is done. Why wait?"

He was a man with whom intimacy was extremely difficult, and though I knew him for many years I often had the feeling that I scarcely knew him at all. But the divisions of his life were apparent even to persons whose acquaintance with him was as casual as my own, and who were sufficiently interested in the man as a human being to wonder and speculate upon those secret sources of inspiration that urged him in restless pursuit of an ideal that he may never have attained.

In his mid-years he had come to a temporary pause in his development; his nose lifted from the grindstone and he seemed to be turning and twisting eagerly to learn something of the physiognomy of the world—appraising the value and observing the shape of things passed unseen in those intense and busy years when the foundations of his great fortune were being laid. Some of these things he now desired, considering them his rightful due; and he seemed uncertain as to precisely how they might be obtained.

For one thing his social life had been greatly neglected. So he gave an enormous party to which were invited all of the gay, and brilliant, and charming people whose names appeared upon the lists compiled by the town's professional social mentors. Compared to the magnificence and Alexandrian splendors of Eastman's grand fete, all other social entertainments given in Rochester since the city was a clearing in the primeval forest paled into insignificance. It was fabulous. It was an Arabian Night. Even Rochester residents who occasionally attended the lavish soirees of New York's "400" admitted that they had never seen its equal.

Since his house was inadequate for the entertainment of the thousand guests who had been asked, two temporary buildings, each forty feet high from its scraped and polished floor to its roof, were constructed in the space between the house and garage, one a refectory, the other a dance hall. The garage itself was transformed into a wisteria garden. Here the carpenters, steam-fitters, painters, florists, all who had contributed their skills and energies to the success of the ball, and their wives, were entertained at supper and invited to co-mingle with the regular guests in the enormous dance hall.

A local caterer with a staff of scores of uniformed pages served, and bottled champagne was the drink of the evening. Eighty musicians were hidden behind a bower of cut flowers on a platform over the dance floor and a small orchestra played in the conservatory of the house. Thousands of American Beauties made the base of the floral decorations, and the walls and ceilings of the temporary buildings were hung with Southern smilax and pink and yellow wisteria. The soft immaculate white of a fresh fall of snow that lay over the broad estate was heightened by enormous floodlights, and a fairylike character was given to the scene by an artificial moon which spread its broad yellow beams from the upper branches of a great elm.

The green vines which interlaced the façade of the house were dotted with hundreds of colored lights, and the guests passed from street curb to the massive front door, which swung open behind the white pillars of the colonnade, through a marquee hedged inside with boxwood.

The guests arrived in droves, the curiosity of many of them feverishly excited by this first opportunity to inspect the great Georgian mansion, faced with tawny brick, prodigal of bath and bedrooms, halfway out East Avenue, that was then—and still is—one of the show places of the city, reverently pointed out by native Rochesterians to visiting aunts, uncles, in-laws, and firemen.

But for Eastman the experience was hardly a satisfying one. The crowd milled through the house like Cook trippers, awed by its chill perfection and vast austerity. They admired with "o-o-o-oh's" and "a-a-a-ah's" of wonder the expensive furniture and elaborate decorations. They danced to the music of musicians who relieved one another with no more interruption than the shifting members of a six-day bicycle team. They thought the Taj Mahal could be no more gorgeous; and in many instances they came away without having seen the small, pale-faced man with the steel-rimmed spectacles who had been their host.

It was not the last great party Eastman gave, but it was the last but one of such proportions. The next day he turned his house and the marquees over to five hundred children, sons and daughters of the city's "better families," who in the unrestrained exuberance of early and mid-teens committed such wanton depredations that the affair was a hush-hush scandal in Rochester for months, and Eastman, justifiably indignant, declared that that sort of thing had ended for him for all time. For now he apparently sensed that he needed social direction and advice if his entertainments were to be something more than a mob scene from *Ben Hur.*

This direction and advice came in time from Mrs. Edward W. Mulligan, wife of Eastman's personal physician. She was a woman of charm, intelligence, spirit, determined opinions, and a keen—if sometimes over-zealous—sense of civic duty; and with her husband in professional attendance upon Eastman, she became in a way the unofficial hostess of Eastman House.

And then began a series of musical entertainments that continued all through that period of Eastman's life when he seemed determined to develop those sides of his character and personality that had received little attention in his early manhood.

Although he had no ear for music, no skill with any instrument, no voice, music had such a singular fascination for him that he had installed a mammoth organ in the conservatory of his home, upon which several mornings a week a professional organist played a program of classical music while the master of the house was engaged with his toilet and breakfast. Eastman felt that the music helped to put him in readiness for his daily routine at his plant, and thus had a utilitarian purpose; and it was this conviction that very likely encouraged his later devotion to the art and inspired the huge gifts that were intended to cultivate an appreciation of music among the masses.

The working hours of his own and other industrial employees were gradually being shortened, and he was doubtful about the benefits working people might derive from this increased leisure. Often he had seen his own employees report for work after a week-end holiday in a condition that prevented them from maintaining the production standards that were virtually a passion with him, and he knew the poet's line—

*For Satan finds some mischief still*
*For idle hands to do.*

At that time Rochester had instituted a program of weekly
band concerts in the city parks, and Eastman was impressed by
the orderly and attentive attitude of the large crowds that
turned out for these entertainments. It struck him that perhaps
one way to keep the common man satisfied and contented was
to bemuse him with the Orphean strains.

But if this new manifestation of interest in music by the
masses was to continue, the people needed to be instructed in
an appreciation of music; and with this notion in mind he first
began, through a series of Sunday musicals in his home, the
musical education of his peers, and later broadened the scope of
instruction by the establishment of the Eastman School of
Music, the formation of a Philharmonic orchestra, and the
erection—at a cost of several millions of dollars—of the Eastman Theater, in which symphonic music by a sixty-piece orchestra was offered more or less gratuitously to audiences that
came primarily to see popular movies.

Eastman's Sunday musicals became something of an institution and a Rochester tradition. Fifty or sixty selected guests
were asked. The music began promptly at a set hour in late afternoon and continued for two solid hours, an organist alternating
with a string quartet or an occasional vocalist, while the audience sat stiffly on folding undertakers' chairs in the conservatory
of his home. The program was followed by a supper of simple,
excellently prepared food, served at a number of small tables
through the lower part of the house. As soon as the guests had
eaten they were expected to depart.

The high-church ritual of these affairs made them an ordeal
for all except the most devoted music lovers. Eastman believed

that the ingestion of music was not a simple process, but one
that required some pain and the strictest concentration. And
once when a woman guest of unusual temerity suggested that
there be less music and more talk and sociability, he answered
brusquely, "If these people I ask don't care about music, they
needn't come. I'm going to have music."

But the people asked continued to come, suffering, as one
irreverent Philistine explained, "the trial of over-exposure to
culture." It would have been frightening to decline. Few had
the courage to do so.

Though Eastman's guests were mostly socially eligible, they
were often unacquainted with their host. One young man,
grandson of a former president of the United States, who with
his wife lived for a short time in Rochester, one day to his
surprise received an invitation to one of these affairs.

Having little desire to attend, but knowing that the invitation
was tantamount to a royal command, the young couple drove
over to Eastman House. The curb and the winding drive that
led to the house were free of cars. Realizing that they were
several minutes ahead of the hour named on their cards they
continued for two or three miles out East Avenue, wheeled
about, and returned.

The drive was now choked with cars, for experienced guests
knew that Eastman was a stickler for punctuality and so arrived precisely on the dot. Chagrined to find that they were
late, the young people parked their car in the street and hurried
to the enormous colonnaded entranceway.

A Negro butler met them at the door and under the reproving
stares of the other members of the audience they were shown
to chairs in the conservatory, upon which they squirmed un-
happily for two hours, later to be rewarded with a supper of
baked beans, brown bread, salad, and bottled beer.

The supper over, Eastman met his departing guests in the cold grandeur of the long marble-floored corridor at the front of the house. There was no forced cordiality in his salutation. His pale face was as inscrutable as a plaster mask.

"I am Mr. So and So," the tardy guest explained, putting his own hand into that of Eastman's, which was as cool and impersonal as a glass door-knob. "Thank you so much for asking us."

The eyes of the great industrialist lighted with a glint of angry recognition. "Yes," said he in a flat voice. "You're the young man who arrived eight minutes late."

It was the first and last invitation the pair received from Eastman House.

# CHAPTER XII

# WANDERLUST

THOUGH I lacked the adventurous spirit that prompted three or four of my friends to enlist in the Canadian Army, I decided early in the second year of the first World War that I did not want to live through the greatest conflict in history knowing no more about it than I read in the cable dispatches. I asked Mr. Adams for a leave of absence, and in November 1915 sailed for England aboard the ancient American liner *St. Louis*.

It was a grim, gray, unpleasant passage. The *Lusitania* had been sunk months before. There was no certainty that Germany's war lords, more arrogant than ever as the result of the growing success of their arms in France and Belgium and their broadening submarine warfare, would continue to respect the neutrality of American shipping. There was no gaiety or entertainment aboard our ship, and the accommodations were far from luxurious. The small passenger list was comprised mostly of persons who had pressing duties or urgent business in England and France. Several of my fellow-passengers were women and children. This fact did not lessen the feeling I nurtured that I was engaged upon a perilous adventure. In moments of regret at having left the pleasant life of my home city to chance the dangers of a war in which my country was not yet a participant, I found sad consolation in speculating upon the tributes to my heroism I felt sure the Rochester papers would pay to me if our ship was sunk in mid-ocean.

I recall standing one morning with an English steward on the deserted and gale-swept deck, staring out at mountainous wintry seas. "Tomorrow at this time," he said ominously, as he glanced at his watch, "we'll be exactly at the spot where the *Lusitania* was sunk."

"But they wouldn't blow us," I said, my voice shamelessly apprehensive. "We're neutral."

"Neutral 'ell," the steward replied. "You should 'ave seen the stuff's chucked in our 'old. The bloody Jerries know you Americans are in this thing, even if you won't admit it. Too proud to fight . . ." he turned disgustedly away, and left me to my gloomy reflections.

We serpentined through St. George's Channel and landed at Liverpool ten days after we had left New York, and I went up to London with a young American with whom I had become friendly and who had been assigned to some minor position in the American consulate. Arriving at midnight at a Piccadilly hotel, we deposited our luggage, had a quick look at our double room, and returned to the street. Picking our way cautiously across the circle, the lights of which were very faint as a precaution against Zeppelins, we quickly located the Underground entrance nearest to our hotel. Twice we paced off the distance between this and the hotel, and calculated how long it would take us to reach this subterranean refuge in the event of an air raid. The distance was about a hundred yards. We decided that under the urge of falling bombs, we could cover it in nine seconds flat, somewhat better than world's record time.

In a few days my friend left to take up his duties at the consulate and establish himself in permanent quarters. Alone I roamed the unfamiliar streets and poked into places of historical interest about which I had read. I talked to soldiers returned from the trenches in Flanders and northern France, costermongers, taxi drivers too old to join the colors, waitresses in the coffee shops, poor little ladies of the evening, who seemed more multitudinous than the stars; everyone I could get to talk, trying to understand the war and the common man's attitude toward it. I liked London, and admitted that it was quite a city, even in wartime. But it wasn't Rochester. And now, like most Rochesterians, who are removed from their native bailiwick, I was eager to hear home-town talk and look upon a familiar face. Presently I telephoned Chadwick H. Moore, who was living with his charming wife in the London suburb of Hendon.

Mr. Moore was one native Rochesterian who had left Rochester to return only at distantly separated intervals. He was the oldest of ten children born to the late Mr. and Mrs. Henry J. Moore, whose great red brick homestead, with its private tennis court, its motor cars and motorcycles, its ponies and dogs, and its two acres of beautiful lawns, stood less then half a mile from the place where I was born.

To my knowledge there had never been before, and certainly since the Moore home was abandoned by its original occupants, there never has been a domestic establishment in Rochester comparable to it. It was amazing, it was unique, and even forty years ago its maintenance must have cost a fortune. I was brought up with the younger members of the family. The Moore house was my second home.

The Moore children were "public-school kids" in their early grades, though a butler answered the door and a male cook, in white jacket and white chef's cap, prepared the meals. These functionaries were only two of a staff that included a chauffeur, a gardener, an upstairs girl, a laundress, and a housekeeper.

It is curious to reflect back on it now. In the days when the Moore house attracted not only the youth of the immediate neighborhood, but boys and girls from various other sections of the city, none of us thought of the Moores as wealthy people, which of course they must have been. No one who visited there, no matter what his social position, was ever "snooted" or permitted to "snoot" anyone else. The spirit of the place was completely democratic. One needed only a friendship with one of the Moore children to enjoy its bounteous hospitality.

The Moores' Sunday night suppers made a famous tradition, and not infrequently the normal complement of the household was added to by more than a dozen youthful guests. At the tables that were laid with dainty lace doilies, glittering silver and delicate glassware, a lad who later was to become a lineman for the telephone company might be seated next to the daughter of one of the town's most socially prominent families; the young barrister who ultimately became president of the Eastman Kodak Company might break bread with an apprentice machinist. It was a great American home; in many ways the greatest I have ever known. The entertainment offered was as varied as the hospitality was genuine. I had my first auto ride in the Moores' red Rambler, my first sailing experience on the *Genesee*, a yacht owned and sailed in defense of Canada's cup by one of the older boys. I was taught to swim by the Moore's private instructor, and played my first tennis on their court.

I knew Chadwick Moore well, though he was several years my senior. He had moved from Rochester to London five or six years before the war to establish John C. Moore, Ltd., an offshoot of the family firm, John C. Moore Corp., manufacturers of patent office ledgers. He was surprised that I should be in London in wartime and insisted that I leave my hotel for his home.

From then on I saw London under the most favorable auspices. Besides his house in Hendon, Mr. Moore maintained chambers in the Temple in the City. Although the proprietor of a successful business, his tastes ran more to literature and politics than industry. He knew a number of journalists, politicians, and military men in London, to whom he was at pains to present me, and my brief talks with several of these made good newspaper copy.

Mr. Moore wanted the latest news of his family and friends in Rochester, which I enthusiastically supplied to the best of my knowledge. But to my amazement I learned that he had no desire to return to his home city, and had resolved to live out his life as a voluntary exile in England. But he knew a lot about Rochester people, we talked a great deal about them, and he told me a story about Eric, one of his younger brothers, which may bear repeating.

Eric Moore was the gayest blade of the whole Moore tribe. He was the yachtsman and the owner of the *Genesee*. His great friend since early youth was the late William (Peck) Farley, one of the most brilliant wits in Rochester and a yachtsman himself of no mean skill.

Beginning his business career in the family factory, today Eric is president of John C. Moore Corp., and the only Moore directly associated with the firm. As a young man learning the business he worked for a time in the bindery of the plant. During this period he and Farley became acquainted with a bookkeeper employed by the Sibley, Lindsay and Curr Company, one of Rochester's leading department stores. The bookkeeper was a staid and orderly man whose hobby was mathematics. Experimenting in this science, he had devised a system for beating roulette. It was one of the "progressive" systems, which seem infallible on paper, and the failure in practice of which has sent many a man to the poorhouse and not a few into hospitals for the insane.

Farley and Moore asked for a demonstration of the system, which the bookkeeper was only too willing to make. One noon when Father Moore was at lunch, the young men took the bookkeeper to a secluded corner of the bindery, where the latter set up a miniature roulette wheel. Permitting the boys to operate it, he bet pennies against them. The wheel lost consistently.

This first demonstration was followed by many others, each made during the noon hour in the Moore bindery. The bookkeeper's luck varied scarcely at all. Eric and Farley were fascinated. The bookkeeper explained to them the involved details of his system, and they bet against the wheel, which the owner now spun. As players they invariably won.

The bookkeeper's system became an obsession with the young men and they talked about it constantly. It looked like the finest get-rich-quick scheme they had ever heard of. They were sure they had a fortune in pocket if they put the system to practical use. And why not do so? So each contributed $500 to send the bookkeeper to Monte Carlo to tap the mines of Golconda. He was gone six weeks. Chadwick Moore, who had learned of the expedition Eric and Farley had financed, not desiring to disclose this knowledge to his own brother, asked Peck what the bookkeeper had brought back.

"A wonderful coat of tan," Farley answered gloomily. "He said he had a very nice vacation. I guess they must have heard about his system at Monte Carlo."

Excellent host and hostess that they were, the Chadwick Moores made no insistence that I subscribe to a fixed program of entertainment, and I was often "on the town" on my own. In Hendon I made the acquaintance of Jack Johnson, famous Negro boxer, who was featured in a Hendon music hall. Johnson had lost the world's championship to Jess Willard in Havana the preceding April, and had gone to England to escape trial in the States on a white-slavery charge.

Johnson's waistline was a great belt of loose blubber, and he was badly out of condition. It was not difficult to imagine why he had lost in Havana, for it seemed impossible that he could have acquired all that fat in the comparatively short period of seven months. He was an arresting figure, nevertheless. He wore the flashiest clothes and drove the flashiest motor car and for all his enormous girth, in the boxing ring he was as quick and graceful as a panther.

He was a good-natured, pleasant sort of giant, loving rich food, crowd adulation, and the fleshpots. We became quite good friends, and occasionally I accompanied him and two or three English chorus girls, who were members of the show, on midnight rides around Hendon. The girls seemed to have no prejudicial feeling about Johnson's color and like myself enjoyed the reflected glory of being in the company of the man who had once been heavyweight champion of the world.

On the stage Johnson's closing number was a three-round boxing exhibition with Georgie Gunthner, a Creole welterweight from America. The night Johnson introduced me to Gunthner, the Creole, instantly realizing that I was an American, asked eagerly, "Where yo' from in the States, boy?"

"I'm from Rochester, N.Y.," I answered proudly.

"Rochester, N.Y.!" Gunthner exclaimed. "Yo' know Mike Donovan?"

"Indeed I do," I said.

"When yo' go back," Gunthner said, "yo' go right away an' tell ol' Mike you see Georgie Gunthner in Lun'un. Fought Mike six rounds in Phee-le-delphia. Toughest white boy ah ever fought."

When I returned to Rochester in the spring I called on Donovan, who was serving as a hoseman with a downtown fire company. I told him Gunthner had sent his good wishes and asked to be remembered.

"I remember the black so-and-so too well," Mike said wrily. "He busted two of my ribs in that fight in Philly. Jack Blackburn broke three. I shoulda drawn the color line."

I remained in London less than two months, and shortly before Christmas sailed across the Channel to France. Before I left I visited briefly with a man who had come from my section of the state and had been sports editor for the *Rochester Herald.* I had never known him before. His short Rochester newspaper experience had ended before I started as a reporter. But I knew a good deal about him. His name was Lyman J. (Ladd) Seely, and I was told that he was having a fabulous success in London.

With his other talents, Seely had an excellent voice and had once studied in Florence, Italy. Returning to his native village of Hammondsport, which lies southeast of Rochester, in the heart of New York State's wine country, he became interested in the aeronautical experiments being made in that village by Glenn Curtiss. Curtiss had already built and flown a few airplanes. Soon he had an airplane "circus" on the road. He and Seely became close friends, and for a time Seely acted as Curtiss' press agent.

When the war broke out, Seely persuaded Curtiss to send him to England as representative of the Curtiss Company. He arrived in London in the autumn of 1914. A man of charm and social presence, he quickly made many and important contacts. One of these was with Charles M. Schwab, head of the Bethlehem Steel Company.

Curtiss' planes, which the British urgently needed, at first were slow in reaching England. But Seely let no grass grow under his feet. Soon he was representing not only Curtiss, but large American steel interests. He took a fourteen-room house in St. Alban's Road, in London's fashionable West End, acquired two Rolls Royce cars, and maintained a large country place twenty-five miles from town.

Calling at the house in St. Alban's Road, I was fascinated to observe the manner in which a former *Herald* sports editor had come on in the world. The door was opened by a footman in resplendent livery and behind him stood another servant who received my wraps. My eyes popped at the luxury of the place. I had never seen a more elaborately appointed home. Seely entertained constantly, and many men prominent in the war news were guests at his house. Reputedly he had already made two million dollars, and he was playing his new role of millionaire with grace and spirit. He greeted me in a friendly manner. When I attempted to draw him out about the "good old days" on the *Herald*, he seemed vague and preoccupied. I sensed that he did not consider them very "good old days" and that his present mode of life was much more to his fancy. I couldn't blame him for that. When our conversation halted and almost lapsed, I quickly left.

# CHAPTER XIII

# PARIS FOR OYSTERS: 1916

THOUGH I possessed a French visa, when I attempted to book Channel passage from England I was held up at every turn. France was having a difficult time of it in the early winter of 1915, and the authorities were understandably reluctant to permit sight-seeing Americans to roam at will about their country. I finally hit upon the notion of having Dr. Ralph R. Fitch, who was operating an American hospital for the French, accredit me as a hospital worker.

Dr. Fitch was a prominent Rochester orthopedic surgeon. He had married a wealthy Rochester widow who was deeply in sympathy with the French cause. Early in the war Mrs. Fitch had contributed from her own wealth and solicited funds from Rochester friends for the establishment of a hospital in a resort hotel at St. Valery-en-Caux, a Channel town some distance below Dieppe. The hospital was put in charge of her husband, a competent administrator as well as an excellent surgeon.

I had never met Dr. Fitch. But I sent him a cable message, explaining that I was a fellow Rochesterian, and asking if he would permit me to work in his hospital and arrange with the authorities to allow me to enter France. A favorable reply came in three days. Two days later I landed in Dieppe, after a stormy and nervous crossing, and proceeded at once to St. Valery-en-Caux.

The hospital was staffed by American nurses and aides, one of whom had come from Rochester, and a few French workers.

The wards were filled with French soldiers, brought in from
the fighting in the Champagne section, most of whom had
suffered wounds requiring orthopedic treatment. For the most
part the cases were not desperately serious, and the atmosphere
of the place, with Christmas coming on, was spirited and hope-
ful.

I was given no pay for my services, a condition that I
thoroughly understood before I arrived. My first job, and practically the only one I had, was in the hospital's storeroom. It was
useful but unexciting work. But in the peaceful little French
town, a long distance from the front, I felt as remote from the
war as though I were living in a village in my native western
New York.

Christmas was a happy occasion. The war was not going well
for the Allies, but the spirit of the holiday season made us
almost forget the reverses being suffered on the fighting fronts.
We decorated the wards with greenery and holly, and sprigs of
mistletoe were so placed that not only many of the young
patients, but some of the male hospital workers, received kisses
from the pretty nurses. We had American turkey, with fixin's,
for Christmas dinner, music and entertainment. It was good to
see the cheer that came to the little *poilus* as the result of our
Christmas preparations and program.

I was not unhappy but extremely restless at St. Valery-en-
Caux. I wanted something to report in my newspaper stories
besides hospital routine and the attitude of mind of the French
wounded. After New Year's I informed Dr. Fitch that I was
leaving the hospital. He was angry and told me pretty sharply
that I was acting shabbily (which was very true) in running out
on him after he had brought me to France. But I had only a
limited amount of money, and the period of my stay abroad
depended entirely upon my exchequer.

One day, early in January, with a chilly good-by from Dr. Fitch, I started for Paris. On the train I met a British Tommy who advised me that if I left the train at a certain station, somewhere near Rouen, as I recall, I might manage to get up close to the Somme sector. It was poor advice, as I learned an hour after the train had gone on without me. I was lugging my heavy suitcase through a small hamlet, hoping to engage some motorist who would carry me close to the front, when two French soldiers, directed by a fiery mustached non-com, took me summarily into custody.

I was ill equipped to argue my case. My French was limited to "*Oui, oui,*" and none of the trio appeared to know a word of English. They seemed, anyway, in no mood to parley. With the non-com shouting excitable commands and making wild gesticulations, I was rushed to a small shed-like structure, which resembled the portable election booths used in Rochester, except for the wide interstices in its siding, and shoved through the door. There was no heat in the place, no furniture except a couple of battered chairs and a small table. One of the two soldiers, rifle at shoulder, stood guard at the single entrance.

I suppose some explanation had been given to me as to why I had been placed under arrest, but I could only guess at the reason. I appealed by sign language to the guard. My reward was an icy stare. I was cold, hungry, and extremely apprehensive. After a couple of hours the guard in front of the one-man jail was changed. In another hour a second non-com of higher rank than the first appeared. He went through my suitcase with microscopic care. He then minutely examined my pockets, which so far had not been searched. He studied my passports and credentials with the expression I had seen on the faces of Rochester detectives when superficially turning through the effects of a confessed murderer. He made me open my mouth and peered intently at my teeth, and I had the un-happy feeling that any moment he would reach in and attempt to dislodge the fillings.

When he finished he shrugged, muttered something in French, and departed. There was another long wait. Then another non-com appeared. This one had a meager familiarity with my native tongue. He asked me, since my papers read that I was a hospital worker, why I had left the hospital to which I had been assigned; and, much more pointedly, why I had left it in less than three weeks after I had arrived in France. I tried to explain. He seemed to try not to understand. He left, and I was again alone, except for the rifle-bearing guard.

I knew that it was hopeless to demand the right of counsel or to remind my captors that habeas corpus was one of the noblest writs of English common law. This was war and the ordinary formalities of the law apparently had been abrogated. I was not a soldier, but a civilian. Yet it was entirely possible—even probable, I was beginning to believe—that I would be haled before a drumhead court, and made to look like a punch-board by a firing squad. At this thought my heart ran dry and I suffered grievously from palpitation of the pluck.

The short winter's day ended and night fell quickly. No light or food was brought to the place of my confinement. My fears were very active. I speculated upon many things, but mostly upon the gross stupidity that had caused me to poke my nose into someone else's war. I had never felt so utterly desolate. The stomping of the guard's feet made the only sound in the dread chill night.

It must have been close to nine o'clock and I had been thus confined for nearly twelve hours, when three soldiers, led by a youthful lieutenant, entered the shed. One of the soldiers carried a lantern.

"You weel come now," the lieutenant said, not unkindly. A
soldier picked up my suitcase. I attempted to question the lieutenant as to where I was being taken. His only reply was a light
laugh. An army motor lorry stood a few hundred feet from the
shed. The lieutenant and one of the soldiers got in beside me.
I thought surely we were bound for a place of execution. We
drove crazily over a slatternly road for ten minutes and stopped
with violent abruptness at the small railroad station where I had
left the train that morning. Far down the tracks I saw the white
swathe of an engine's headlights.

"*Paris! Quelle chance!*" the lieutenant said.

"Oh—"

He smiled and patted my arm. "Zee Mademoiselles! Cafés!" He touched the tips of his gloved fingers to his lips and
made a sweeping gesture with his hand. I felt like kissing
him.

"You weel go *tout de suite* to zee prefect of police," and he
handed me written instructions in French, which I was to present to the guard on the train, and station attendants in Paris.
The train was in now. I bade the lieutenant good-by, called
"*Merci beaucoup*," and leaped into a third-class carriage. It
smelled vilely. It was occupied by an enormous, greasy, hog-
killing sort of a man with an asthmatic snore, a small and very
restless boy, and two women, one with a large over-ripe cheese
in a hamper. It seemed to me as luxurious as the Super-Chief. I
had escaped the firing squad or the gibbet. I was free again. And
bound for Paris!

The great, gay capital of France was a slowed-down and
sombre city in the winter of 1915–16. There was no music in
the cafés, and the larger and more expensive ones were quiet
and sparsely populated.The cocottes were hungry in the streets,

pleading for coins like beggars. What gaiety you found seemed forced and meretricious.

Only the eating and drinking places of the bourgeoisie retained their popularity. Each early evening the interior of these resorts, and even the terraces outside, if the night was dry, attracted crowds of black-garbed women, soldiers on leave, and older men with sad faces and haunted eyes. There was something spectral about their fellowship. They had come together in a sort of communal desperation. Fear was upon the faces of the civilians. Fear seemed to have permeated the whole city. The soldiers alone gave what spirit remained in this capital of dread.

A few theaters were still in operation. I tried these and found the entertainment dull and lifeless. Out beyond the Champs Elysées a roller rink was still doing business. It was the nightly rendezvous of the young Americans who were driving ambulances for the French. I went there frequently in my first few weeks in Paris. It was good to meet with and talk to my fellow countrymen, who talked about the exploits of Eddie Mahan, Harvard's All-American fullback; the World Series, the shows on Broadway; who used the American idiom, and liked ham and eggs and apple pie, and were confident that if and when America entered the war we'd kick the living hell out of this stalemated trench warfare, and make the thing a moving, quickly finished fight, no holds barred.

I was stopping at the Grand Hotel. It was too large and too expensive, and I quickly learned of other places that would have better suited my tastes and pocketbook. But since my difficulty with the French military I was under strict orders not to change my residence without first gaining permission from the prefect of police to do so, and I was sure that this would involve a lot of official red tape.

A man named Perkins from Cleveland was a guest at my hotel. I met him one morning at breakfast and we became good friends. He represented an American steel company in some capacity, the nature of which he never divulged to me. He was not wallowing in new wealth like Ladd Seely in London. He was a serious, conscientious man, in his mid-thirties, who had never been in Paris before, liked little that he had seen, and talked sometimes to boring lengths about his wife and two daughters back home.

I was fond of Perkins. We were kindred spirits in our provincial attitude toward our respective home cities. He thought Cleveland was the greatest place on earth. I admitted that it might be a great city, but I was confident that as a desirable place in which to live it was second to Rochester.

We made a practice of dining together two or three times a week, tried a couple of music halls, and once went to Maxim's. Perkins had little interest in Paris night life. He was a strongly built man who had played football at some mid-Western university and been educated as a mechanical engineer. He had solid, homely virtues, but little sense of humor. He thought the morals of the French degenerate and their plumbing atrocious.

One day Perkins received a message from a friend of his named Clasgens, who represented a rival steel company. Clasgens had arrived in Paris only two days before, and he wanted to get together with his friend and friendly competitor. We three met that night for dinner. Clasgens was the exact antithesis of Perkins. He was obviously a gay blade who had eagerly anticipated his first visit to Paris. He was younger than Perkins, but three or four years my senior. He wanted to see the town and see everything. Home, Sweet Home, he told us with a grin, was all tommyrot to him. He had a wife in Pittsburgh, but now he was in Gay Paree. Oops la-la! After dinner he insisted that we accompany him on a tour of Montmartre. The notion was, I saw, distasteful to Perkins. Under persuasion he consented.

I was always puzzled by the number of slinky, rat-eyed guides who were available in Montmartre, when all other Frenchmen of similar age were in uniform. They made me wonder if commercial vice, in a city that traded so extensively in it, was a preferred occupation. They would skulk out from the façades of darkened buildings, leering and making loose-lipped promises of sinful adventures. They were a breed unto themselves and in wartime particularly detestable. One of these vermin accosted us the instant we turned into the rue Pigalle. Clasgens engaged him at once.

"Give us the full treatment," he told the fellow, adding with a drunken leer, for he had fortified himself with numerous *pousse-cafés*, "ain't had so much fun since Aunt Kate died."

In a few minutes, Perkins volubly protesting that we were making damn fools of ourselves, we entered a shuttered house to receive the showy welcome of a huge-bosomed madam in a red evening gown. She held a lighted cigar in her bejeweled fingers and the short, wiry, black hairs that sprouted from the first of her triple chins, given proper cultivation, would have qualified her for the bearded lady in a side show.

With an expansive gesture she directed us up a circular staircase, the walls of which were decorated with gilded baroque work. The stairs turned at a landing, and on the wall above this hung an enormous gilt-framed mirror, surrounded by numerous tinny-looking *objets d'art*.

The guide was in the lead, turning and beckoning us on with his hand. The eager Clasgens directly followed. Perkins and I drew up the rear.

The stairs opened immediately into a sort of a ballroom. On the floor of this a group of perhaps half a dozen girls were dancing the can-can in the nude. They looked very young, no more than in their mid-teens. The guide was waiting at the edge of the stairs until we all made our ascent. Perkins was the last to reach the ballroom floor. One look at the performance and his purpling face contorted into muscular ridges.

"You low-lived pimp," he cried. "I got a daughter the age of those girls."

With these words he brought a haymaker up from his shoe tops. It caught the guide squarely on the chin. He twirled, verily I believe, three times, like a dervish. His knees buckled. Then he seemed to spring like a diver and slide downward along the side of the stairway wall. His head banged against the frame of the great gilded mirror, which fell with a terrific crash, the glass spouted out in a thousand glistening shards. And then all of the other ornaments tumbled upon the crumpled figure of the guide, whose head—which miraculously escaped more than superficial cuts—appeared through the mirror's flimsy backboard, for all the world like the head of a man in a cabinet bath. Only this head was deathlike in sleep.

The thing was done in a twinkling. But the original commotion was as nothing compared to the pandemonium that followed. The madam's screams were as blood-curdling as those of a horse in a burning stable. The can-can dancers had retreated, but now were re-appearing, each partly covered with some piece of apparel, as though fearful to face doomsday unclad.

The spectators, perhaps a dozen in number, had rushed to the stairway, adding the cries and wild gesticulations of the excitable French to chaos that confounded chaos. Other inmates of the house arrived from various quarters to heighten the mad cacophony of wails and terrible incriminations.

And now someone had flung up a window and screamed, I

suppose, what in French is equivalent to "Police!" It was a
bawdyhouse we were in, but the status of such in Paris guaran-
teed rights that are inviolate. It was the right of no outraged
steel salesman from America to bop a pimp on the chin and
create a disturbance worse than a Zeppelin raid.

Two, then two more, then half a dozen gendarmes, with their
comic-opera swords, burst through the front door. The huge-
bosomed madam's anger and outrage were magnificent. She
was a Vesuvian eruption of denunciation, protest, and demands
for redress, her words as burning hot as lava.

Calmed by the violent venting of his emotions, Perkins stepped over and around the debris on the stairs, and the guide's
death-head, and stood in a corner of the lower hall nursing a
bruised fist. He was quiet, but alert for any attempt at reprisal,
which I felt sure he would have dealt with competently. The
thick, jerking forefinger of the madam indicated the culprit.
The gabbling police surrounded him.

Having experienced one encounter with French authorities,
I held my tongue and made myself as inconspicuous as possible.
Not so Clasgens. Though his evening had been spoiled by the
impetuosity of his friend, he was loyal to the core. As the gendarmes ganged up on Perkins, he leaped among them.

"No, wait a minute—wait a minute," he exhorted belligerently, his attitude understandable to the police, if his words
were not. "There's going to be no trouble here (as though there
weren't plenty already), and if there is, by God, there'll be a
couple of dead frogs. It was all a mistake. My pal momentarily
forgot himself."

So far no hand had been laid upon Perkins, and that was
fortunate for several reasons. But the police were stern. Near
murder had been done. You could see that by looking at the
guide, not even a hair of whose head had yet come to life. This

was a matter for investigation by higher authorities. Would we come peacefully? Or under duress, in the wagon? The police and Clasgens held a parley. I kept out of it, knowing my French would add nothing constructive, and Perkins remained moodily silent. In the end it was decided that we would go.

"But they won't put any cuffs on me," Perkins announced, with a sudden return of spirit. "No cuffs. I won't stand that. Not from those funny-paper cops."

So he went without cuffs. The three of us made a neat, compact little trio, gendarmes to the right of us, gendarmes to the left of us, and one each fore and aft. The huge-bosomed madam wailed in our wake. The guide, who had been doused externally with water, and internally with cognac, was led by two male attendants of the resort. He stumbled along in a sort of trance, one hand pressed to his swollen jaw.

We reached a near-by station house. It was midnight now. The French police official before whom we were arraigned, who looked like a younger Papa Foch, spoke no English. None of us spoke workable French. The bilingual conference was noisy but ineffective. Perkins became sullen and obdurate.

"T'hell with it," he exclaimed angrily. "If they're going to lock us up, let 'em lock us up. I never wanted to come to this God damn country anyway. But if they want any steel for their plants, they better get on the phone and get someone to spring us. Wonder if these French jails have inside plumbing?"

Clasgens, cold sober now, showed his card to the official "Steel, steel, steel," he said, and pointed to the name of the company he represented. Neither his words nor the name on the card impressed the official. It looked as though we would do a night in stir.

Then Perkins brought some credentials from his pocket. On one of these was the name of the head of a French purchasing commission. With patient pantomime he presently persuaded the police official to telephone to this man. There was a long phone confab, at the end of which the official's attitude changed markedly. He motioned us to chairs and told the still screaming madam to shush down. In an hour a military motor drew up at the station house. An officer who spoke English entered, followed by an aide. The officer explained that he represented the member of the purchasing commission who had been phoned. And how, please, might he be of service?

Clasgens did the talking. He was eloquent in his own tongue. It required a noble effort on my part to keep from laughing outright. He and his friend, Monsieur Perkins, "and this distinguished American journalist"—and he pointed to me—had been out for a stroll along the boulevards. The Colonel—I am sure the young officer was no more than a lieutenant—knew, of course, the vital mission upon which Monsieur Clasgens and Monsieur Perkins were engaged. It was steel that they were bringing to France; steel that was desperately needed by the French munitions works.

Well, it seemed, that in course of this stroll, one of our party had expressed a desire for oysters. Unfamiliar with Paris, Clasgens himself asked this young man—pointing to the guide—where oysters might be obtained. The young man said he knew of a lovely oyster parlor. And where had they ended? Not in an oyster parlor, but in a house of ill fame. He shook his head sadly, and rubbed a hand over his eyes, as though they were again exposed to the wicked spectacle of six nude dancing girls.

"My friend, Monsieur Perkins, is a deacon in his church in Cleveland. He, like the rest of us, is a good God-fearing man. We were outraged to learn of the ruse that had been played upon us. My friend, Monsieur Perkins, lost his head."

To tell it now seems flat and dull. To have heard Clasgens

in his plea to the young officer was convincing proof that he had mistaken his vocation, and that the stage, the pulpit, or the courts of justice should have commanded his talents.

The young officer wheeled sternly on the police official, and sputtered briefly in French. What he said, of course, we never knew. But we were bowed out of the station house and returned to the street. The young officer solicitously asked if he might carry us to our respective hotels. We thanked him, but declined his invitation.

In the next block we hailed a taxi and rode back to the Boulevard des Italiens.

"We'll have to get a new guide, and find another place tomorrow night," Clasgens said.

"You'll find it alone. I'll be in my hotel room, writing to the family," Perkins answered. He rubbed the knuckles of his right fist reflectively. "Cripes, did you see that pimp hit things? He was like a bowling ball making a strike. Cripes, I guess I don't know my own strength."

In the spring of 1916 I returned to Rochester and my job on the *Democrat and Chronicle*. My experiences abroad had hardly been sensational. However, one day toward the end of my stay in France I did pass a few hours in the trenches in the Boulogne sector. The trip was arranged for me through the good offices of a couple of friendly American newspaper men, who had been accredited to the French Army. The front was extremely quiet. What little action there was was confined to a desultory interchange of artillery fire, the German shells flying high over our heads and landing far behind the trenches through which I was being escorted.

I made a good deal of this expedition in the newspaper story I wrote home about it. When I returned to Rochester I found that many people were impressed by my experiences, and that I was looked upon as a sort of expert on the war. This pleased my vanity, and I am afraid inspired me to tell things that were more in the nature of fancy than fact. I had become not unlike some of the very precious, very special correspondents of the last war, who filled their copy with *I, I, I's*, neglecting the struggle they had been assigned to write about to describe their personal experiences, and whose stuff might have been printed under the appropriate title, "The Rover Boys Go to War."

Soon I settled back into my normal Rochester routine, and found it extremely pleasant. I am not by nature a traveler. I have never suffered greatly from wanderlust. Rochester had a particular appeal to me that spring and I was grateful that I had been permitted to return to its peace and security after several months in two countries pinched and terribly torn by war.

But there was a growing feel in the air, which at first I attempted to ignore, that the United States could not permanently avoid becoming involved in the European struggle. The small Channel steamer *Sussex*, in which I had crossed from England to France, had been sunk with a loss of twenty American lives. Though this was in no wise comparable to the tragic total run up at the time the *Lusitania* was torpedoed, it was an outrage that gave added support to the argument for American intervention. President Wilson was being savagely attacked for his policy of delay, appeasement, and note writing. I soon sensed that if the war was not quickly over, and there seemed little likelihood that it would be, I would probably return to France in the garb of an American soldier. Yet nearly a year passed before we declared war. Another year passed before I was again in France. I remained there nearly twelve months.

# CHAPTER XIV

# HOME AGAIN

U PON MY discharge from the Army I did not return to the *Democrat and Chronicle*. My range of experience had been widened by two trips abroad and I felt that I was destined for greater things. New York seemed the place for a newspaper man with soaring ambitions, and I was scarcely out of uniform before I was knocking at the door of the *New York Tribune*.

The *Tribune* had no opening. It owed its first obligation to employees who had left the paper to join the armed forces, and in 1919 these men were returning in droves. The city editor questioned me about my experiences, took my name, and told me to keep in touch with him. I tried other metropolitan dailies with similar results. Still determined not to resume my newspaper career in Rochester, I obtained a job as rewrite man for the *Detroit Free Press*. I was aided in this by Will Richards, who had joined the *Free Press* staff shortly before the war, and had become its star reporter, and an ultimate sharer of the Pulitzer Prize for Journalism.

Richards and I lived together in a small apartment. I enjoyed our personal association but soon found, as so many native Rochesterians have discovered, that I was neither happy nor contented outside of the borders of my home town. In the end I applied by letter to Louis M. Antisdale, publisher and editor of the *Rochester Herald*, for a position on that paper. When my application was accepted I returned to Rochester.

Rochester had five daily newspapers during the first decade and a half of the century. Three of these were printed in the afternoon. The *Herald*, avowedly independent, but actually a strong supporter of the Democratic Party, competed in the morning field with the *Democrat and Chronicle*.

Antisdale possessed unusual newspaper abilities and he was an editorial writer of the first rank. The paper was not a great financial success, and in the later years of its career only the personality, character, and talents of its editor and publisher kept it afloat in an increasingly difficult sea of newspaper competition. Yet in many ways it was an excellent newspaper and a good antidote for the hidebound Republicanism of the *Democrat and Chronicle*, to which it furnished spirited editorial competition.

Antisdale lampooned the sacred cows of the city unabashedly and with vigor and style. His brilliant pen constantly attacked the powerful Republican machine and the despotism of its leader, George W. Aldridge; and the cartoons of John Scott Clubb, an astute political observer and an outstanding draughtsman, perfectly complemented Antisdale's scorching editorials. Antisdale was at his best when he was bitter and vitriolic. But Clubb's cartoons were inherently good-humored, and even Aldridge, whom they most frequently caricatured, derived considerable amusement from them.

Like all other cities in America, Rochester shared in the daffiness and license that marked the decade that began shortly after World War I and ended in the thunderous crash in late October 1929, when Wall Street laid its gigantic egg. It was the age of the flapper and Flaming Youth, the blind pig, atrocious manners, the hip flask, the bootlegger, and wild speculations in stocks. It changed the social habits of the entire race, encouraged disrespect for the laws of the land and the constitutional authority of the courts, and elevated mugs, murderers, and swindling millionaires to a sort of greatness.

Participating in the Corybantic frenzy of the day, because of the nature of their work, newspaper reporters were also objective observers of what history may report as the greatest social revolution in American life during the twentieth century. Indeed in a way they were the minor historians of this transformation and violent dislocation. They heard much that they could not prove and saw much that they could not print. But they penetrated deeply into the human midden heap the war had stirred and got the smell of it up their nostrils and the taste of it in their mouths and whooped it up like the Cherokees most Americans had become during one of the craziest periods in the entire history of the country.

The *Herald* at this time was a lively, alert, and enterprising newspaper that quite precisely reflected the spirit of the times. It was vigorously edited by its able publisher, and staffed for the most part by young people of keen awareness, who displayed a finer esprit de corps and more genuine loyalty to their paper than I have observed in the twenty years I have continued in newspaper work since the *Herald's* demise.

Antisdale kept on top of the news and campaigned vigorously for political and social reforms. There was no pussyfooting in his editorial policies, and he printed the news without fear or favor. He was caustic, severe, and fear-inspiring. But he had a genuine interest in the welfare of his employees, and his reporters knew that he would staunchly support them against all outside complaints, once convinced that they had acted properly in the pursuit of their duties. This virtue, not as common as it should be among editors and publishers, was one that I came to appreciate very early in my association with "Uncle Louie," as Antisdale was called by his employees.

During the brief period when the Mullan-Gage Act encumbered state agents of the law with the responsibility of enforcing the Eighteenth Amendment, the magistrate's court, which I daily covered, each morning was cluttered with cases of speakeasy proprietors whose resorts had been raided by local police.

The arraignment of these offenders in a local court gave them greater prominence than if they had been haled before a Federal judge in the obscure confines of the Federal Building, and usually several members of the Committee of Twenty-Five, a blue-nosed junto dedicated to the cause of Prohibition, were on hand to see that there was no monkey business or out-of-court fixing.

One of the most active and fanatical members of this committee was a clergyman of some prominence who seemed to believe that the sale of a pint of bathtub gin was a crime comparable to setting fire to an orphan asylum. Either utterly ignorant or completely disdainful of the rules of evidence, he believed that the mere arrest of a man on a charge of traffic in illegal beverages conclusively established the prisoner's guilt, and he was intolerant of any delay in the pronouncement and execution of sentence.

When court convened each morning the worthy reverend occupied a seat in the front row of the spectators' benches. At its adjournment he insisted upon a detailed explanation from the judge if the latter had decided that the evidence against some liquor law violator was insufficient to hold him for further examination. He was a self-appointed watchdog of the court and a pest to court clerks and reporters.

I myself had had two or three brief passages at arms with the clergyman as the result of his imperious demand that I give first prominence to Prohibition cases when the real news of the session might have been made by an alleged murder or arsonist, or Black Tom, the Cat, a porch climber with a list of burglaries behind him that read like a street directory. But one morning the minister came to me with a new appeal.

It seemed that among the prisoners called to the bar were two of his own parishioners, each of whom was charged with grand larceny and forgery in a matter involving the theft of several suits of clothing from one merchant and the passing of forged checks to the total amount of more than $300 on another.

"There is nothing vicious about these young men," the clergyman said to me. "Their trouble is that they unfortunately have fallen among bad companions. The clothing they have— er—taken will be returned. The merchant who cashed their checks will be fully reimbursed. I want no mention of this in your newspaper. These poor lads—" and tears filled the good brother's eyes.

I was surprised that a man who often insisted that liquor violators expiate their sins by long penitentiary sentences should display such commiseration for two young men who he virtu- ally admitted were guilty of what seemed to me the greater crimes of larceny and forgery. But I explained mildly that it was my duty at least to make mention of the fact that the pair had been arraigned.

"It isn't your duty to do anything of the kind," the clergyman insisted angrily. "Human values are involved here. An irrepa- rable wrong will be done these young men if the stigma of theft and forgery is put upon them. They will never go to trial. This matter will be adjusted out of court."

I did not argue the issue. But in my report of the day's court proceedings I told the story of the clergyman's parishioners, and irked by his presumptuous attitude, added with malice prepense, "The arraignment of the two young men on charges of grand larceny and forgery was marked by a curious reversal of form on the part of the Rev. Mr. So and So. Ordinarily Mr. So and So is in court to insist that all violators of the Eighteenth Amendment be severely and summarily punished. Yesterday he pleaded clemency for his parishioners and told this reporter that their cases would never go to trial, since the clothing they are alleged to have stolen is to be returned and the merchants who cashed the checks they are alleged to have forged is to receive full restitution."

I had scarcely entered the pressroom adjacent to the court chambers next morning when the clergyman descended upon me with blood in his eye. "Young man," he shouted dramatically, a monitory forefinger wagging in my face, "You'll rue this day. I've been trying to contact your employer. He isn't yet available. When I reach him, you'll be out of a job."

My own temper a little out of hand at this point, for the first time in my life I spoke disrespectfully to a wearer of the cloth. "Aw, go to hell," I said, and slammed the pressroom door.

Though I had not been the least alarmed by the clergyman's absurd threat, I instantly regretted the manner in which I had replied to it, and suffered growing pangs of conscience and apprehension. I knew that the Committee of Twenty-Five enjoyed the support of the entire reform element in the city, and I was fearful as to how my new employer would react to the report I was sure he would receive of the unseemly and blasphemous manner in which I had spoken to a prominent ecclesiastic.

When court adjourned I returned to the *Herald*'s city room. It was then shortly after noon and Antisdale had entered his office for the first time. I was trying to concentrate upon my work when the copy boy whispered that Uncle Louie wanted to see me. With considerable trepidation I presented myself at his desk.

"Clune," said he, "my wife has been badgered all morning with telephone calls from Rev. So and So and other members of the Committee of Twenty-Five. She didn't waken me—I never answer the telephone before noon—but she said all of these calls concerned you and something you had written in today's police court column. What—"

He was interrupted by the ringing of his desk telephone.

"Yes—yes," he said, "this is Mr. Antisdale."

The voice on the other end of the wire was high and rasping and angry, and the tone quality was such that I could hear each word as distinctly as though the receiver were at my own ear. It was my friend the clergyman. My fears leaped. He related all of the details of our encounter, tore my character to shreds, and as Antisdale listened without a word of interruption, ended with the damning charge, "That loafer, Clune, told me—*told me to go to hell!*"

There was a momentary pause. Then Uncle Louie cleared his throat and made reply.

He began in temperate tones and with a precise choice of words. But as he got through his prelude and into the body of his speech and presently into the peroration, his voice rose to a thundering crescendo and his style and manner seemed to me as magnificent as Demosthenes' denunciation of Philip.

"Mr. So and So," he concluded rhetorically, "the *Rochester Herald* is part of that great, sacred, and glorious institution, the free press of America. It is the defender of the oppressed, the champion of human rights, the trumpeter of justice. I bitterly resent your mean, unworthy, pettyfogging attempt to divert it from its noble purpose. By your own admission you virtually ordered a reporter for the *Herald* not to print a piece of legiti-

mate news. That I consider a gross affront, an egregious imperti-
nence. Only the fact that you are a wearer of the cloth
constrains me from repeating what you claim Clune said to you
and telling you to"—Uncle Louie sputtered for a moment, and
his free hand plucked sharply at the gray hairs of his short
mustache—"to—to go chase yourself! You are never again to
annoy me with a complaint of this character!" and he slammed
the receiver on the hook.

I waited. Antisdale's face was flushed by the agitation of his
emotions and verbal exertions. He looked up, expelled a
"pooh!" through his lips, and said: "Better go back to your
work, son," and as I turned, with a grateful "Yes, sir," he added:
"I'd be a little careful in the choice of my language when dealing with the clergy, even when they're wrong and you're in the
right. Being in the right should give you the superior dignity."

I was whistling as I returned to my typewriter and my step
was as light and airy as a dancer's. Two years later, when Harry
Gray, editor of Hearst's *Journal-American*, offered me a flatter-
ing salary increase to join the staff of that publication, I recalled
the gallant manner in which Mr. Antisdale had defended me
against the clergyman's charges and had no difficulty in decid-
ing that I preferred to remain on the *Herald.*

There were other subsequent incidents that strengthened
my faith in Antisdale and increased my loyalty to an employer
who well merited it. One of these concerned the late Thomas
F. Swanton, president of the now defunct National Bank of
Commerce, a close friend of the publisher and a man to whom
he was financially obligated.

Swanton was a character in banking circles and a veritable
Czar in his own organization. Although he wore handsomely
tailored clothes and lived lavishly, the aura of ultra respecta-

bility—as evidenced by a gold-headed cane, a silk topper, and a Prince Albert—that radiates around the bank president of legend and tradition, was entirely lacking in him. He was brusque often to the point of coarseness; a lover of strong waters, a middle-aged playboy, a daring plunger, picturesque, as hard-boiled in manner and speech as a dock hand.

Returning from a party one afternoon with a particularly edgy temper, Swanton engaged in a sharp altercation with his chauffeur and the angry words exchanged between the two men quickly led to a flurry of blows. The banker was a stocky, barrel-chested man with an over-larded abdomen. He was not lacking in physical courage, but he was in no condition for violent combat. After a brief scuffle in his backyard drive, the chauffeur grabbed him by the scruff of the neck and the seat of the pants and bum-rushed him into the garage, slamming and locking the door after him.

Purple with rage at this affront to his dignity, Swanton stormed and shrieked like a madman. Desperate to escape, he flung up one of the narrow windows of the garage and attempted to squeeze his considerable girth through its inadequate opening. To facilitate this effort he had mounted to the top of a wooden box. After he had thrust his head and shoulders through the window, the box slipped from his feet, further egress was stymied by his protuberant abdomen, and he was left in the unseemly position of a boy laid over a barrel.

Standing outside, the chauffeur taunted him with disparaging words and occasionally added injury to insult by sharply rapping the banker's large head with his knuckles; and all this time Swanton rent the chaste air of the fashionable neighborhood in which he lived with fierce threats and incriminations, couched in language of the deepest blue, until the aroused neighbors sent a call for the police.

The minions of the law arrived with sirens wailing. A crowd that believed a homicide was being done was attracted to the scene. The police unlocked the garage door and dislodged the kicking, squirming banker from the window casing. Resorting to everything except hypodermic injections and the Tibetan devil dance in an unsuccessful effort to quiet him, they led him screaming into the house. The chauffeur was questioned, but not held, and a brief routine report of the police call was written in the complaint book of an outlying precinct station.

The police apparently considered the matter too trivial to pass on to the newspapers. But in the course of my tour of the police beat I discovered the report in the complaint book, questioned the officers who had responded to the call, and with some fictional license, embroidered out of the incident a humorous yarn of which I was not a little proud and which even elicited a belly laugh from the city editor.

"But I can't run this," he said helplessly. "It would make Tom Swanton the laughing stock of town. You know as well as I, Swanton and the boss are pals. Swanton helped Uncle Louie clean up on that Eastman stock deal."

Fearful of this, I was nevertheless deeply disappointed. I had given the best I had to the story on the long chance that it might get by. But I supposed a newspaper publisher, like any other man with a sense of appreciation, could hardly be expected to pillory a friend who had helped him turn a profitable stock transaction.

"Well, okay," I said resignedly. "But it's news and I wrote it. Why don't you show it to the boss?"

"By God, I'll do that," the city editor said suddenly. "After all, I'm not supposed to know about Uncle Louie's deals with Swanton. If he throws it out, that's his business."

I thought no more about the matter. But the next day, to my

surprise and delight, the story appeared under a two-column head on the first page of local news. Not a word had been deleted.

Antisdale was in the city room when I arrived that afternoon, and I heard the city editor call to him. "You're wanted on my phone, Mr. Antisdale," he said; and added, with a surreptitious wink at me. "The party seems sort of excited."

"Oh, it's you, Tom," Antisdale said, and then he was silent for some time. He had no opportunity to speak. The loud and excessively profane voice on the other end of the line was damning the *Herald* from Hell to Harlem and wondering what in the name of Jesus H. Christ Antisdale was thinking of to permit such a story to be printed. Holding the receiver an inch from his ears, to save his ear drums, Uncle Louie plucked at his mustache, and his eyes twinkled with amusement. He was thoroughly enjoying Swanton's violent diatribe. Presently he edged in a word of his own.

"Well, you know, Tom, I sit here twelve hours a day, but I can't see everything that goes into the paper," he said in a tone intended to soothe the savage breast. "It won't happen again. And do try to keep on good terms with your chauffeur."

He turned from the telephone and the nearest thing to a grin I ever saw him display played for a moment over his features.

~~~~~~~~~~~~~~~~~~~~~~~~~~~~~~~~~~~~~~~~~~~~~~~~~~~~~~~~~~~~~~~~~~~~~~

# CHAPTER XV

# UNCLE LOUIE'S HERALD

I HAD A fine time working for the *Herald*. It was good to be back in my home town, the scenes of which were familiar to me, where the people were friendly and accessible, and in the employment of a publisher uninhibited by the taboos I had found it necessary to respect while working for the *Democrat and Chronicle* under the regime of Matthews and Pond.

Antisdale's first purpose was to print the news, no matter whom it affected. Because of his determined prosecution of this policy he and the *Herald* were often in hot water. But there were no libel suits, only threats of libel suits, and while the paper had its bitter enemies, these were vastly outnumbered by loyal friends and a reading audience that preferred its lively news reports and controversial editorials to the hidebound conservatism of the *Democrat and Chronicle*.

The spirit of the *Herald*'s city room was kept at high pitch partly because of the youth, freshness, and enthusiasm of the people who worked there. Several of the reporters had better than average talents; the most notable of these was George S. Brooks, who had originated on a farm in Wyoming County, forty miles south of Rochester. Before the war he had matriculated at the University of Rochester, but was dismissed early in his freshman year because of his failure to make passing grades in English. During the war he served in France as a mule skinner with a supply train, and returned to obtain a job as reporter for the daily paper in Batavia, N.Y., a city of 18,000 halfway between Rochester and Buffalo.

Brooks could butcher a hog, quarter a beef, castrate a cock, or turn his hand creditably to almost any task of husbandry. But his interests were entirely urban; and despite his back country youth and training, he had a great deal of erudition, a fine writing style, a keen wit, and an inordinate zest for newspaper work.

He was a lover of good food and good drink, but his appearance belied his tastes. He wore scholarly-looking spectacles and clothes of such modest design that I sometimes believed they were fashioned with the deliberate intent of deception; and his whole aspect was so ministerial that his friends on the police force fixed upon him the entirely inappropriate appellation of "Bishop."

Brooks remained on the *Herald* only a few years, but during this time a friendship developed between him and me that has continued ever since. He left first to take the editorship of *McClure's Magazine*, which enjoyed a brief revival under the auspices of its original founder, S. S. McClure; then to write the brilliant Broadway play, *Spread Eagle*, in collaboration with Walter B. Lister, and successively to hire out as a Hollywood scenarist and make a fine success of slick-paper fiction.

To Brooks city newspaper work was the rich fulfillment of his dreams and hopes; never have I known a young man to come into the business with more energy, enterprise, and eagerness. For a time he helped on the police run and later was regularly given this assignment. Nothing could have pleased him more. He delighted in his association with harness bulls and detectives and was constantly in their company. Each working day was a new and shining adventure which he played out fully to the last exciting minute.

He bubbled over with police stories. Those that lacked the support of facts required by the *Herald* he began to write as fiction. He was an indefatigable worker. His daily stint ended at midnight; I worked mostly during the daytime hours, and at the close of court each morning I proceeded directly to the city room. It would be deserted at that hour except for Brooks. The *Herald* office was not elaborately equipped, and Brooks's typewriter reposed upon a sewing machine stand. The machine itself of course was gone, but the pedals remained, and these Brooks pumped vigorously as his fingers flew over the typewriter keys intent upon the composition of some fictional police adventure.

He was selling occasionally to the pulp magazines, as I also was doing. Then one day we contrived a collaborated piece of fiction which, upon its completion, we promptly mailed to *The Saturday Evening Post*. It came winging back like a homing pigeon. Undaunted, we remailed it to *Collier's* and in two weeks were rewarded with a magnificent check for $400.

It was manna from the gods and called for a Lucullan celebration. Brooks was something of an epicure, with at least an empirical knowledge of bootleg wines, and all details for the fiesta were left in his charge. The dinner was a roaring success. It was held in Powers Hotel and the waiters, whom Brooks had prodigally fed before the guests took their places at the festive board, were as attentive as Nubian slaves at the banquet of a Roman emperor. George and I were millionaires for the night and those who enjoyed our bounteous hospitality clamorously agreed that we were also jolly good fellows. And we promised that the occasion was not to be the last of its kind.

"This fiction racket's a cinch," we told one another confidently. "Now that we know the pattern, the rest will be a cakewalk." And straightway we organized a fiction factory.

Our first move, following the banquet, was to rent a down-town office equipped with typewriters, tables, chairs, and a steel cabinet for the filing of research material and plot germs which we believed would develop like hothouse bulbs. We planned a factory schedule. I arrived at the office at seven o'clock each morning and devoted three hours to creative labors before taking over what now seemed to me the prosaic duties of the magistrate's court. Brooks relieved me at that time and continued until it was necessary for him to report in the *Herald* city room. Twice a week we held a "story conference."

We worked swiftly and adhered faithfully to the routine we had fixed for ourselves. Usually we kept two stories going simul-taneously, one partner turning his first draft over to the other for revision, and vice versa. We were shooting for quantitative production, and our output was enormous. But unfortunately, after our first effort, nothing that we wrote was found accept-able to the high-paying slicks, and when we rather patronizingly submitted our rejects to the pulps, they too found them want-ing. We tinkered, rewrote, ponderously deliberated, and fell behind in our office rent. After three or four months without a sale we disbanded the partnership, closed the office, and in a chastened spirit turned to the study of the works of Guy de Maupassant, convinced that there was still something we didn't know about the short story.

Glenny Harris was one of the younger members of the *Herald* staff. Unlike Brooks, he possessed no unusual newspaper talents. Indeed, he was singularly unfitted by training, inspiration, or experience for the job of reporter, and how he continued for two years on the *Herald* payroll has always been a mystery to me. I suspect, though, that he had ingratiated himself into the city editor's favor at a time when the staff was undermanned and that the city editor, liking Glenny—as almost everyone who knew him did—was so beguiled by his charm and fascinated by his Rabelaisian escapades that he hadn't the heart to fire him.

Though he was married at the time, he carried no pocket photograph of the little woman, and I am sure he considered his connubial covenant a great error. His curiosity about women was insatiable; in affairs of the heart he was as loose-gaited as a jackrabbit, and he seemed to have no sense whatever of marital fidelity.

The son of a prosperous small-town businessman, he had been educated in a fashionable preparatory school, where he had been thoroughly indoctrinated in the theory that "manners make the man," and drunk or sober I never heard him utter an improper word or display anything except the most punctilious deportment. He was tall, well-built, beautifully groomed and carefully dressed, with a red, fleshy, well-constructed face, and large, brown, incongruously innocent eyes that protruded so far from their sockets they might almost have been knocked off with a stick.

He had engaged in various occupations, and once had had a reasonably profitable business of his own, before he showed up in the *Herald* office, and he had inherited a modest patrimony at the time of his father's death. Proceeding west on a transcontinental luxury train, he had become enamored of a fair passenger bound for San Francisco, had persuaded her to take in the beauties of Lake Louise, and the pair had remained there throughout the season, gazing at the mountainous prospect and reading Shelley in bed. "It was strange," Glenny said, with the embarrassed laugh and apologetic shake of his head that accompanied every admission of wrongdoing, "how much time we passed in bed. The beds in that hotel were wonderful."

But the lady was a luxury, and an expensive one, and to maintain her in her accustomed manner Harris in time found it necessary to wire a New York broker instructions to sell some of the holdings that had come to him through his father's estate. This order was frequently repeated, with the result that by the time the Lake Louise season closed most of his fortune was expended in the prosecution of his love, and he bade the lady a fond adieu and returned East in a sadly depleted condition.

"It was worth it," he admitted. "We had a splendid season. I learned most of Shelley's *Adonais* and all of the *Ode to the West Wind*. My friend was a bear for Shelley. And I learned other things that weren't in the book."

What persuaded Harris to attempt newspaper work I do not know, though he occasionally half explained that he had "always wanted to write." But he made no effort along these lines outside of the newspaper shop, and did very little writing in it. He did possess some slight skill at ferreting out certain kinds of news, but his stories were so poorly written that they needed a good deal of revamping by the copy desk. I think he was mostly attracted to the business by the freedom he believed reporters enjoyed, and the hours he wangled from his working day usually were passed in the company of some fair charmer in a cozy speakeasy.

Midnight was the hour at which *Herald* reporters knocked off work, and Glenny customarily made his second nightly appearance thirty minutes before quitting time. After languishing for hours in some illegal pub, he would bound off the elevator, and stride briskly across the city room, as though he had a red hot story that would need swift handling to beat the deadline. He would strip off his coat, roll up his sleeves, sidle over to the city editor, and whisper apologetically into his ear, "Chet, that thing you sent me on didn't quite pan out," and for the next half hour he would industriously preside over the hand-operated dumb-waiter in which copy was lowered to the composing room.

The city editor rarely questioned him as to why the story to which he had been assigned "didn't quite pan out," for it was never a matter of first importance, and at that hour space was so tight that only the liveliest spot news could be fitted into it.

Harris was an inveterate playboy, to employ a popular term of the day, and his companions were mostly a fast and raffish crowd of get-rich-quick-Charlies, who made the welkin ring, not only on Saturday, but every night of the week, and who carried Glenny along as a sort of remittance man, for his salary was entirely inadequate to meet the Dionysian indulgences of his friends. But they found him charming and entertaining and perhaps felt that his faultless manners lent a stamp of class to their own ribald and rowdy goings-on.

He was devoted for a time to a pretty hairdresser whom he showered with attentions. In so doing he excited the vindictive temper of his wife, who threatened to "throw acid in that Madeline's face the first time I see you with her." This dire threat was never carried out. Tiring presently of her husband's infidelities, one day Mrs. Harris packed up and left, and then Glenny really was on his own, and made the most of his new freedom.

I recall one New Year's Eve when he was starting out for a celebration and slipped on the icy sidewalk and seriously injured one of his ankles. The pain was too great to permit him to rest his weight upon the injured member, and against my earnest advice that he see a doctor rather than go to a party he insisted that I call a cab, into which the driver and I bodily lifted him. His ankle had already swollen to twice its normal size, but with pain-twisted lips he announced gallantly, "Madeline expects me. A Harris never failed his woman."

Propped up on a divan, he found relief from pain in the flowing bowl, remained until all hours, and next day failed to appear for work. That afternoon I called at the place where he lived. It was a small stone-fronted apartment hotel in a downtown neighborhood that was largely populated by ladies of questionable morals. It was owned and operated by a middle-aged widow with dyed blonde hair, an hour-glass figure, and a general aspect of shabby elegance. She told me that she had removed "poor, dear Glenny" into her own apartment, where she could give him "motherly attention," and there I found him ensconced in a great four-poster bed, under a faded brocade canopy adorned with cupids and satyrs, sipping a milk punch, his injured ankle in a cast.

"I had the doctor this morning," he explained. "The blame thing's busted. I'll be laid up for weeks. Mrs. Warwick"—he flourished a hand at the blonde chatelaine—"is a perfect gem of kindness." He moved his leg slightly and winced. Mrs. Warwick was instantly at his side. "You dear, dear boy," she said, almost tearfully, as she laid a bejeweled hand on Glenny's brow. "How I wish I could share your suffering."

When she left to prepare a "little snack," Glenny said: "I didn't want to inconvenience her, but she insisted that I move in here until I'm better. She's one of nature's noblewomen, and what food she serves! I had a steak this noon as tender as a mother's heart. We're having squab for dinner. We eat together up here in the apartment. It's very comfortable. Don't know how an old reprobate like me warrants such high-grade attention," and his large brown popeyes were as soft as a faun's.

I left when Mrs. Warwick returned with the "little snack."

It consisted of a plate of sandwiches, a cup of hot broth, and another milk punch. "You've got to eat, dear Glenny, to regain your strength," she said.

Harris was invalided in the lap of luxury for several weeks. This might have been an opportune time for the city editor to drop him gracefully from the staff. But when he was able to move about with the aid of a gold-headed cane that had belonged to Mrs. Warwick's late lamented, he was warmly received in the *Herald's* city room. He told me then that he had a "little something going for him on the side," and it turned out that Mrs. Warwick had persuaded him to accept the "assistant managership" of her establishment.

This automatically provided him with a rent-free room and free food in the basement restaurant, and the duties were so slight that they in no wise interfered with his equally slight duties on the *Herald.* Things were going along swimmingly for Glenny, and he often reported to me the progress he was making in his new job. One day he said:

"You know that corner where our apartment stands is—well, a not too desirable section of town. Those women around there"—and he tossed his hands with a little gesture of distaste. "I found, I'm sorry to say, that even some of the young women in our apartment were not all that they should be. Some of them"—his voice lowered to a whisper, as though deeply ashamed of the revelation—"were prostitutes!"

"But how do you know, Glenny?" I insisted. "How could you be sure?"

He wagged his head, in that embarrassed way of his, and made his apologetic laugh. "It's disgraceful, I know. I'd ought to be ashamed of myself—and don't think I'm not. But I—I—" his voice again fell to a whisper—"to tell the truth, I slept with four of 'em, and sent each one a-packing in the morning. So long as I'm going to have anything to do with the place," he added, in a firm voice and with a righteous squaring of his shoulders, "it's going to be high class and decent."

Glenny enjoyed the loving favor of the proprietress for several months, but inevitably his indiscretions terminated their relationship. Returning late one night to his bed and board, he brought with him a heavy jag and his pretty hairdresser. He was still fog-bound in the morning, and made the grave error of taking Madeline into the basement restaurant, where the pair were discovered by Mrs. Warwick as they were about to attack a double order of ham and eggs.

Realizing that Madeline had been Glenny's overnight guest, the proprietress made, as Glenny put it, a "very unmannerly scene," and practically threw her "assistant manager" and the hairdresser into the street, with the dramatic adjuration that Harris never darken her door again. It was a cruel blow, and he complained sadly that Mrs. Warwick was a narrow-minded woman, with no tolerance whatever for the frailties of the flesh. "And after all I did for her, too," he said, almost lachrymously, "in getting those prostitutes out of the place, and making it decent and respectable."

Forced now to pay for his keep, Glenny soon became dissatisfied with his newspaper salary. His extravagant tastes led him into financial difficulties, his checks bounced, his debts threatened to inundate him, and it was not long before he left Rochester for New York. He died a few years later from pneumonia, contracted when he left some midnight carousal during a blizzard and fell asleep in a snow bank.

# THE JOY CHRISTIANS

"**B**ISHOP" BROOKS'S title later became more than a policeman's jape, for he was elevated to the bishopric of the Joy Christians, founded by A. Stanley Copeland, whose subsequent prosecution by the government makes an interesting chapter in the history of Prohibition in America.

At the time this short-lived religious sect was organized, brewers and distillers were microscopically examining the dam-like walls of the Volstead Act for leaks that might permit a legitimate flow of intoxicating beverages into their casks and bottles. The walls seemed solid and impervious. Copeland had no interest in commercial traffic in spirits. His tastes were not bibulous. He was fundamentally a water drinker. But he passionately believed that Prohibition violated the sacred teachings of Christ. This sacrilege he was determined to end.

His idea was startling in its simplicity. As a devout Christian—which he undoubtedly was—he concluded that he must believe that Christ's every act was performed for the guidance of all men who subscribed to His teachings; that each of these acts was recorded in order that all true Christians might more precisely follow in the footsteps of the Saviour. As written in the New Testament, Christ performed the miracle of changing water into wine at the wedding feast of Cana. Copeland believed that it was not only his right, but his duty, to celebrate Christ's joys as well as His sorrows. Since the former included the drinking of wine, he applied for a Federal wine withdrawal permit, which would allow him to use wine for his private services, and in time this was granted.

Copeland was a fanatic. His assorted followers were neither fanatical nor conscientious. They had joined the order mostly for the privilege of drinking wine, and few other than their leader had any interest in the religious purposes of the Joy Christians. All but Bishop Brooks, hand-picked and ordained by Copeland, deserted him at the time of his arrest and left him as friendless as they had found him when they eagerly flocked as venal converts behind his banner.

Copeland was thirty-seven years old, the son of a well-known Methodist hymn-writer and preacher. For several years before the adoption of the Eighteenth Amendment, he had been affiliated with the Prohibition Party. He was interested in the definition of "intoxicating beverage" as one containing more than one-half of one per cent of alcohol. It was characteristic of the man that after "intoxicating" was defined, he experimented for three years to determine to his own satisfaction what percentage of alcohol made a drink intoxicating. Aided by a knowledge of analytical chemistry, Copeland made his first tests in a laboratory. The formulas he concocted there were later administered to several acquaintances, whose reactions proved to Copeland's satisfaction that he knew when booze was booze and when it wasn't. From these practical tests he concluded that to be intoxicating a drink required between four and one half and five percent of alcohol.

The procedure followed in arriving at these deductions seemed to a man of Copeland's curious mental make-up the most natural thing in the world. He never made hair-trigger decisions. It is doubtful indeed if he ever expressed an opinion on any subject without first devoting to it considerable thought and study. Since he had found to his own satisfaction that a drink containing two, three or even four per cent of alcohol was not intoxicating, he felt that to "make the law right," as he put it, the Volstead Act should be altered to permit drinks with an alcoholic content of four and one half per cent.

Copeland first made newspaper headlines when he was thrown out of the Baptist Temple in Rochester as he attempted to address a Prohibition gathering in the Temple's auditorium. The meeting was led by an under-sized, gasconading professional mouthpiece of the fanatical "drys," Clinton N. Howard, whose flowing Windsor tie, black-hander's hat, and stentorian shouts for reform had made him a conspicuous figure in Rochester for many years. Self-styled the "Little Giant" of the Prohibition forces, Howard had a carnival grifter's gift of gab, a hammy sense of histrionics, and a considerable following of local do-gooders with dandruff on their coat collars and poor digestive function.

Armed with facts and figures, Copeland sat quietly in the Baptist Temple until Mr. Howard had concluded his speech. The "Little Giant" then asked for comments from members of the audience. Copeland was instantly on his feet. He told about the experiments he had conducted and suggested that all who were interested in honest enforcement of the Volstead Act campaign vigorously to have the law amended to comply with the facts his experiments had revealed. Outraged at this heresy, Howard then caused Copeland's ejection from the hall.

It was this summary act that inspired Copeland to formulate the Joy Christians' creed:

"I believe in Jesus Christ, the Son of God, and in the perfection of His divine character and acts, including, according to the Bible, the making, giving and drinking of alcoholic wine in good fellowship; and promise to remember Him when partak-

ing in those social pleasures which His enjoying and commend-
ing guarantees to all true believers in Him."

His next move was to collect the opinions of the best available
church authorities on wine. Well equipped with data obtained
through both his scientific and spiritual research he challenged
Howard to a debate. Howard ignored the challenge except to
imply in a statement to reporters that Copeland was not in full
possession of his mental faculties. Copeland retorted that
"Clinton Howard's only argument for Prohibition is that he
once promised a deceased relative he would support it, so it
would hardly be expected that he would be willing to debate
the facts of the issue." Howard's cohorts called upon the police
to arrest Copeland.

Several ex-saloonkeepers offered Copeland financial backing.
When he explained to them that he had no interest in the
return of the saloon, but only in the legalizing of light wines,
these offers were instantly withdrawn. Copeland's employers
then decided that the efforts he was exerting in the propagation
of his new faith had destroyed his usefulness, and he was out of
a job.

His spirit still undaunted, Copeland induced a number of
men to sign cards attesting to their belief in his creed, and on
December 3, 1922, he convoked the first Joy Christian meeting
in the Rochester Labor Lyceum.

"We can put the rollers under the Pharisees' religion," Copeland assured his audience, which consisted of a saloonkeeper,
a ward politician, two newspaper reporters, a labor leader, three
policemen, and half a dozen cranks and drunks who had blun-
dered into the room.

The policemen were there on Howard's threat to "hold the
police responsible" if Copeland passed out his thin red wine to
the "congregation."

The speaker pictured Christ sitting down to "meat and drink with publicans and sinners" and drinking the wine set before him. "The Pharisees would not drink with the sinners, as did the Saviour," he continued.

"Yes, I'm a sinner," interrupted a man in the audience, getting the better of a hiccough.

Copeland was oblivious to the interruption. "Perhaps they drank secretly in their own homes," he remarked, his mind on the Pharisees. "Perhaps Mr. Howard, who thinks I am crazy, drinks secretly in his home. But I do not believe it. I think if he did he would show the effects of his indulgence by a kindlier and more broad-minded view of life.

"Mr. Howard caused me to be ejected from the Baptist Temple because I referred to the 'lying definition' of intoxicating liquor contained in the Volstead Act. When I said these words I was standing in the pulpit, a place where a man is supposed to receive divine inspiration."

He explained that under the law the government must honor an application for communion wine if the application was made by a religious organization. "And then, if you wish," he added, "you may celebrate your faith in good fellowship as our Saviour celebrated His.

"If you do not believe in this literal reading of the New Testament, you may join with Clinton Howard and be a Pharisee.

"The Pharisee teachers want us to forget the story of the wedding feast, in Cana of Galilee," Copeland went on with lifting voice and growing spirit. "They want us to think it was grape juice that Jesus provided for the wedding guests. But the governor of the feast told the bridegroom, 'Every man in the beginning doth set forth good wine; and when men have drunk, that which is worse: But thou hast kept the good wine until now It was not grape juice that the governor was talking about."

Bishop Brooks, whose most effective means of serving Copeland and the Joy Christians was through the pages of the *Herald*, saw to it that an extensive report of Copeland's remarks was printed, and as the result of this, new demands were made that Copeland be arrested for transporting "communion" wine to his meeting.

Copeland replied that he had transported no wine to the meeting, but that had he done so he would have been strictly within his constitutional rights. He had registered with the County Clerk a formal notice of his congregation and his new religion. On December 6 he made application to the Federal Prohibition Commission for a wine withdrawal permit which was countersigned by Bishop Brooks. Pending action on the application, Copeland called a second meeting of the Joy Christians the following Sunday night. The converts had scarcely risen from their knees at the conclusion of the invocation when police stormed the doors. In full view of his flock they subjected the shepherd to a "frisk," and took from his rear pants pocket a flask of "communion" wine. The wine was analyzed, and on December 15th Copeland was arrested on a warrant charging him with transporting an illegal beverage.

The Joy Christian leader consulted with his bishop, Brooks, who strongly urged Copeland to obtain the best legal talent available and fight the case tooth and nail. In this single instance the two men disagreed. Copeland insisted that he was capable of conducting his own defense and in the end he appeared in court without counsel. He staunchly maintained that his sect, as a "congregation that meets together regularly or irregularly to worship God," constituted a "religion" under the best legal definition of the word, and he asked that a jury of his peers decide the issue. The "drys" now had a change of heart. They no longer wanted Copeland tried in open court. They continued to maintain that he was insane, and presently he was taken to the County Hospital for observation. At a preliminary hearing, Copeland requested that the magistrate order him held in jail.

"Why do you ask that, Mr. Copeland?"

"Because the vermin in the County Hospital annoy me so I fear I may be driven insane if I am kept there."

The superintendent of the hospital rose and angrily explained that there were no cockroaches in his institution.

Copeland favored him with an indulgent smile and took a spectacle case from his pocket. This he placed upon the magistrate's desk. He opened it and several roaches crawled out. "I found these in my room this morning," he said. "I thought I might need an exhibit."

The superintendent relapsed into chastened silence.

Howard made a public statement in which he offered to "do anything in my power to assist Copeland recover his reason." Copeland answered, "Tell Mr. Howard I will do the same by him."

On December 21, the master of the Joy Christians was brought before Judge Willis K. Gillette of County Court for an examination as to his sanity. Copeland tersely summarized the proceedings in these words: "Instead of arguing with me, they locked me up."

Dr. James C. Davis, jail physician, was put on the stand. "Doctor, you gave an interview to the newspapers in which you stated that I was insane, did you not?" was the first question Copeland asked him.

"Yes, I said that you are suffering from religious hallucinations."

"Had you examined me at the time you made that statement?"

"I must explain that," Dr. Davis said. "I was called to the telephone and was asked my opinion about your mental condition. I supposed I was talking to a representative of the District Attorney's office. Later I learned that I was speaking to a newspaper reporter."

"Then," said Copeland, "you admit that you were suffering from a delusion yourself, if I understand you correctly."

The physician swallowed hard and nodded.

Copeland's skillful examination of the witness won the admiration of a packed court room. A portion of this examination follows:

Question: "You said I am suffering from delusions?"

Answer: "Yes."

Q: "Because I said I am inspired to form a new religious faith?"

A: "Yes."

Q: "When the child Samuel, mentioned in the Bible, awoke from a dream in which he was told someone was calling him, and went to that person, do you believe he was suffering from a delusion?"

A: "I don't know."

Q: "If Christ turned water into wine today, would he, in your opinion, be a criminal?"

A: "Yes."

Q: "Do you understand that true Christians are supposed to follow the example of Christ?"

A: "I don't know."

Q: "You don't know? Are you a Christian?"

A: "I am. . . . Yes they are."

Q: "But you believe that they are not supposed to follow Him in all things? You hold that they are not supposed to drink wine, as He did?"

A: "Yes."

Q: "And all others are irrational?"

A: "Yes."

Q: "Then we are supposed to follow the beliefs of the majority rather than the teachings of Christ or the dictates of our own conscience?"

A: "Yes."

Q: "Would you consider the Colonists, who before the Revolution opposed the tyranny of England, were irrational?"

A: "Yes."

Q: "Would you consider the Colonist who gave up his palatial home at Mt. Vernon, his wealth, his position, and his slaves to lead a ragged army at Valley Forge; in a word, do you hold that Washington was irrational?"

A: "Yes."

The judge rapped for order as laughter rose in the courtroom.

"Am I testifying to your mental condition or are you attempting to prove me insane?" Dr. Davis demanded angrily.

"If you will excuse me, I prefer to spare your feelings and not express an opinion on your condition," Copeland answered gently.

At the close of the examination, Judge Gillette pronounced Copeland "mentally sick" and remanded him to the custody of his father. Hoping to fight the criminal charge in the courts and demonstrate his right to worship with wine, Copeland filed an appeal.

When the Supreme Court reviewed the case, the Justice held that Copeland was neither sane nor insane. He was not sane, the Justice maintained, since Judge Gillette had not used the word "insane" in either the decision or the parole. During the nine months that followed Judge Gillette's adjudication, fearful of Howard and his followers, the police refused to issue Copeland a permit to speak in Rochester, on the ground that he was mentally unbalanced.

When he was finally released from custody, Copeland threatened to bring a "show cause" action against the state Prohibition Director if a wine withdrawal permit was not granted. Previously the Director had ignored Copeland's letters. Upon receipt of a sworn statement that a Joy Christian congregation with a bona fide membership had been organized, he signed the withdrawal application.

Copeland received his first shipment of "communion" wine in February, 1923. He sent a bottle, with his compliments, to Judge Gillette, who had declared him "mentally sick." The bottle was not returned.

# CHAPTER XVII

~~~~~~~~~~~~~~~~~~~~~~~~~~~~~~~~~~~~~~~~~~~~~~~~~~~~~~~~~~~~~~~~~~~~

# A TRAMP REPORTER

JIMMY CALLIS dropped from blind baggage as an eastbound New York Central train slowed for the Rochester stop. He was cold, hungry, and clean out of funds. It was a late October night. He had swung up on the front of the baggage car at Ashtabula, Ohio, and all he now desired was hot food in his stomach and relief from the tornado of wind and cinders. A battered suitcase contained his worldly possessions.

A yardman was stumbling through the dark along the track ballast. Jimmy hailed him. "Is this Buffalo?" he inquired.

" 'Tis not, me lad," the yardman answered. "It's Rochester. Buffalo's sixty-odd miles west. Git out of these yards before I sic the railroad bulls on you."

Jimmy thanked him politely. He was a small young man, pert as a wren. His face under the grime of his stolen ride had a choirboy's innocence.

The tramp reporter is now virtually an extinct species, and Jimmy was a tramp reporter. The breed died out when the Newspaper Guild came into being. Publishers, held to rigid contracts with the Guild in the matter of wages and severance pay, are reluctant to hire unknown applicants, blown in on any old wind, who may prove difficult and expensive to dismiss if their services prove undesirable. Then, too, there are fewer city dailies than formerly, and their city room staffs are more permanent and stable.

Shinnying over the railing that separates the station yard from Central Avenue, Jimmy put his feet for the first time on a Rochester sidewalk. He turned south from Central Avenue, crossed Main Street, continued a block in South Avenue, and stopped in front of the Seymore Hotel, John A. Dix, prop.

The Seymore was not a genteel hostelry. It was small, down at the heel, a cut-rate house for burlesque troupes and small-time vaudeville performers. Dix was no mine host in the grand manner. He looked like a tough hombre, and he was. Under the room clerk's desk he kept a handy bung starter with which he rapped the noggins of recalcitrant guests and lobby brawlers. Entering, Jimmy gave Mr. Dix his Sunday smile.

"I'm a little short of funds—" he began.

"Out, bum," Dix roared, and reached for the bung starter.

"Take it easy, pal," Jimmy urged. "You can always use a porter. I'm your new porter."

After a moment's glowering reflection, Dix ordered Jimmy to grab a mop and get busy on the lobby floor. He laid his suit-case in a corner and without removing his hat went to work. That job and a second one of cleaning the curl-rimmed spit-toons got him a late supper and a cot in the hotel's baggage room. A small barroom was convenient to the lobby and Jimmy quickly ingratiated himself into the favor of the man behind the strip. He cadged several drinks and ended the evening in song and wassail in the company of congenial spirits.

Jimmy thought Rochester was a good place to hang his hat.

Next day, spick and span in a sack suit he had taken from his suitcase, he presented himself to Mr. Antisdale, publisher and editor of the *Herald*. He had documents to show that he had worked for several of the leading newspapers in the country. One of these was the *New York Morning World*, and the

*World* was Antisdale's second favorite newspaper. Callis was hired on the spot.

Besides his business suit, Jimmy had a pair of black trousers, a satin vest, and a dinner jacket. Assigned to cover some formal or semiformal affair he invariably showed up in evening attire. He had an air about him. He looked like a clubman, unless you looked closely. Then you noticed the frayed edges of his cuffs, the moth holes in his satin vest, the cracked and lackluster patent leather pumps. He delighted in this getup. The rest of us were tolerant of his little conceit, remembering that Jimmy had once worked for the revered *World*.

For more than a month Jimmy closely adhered to the straight and narrow. He was punctual in reporting for duty and faithful in its performance. Beside his regular assignments, he frequently turned in some of the brightest little human interest stories, which he said he had "just picked up in the street," that the *Herald* had printed in years. Antisdale was impressed. "That young Callis has the touch," he said enthusiastically. "He'll go places." It was not until Callis left that we discovered that he had clipped most of his gratuitous contributions from the columns of the *World* and turned them in with no alterations except a change of names and locale.

In time the tramp reporter's invariable weakness for drink began to manifest itself in Jimmy. At first his jousts with the bottle were sporadic and mostly confined to his leisure hours. But soon he formed the habit, once he had received his office assignments, of flying back to the Seymore barroom, where he passed his time in the company of burlesque chorus girls. Several of us knew about this long before the city editor. If Jimmy occasionally missed an assignment he promptly retrieved his status with the city desk by submitting one of the little gems he had culled from the files of the *World*.

His heavy fall from grace occurred at a celebration arranged by the local chapter of the Women's Christian Temperance Union to honor the birthday of Frances Elizabeth Willard, founder of the order.

The birthday dinner was scheduled for seven o'clock in the ballroom of a downtown hotel, and Jimmy was told to cover it. At five o'clock that afternoon he returned to the Seymore and got into his dinner clothes. He was on his way to duty when the call of the hotel's barroom proved irresistibly tempting. There he found several members of Ed Lee Wrothe's Midnight Maids, the attraction at the Corinthian Theater.

It was payday and Jimmy had a set of fresh new money. The Midnight Maids had a thirst. At seven o'clock the girls reluctantly left good old Jimmy and his free-handed buys for their evening's frolic at the theater. Now in an expansive mood, Jimmy remained. Eight o'clock came and went; then nine. Suddenly Jimmy remembered the white-ribboners who had gathered to break bread and pay tribute to their departed leader. He left in a rosy glow and with a heavy list to port.

The sisters had opened with prayer, gone through a thin soup, rubbery chicken, a limp-leaf lettuce salad, dessert, and coffee, and were giving with the second verse of *I Worship Thee, Sweet Will of God*, when Jimmy's unsure feet paused a moment at the threshold of the ballroom.

The prospect appealed to his imagination. The speakers' table, occupied by local officers and visiting dignitaries of the W.C.T.U., rested on a dais in the center of the room. Below this were the tables of the rank and file. They were mostly large-bosomed ladies of determined countenance and unyielding spirit. They wore white muslin dresses, and the badges of their order were pinned like corsage bouquets at their shoulders.

"Whee-ee-eee," Jimmy sang out, as the hymn ended, and

there was a brief silence as the toastmistress prepared to intro-
duce the first speaker of the evening. Then Jimmy was on his
way.

His course was a diagonal one, set for the speakers' table. It
began with a hop, skip, and a jump, continued with a short
sprint, and ended in a long slide across the shiny ballroom floor
that banged his pumps against the boards of the platform like
a hockey puck. Briskly he thumped the lady chairman on her
muslined back, and stepped back with arms wide extended, as
though to enfold her in a loving embrace.

"Hi ya," Jimmy called, his innocent, choirboy's face brilliant
as a sunbeam. "Hi ya, Carrie Nation!"

What followed after that has always been a confusion of
historical fact and rumor. But it is known for certain that someone at a table in the rear of the hall screamed, "Police!" And
that someone at a nearer table shouted incriminatingly, "the
man's intoxicated!" And there is further documented evidence
that several of the sisters left the table to engage in a foot race
to a house phone in the corridor to solicit managerial aid.

Jimmy was grieved by this spoil-sport attitude. He thought
that a dressed-up dinner should be an occasion for good fellowship, cheer, and lively antic. He was remonstrating with the
lady chairman that it was all in good fun, when a posse of bell-
hops, headed by the grim-faced manager of the hotel, crossed
the ballroom on the double.

Vigorously protesting that his ejection violated the sanctity
of a free press, Jimmy nevertheless was rushed in the middle of
the bellboys' phalanx from the hall, lugged down two flights of
stairs to the lobby, and pushed through the service entrance to
the street with a stern warning from the manager that any
attempt on his part to return would be met with reinforced
defenses.

Jimmy straightened his disarranged clothing, made sure that his black tie was in correct bow, shrugged, and decided t'hell with it.

Then he returned to the Seymore. The mid-evening lull was on. He had two drinks. Lacking a story to write he proceeded to the Corinthian Theater. He mounted the steep stone steps that led to the foyer. The ticket taker passed him through when he gave the password, "Callis of the *Herald*." He climbed to an upper right-hand box, his spirits mounting with his physical ascent.

The chorus was engaged in a lively ensemble and Jimmy knew every girl in the line. In their black tights and gilded bodices they seemed less appealing to him than when he had last seen them in the Seymore barroom. He guffawed at their terpsichorean efforts and made loud and uncouth remarks about their physical characteristics which provoked laughter from the audience but lamentably failed to tickle the risibility of the theater's manager.

In half a minute Jimmy again was seized—this time by ushers—and escorted from the theater in a manner much less gentle than that which had marked his egress from the hotel. He was booted down the stone steps and into the street, in descent an angry cry rising from his lips. "I don't care! I saw the show in Cleveland! It stinks!"

In the meantime Mr. Antisdale was besieged by telephone calls from the irate ladies of the W.C.T.U., the hotel people, and the manager of the Corinthian Theater. The callers laid Jimmy out in lavender. They excoriated Antisdale for permitting a drunken rowdy to represent a supposedly self-respecting newspaper, and for once Uncle Louie retreated under fire. The evidence against Jimmy was impossible to refute. He called me into his office and asked me to try to turn up his errant reporter.

I repaired immediately to the Seymore's bar. Jimmy was there. But no longer a glass of fashion. The rough handling he had received had scratched and marred the gloss of his sartorial perfection. One trouser leg was torn at the knee. His dinner jacket was soiled with street dirt. His black tie, originally in meticulous bow below his Adam's apple, was now askew under his left ear.

"The boss wants to see you," I told him.

He looked at me with moist red eyes, lifted a glass to his lips with a palsied hand, and laid it back on the bar.

"I suppose he's going to tap me out," he said depressedly. "That's life for you. A man gives his all for a newspaper— suffers, as I have, an emotional cataclysm—and runs a little amuck. In a wide experience with them I've found that editors are men with mean souls and no charity."

"Maybe he isn't going to fire you. You better go over and talk with him."

Jimmy shook his head. "No. I've gone through this sort of thing before. I know the pattern and I know editors. My old man always wanted me to learn the plumbing trade, and I went into this lousy business instead. I'm through. There's always another town." He grasped my arm suddenly. "Listen," he said, intensely, and his face was so close to mine that his breath almost made me dizzy. "I've got a little tab in this hotel needs to be squared. Let me have ten bucks."

Since it was payday, he knew I was solvent. And there was a sort of desperation in his voice that made it difficult to refuse. I gave him the ten—a third of my weekly wage.

"I'll send it to you from the next place," he promised. "I know of an opening on the *Boston Post*." He stepped away from the bar, squared his shoulders, and with an elocutionary gesture, announced to the assembled bibbers. "Friends, I am

leaving your fair city. But leaving as I entered—pure and right-
eous! A gentleman, always!"

With as much dignity as his shaky legs could command, he
left the barroom at my side. Outside we shook hands and I reported back to Antisdale.

"Too bad about Callis," he said. "I was going to dock him,
and lay him off a couple of days. I wouldn't have the heart to
fire him on the complaints of a burlesque manager and the
W.C.T.U." He shook his head regretfully. "The young man
was good—very good. You know, some of those human-interest
stories of his were almost as well written as those fine pieces the
*New York World* occasionally prints."

~~~~~~~~~~~~~~~~~~~~~~~~~~~~~~~~~~~~~~~~~~~~~~~~~~~~~~~~~~~

# CHAPTER XVIII

# THIM DARTY THINGS

---

THE OLD Lyceum Theater has been razed these several years; the Temple, once the home of big-time vaudeville, today is a second-rate picture house; the Corinthian, the historic temple of burlesque, has been torn down and the space it occupied made into a parking lot. I had many happy times in each of these theaters. I miss them all. In some ways I miss the Corinthian more than the other two.

After the war burlesque changed appreciably. During the pre-war glory of the Columbia Wheel, comedians invariably were billed above the leading feminine members of the troupe. When the postwar Mutual Wheel began to send its shows into the Corinthian, the comics were definitely relegated to second position. Their gags, which once had been original and amusing, now became dull and very dirty, and the only possible excuse for their presence in the cast was to fill the stage and occupy the time during those minutes when the ladies of the ensemble and women leads were changing what, with considerable license, might be described as their costumes. The stripper had come in. The sweet soubrette who sang songs about unrequited love and dear old mother went out. If a woman didn't strip she had no chance; if she didn't strip almost total, she won no more than apathetic attention from audiences to whom Ann Corio's navel was as familiar as Jimmy Durante's nose.

I own that I was startled myself when I first observed the

160

nudity displayed in the modern burlesque show, and I often wondered how old Dinny McCarthy, were he alive and functioning, would have coped with the situation.

Besides his regular duties as police sergeant at City Hall, Dinny had served each Monday afternoon as censor for the burlesque show. He must have been an unusually moral man, for he was an exceedingly severe censor.

His coign of vantage was the best seat in the house, a front-row chair in a stage box. He would lumber up the stone steps of the theater, pass heavily through the entrance without a word of greeting to the doorman, move ominously down the side aisle to his customary seat, and sit throughout the performance with his brick-red, heavy-jowled face as stern and unyielding as the death mask of Rameses II. His ponderous countenance never relaxed; he never compromised with his conscience. He was the dread ogre of every performer on the wheel and a constant thorn in the side of John L. Glennon, the house manager.

There were rare occasions when Dinny failed to assume his censorial throne until the Monday matinee was half over, and pending his arrival the show proceeded as written and arranged. The instant the bulky figure of the sergeant passed the doorman, a box office look-out pressed a button that rang a tiny bell backstage, a signal that meant, "For God's sake be careful. McCarthy's in."

I was covering the show one afternoon when the young women of the chorus appeared in Highlanders' costumes which, I am morally certain, would never have excited the most demented member of the audience to commit a sex crime. But their legs were bare from a point an inch or two above their knees to the tops of their calf-high plaid socks, and Dinny's closed fist thundered on the rail of his box. "Stop it! Stop it!"

he bellowed in a field marshal's voice. "Have thim darty things go back and make themselves dacent."

The command of course was obeyed and a sentimental tenor was thrown into the breach as the chorus line retreated. He had little chance. The audience howled and catcalled and demanded the return of the bare-kneed ballerinas. The natural crimson of Dinny's face darkened to an apoplectic purple, but he never weakened. When the chorus next appeared the girls were bundled up like Arctic explorers.

This was the final straw, and Glennon and his assistant, Frank L. Smith (now manager of the EastmanTheater) decided on an act of reprisal. Under the *Help Wanted* column in the classified section of next Sunday's *Democrat and Chronicle* an appeal was made for one hundred laborers. The wage announced was astonishingly high, and all applicants were asked to report that day at No. 5 Arnett Street.

The house at No. 5 Arnett Street was the home of Sergeant McCarthy, although his name did not appear in the advertisement. But long before the hour of early mass, residents of Arnett Street were aroused by what had all the aspects of a mob scene. Scores of heavy-handed sons of toil were milling through the quiet residential street fighting to reach the door at No. 5, and Dinny must have thought he was being serenaded by an enormous company of Swiss bell ringers. For no sooner would he dismiss one applicant with the stentorian announcement that he wasn't a labor contractor, that he hadn't any jobs to offer, that he didn't know who in holy hell had put that ad in the paper, than another innocent applicant would mount the steps and ring the bell, and the whole routine needed to be repeated. The thing kept up all day, preventing the good sergeant's attendance at mass, ruining his Sunday dinner, and keeping him from his afternoon nap; and the bell still rang far, far into the night.

Try though Dinny did to discover his tormentors, he was unsuccessful in doing so. But he took no moral from what had happened to him. The very next day he was back at the Corinthian, this time to rise in righteous might from his front-row chair and demand the end of a wrestling match between Miss Cora Livingston, the lady champion, and some lesser rival, on the grounds that the exhibition was indacent and a threat to public morals, and that any attempt to resume it later in the week would bring about the arrest of the participants and the revocation of the theater's license.

So Dinny McCarthy continued to be John Glennon's heavy cross until he ultimately retired, and a more liberal-minded censor, with a capacity for being amused by burlesque antics, replaced him.

I knew many burlesque people and consorted with them more than with any other members of the entertainment world. When the Mutual Wheel came in, I was enormously curious as to what sort of women these were who, for a stipend—and occasionally for a queen's ransom—consented to remove all of their clothing, except the last three rhinestones of their G-strings, for the edifications of audiences that made no pretense of interest in the aesthetic glories of the human form divine and had come avowedly for an 85-cent-thrill.

The first of these revealing ladies I met was Miss Mildred (Peaches) Strange, a Texan, come to burlesque by way of Cleveland, who for the first few years of the Mutual Wheel was as red hot as Custer's pistol at Little Big Horn.

She was a tall girl, as magnificently proportioned as a Greek

statue, and capable of such amazing bodily contortions that
Major Charles L. Clifford, a regular army officer, temporarily
stationed in Rochester, who usually accompanied me to the
Corinthian, remarked in gape-mouthed awe, "My God, she's
got the labor movement beat a mile."

Clifford, a lean, immaculate, dapper, short-mustached man,
who looked every inch the professional soldier that he was, was
as fascinated as I by Miss Strange, and that night, in company
with Allen Styne, now a secretary at the American Embassy in
London, we dined with her on the roof of the fashionable Sagamore Hotel.

Rather than the tough, hard-boiled Annie we had suspected,
we found her a surprisingly "nice" girl; witty, agreeable, intelli-
gent, a minor authority on the poetry of Alfred Edward Hous-
man; who proved so pleasant a companion that we all three
contributed to her entertainment during the remainder of her
week's stay in Rochester. I saw her many times afterwards, both
on and off the stage, and found no reason to change the impression of her I formed at our first meeting.

For sheer vitality and physical stature I have never seen anyone quite like her in burlesque, and I recall an apt line written
about her in the old *Vanity Fair*. "Surely," enthused the
author, "Delacroix, or Gericault, never found a model as
opulent, as tigerishly vital, as 'that exotic princess of rhythm,
Peaches Strange.' " When I came across that sentence in the
late Frank Crowinshield's slightly lavender publication, I wired
"Peaches" to look it up, and I know that she warmly cherished
it.

Because of the beauty of her body and the wantonness of her
performance—which was quite contrary to her offstage con-
duct and deportment—she enjoyed tremendous vogue. Yet she

never reached the top income bracket occupied by Miss Ann
Corio, Miss Hinda Wassau, and Miss Gypsy Rose Lee, a failure
she attributed, and I think correctly, to her choice in husbands
and backers.

"You've got to have good management in this business, to get
up in that thousand-a-week class," she once told me. "Ann was
married to Emmett Callahan, Hinda to Rube Bernstein, both
very smart burlesque men; and Gyp had awfully clever friends.
I went it pretty much on my own. The managers racketed me
around. But I've had fun and made some money. See this mink
coat." (It was matched mink, and quite handsome.) "Under
it," Peaches explained wrily, "is an $18.22 dress."

In New York's National Winter Garden, in Huston Street;
in the Irving Place, near Fourteenth Street; and later at the
Elting Theater in West 42nd Street, she gave with everything
the exceedingly liberal laws of the time allowed, and the
peculiar style of her "art," imitated by many, was matched by
none.

Once she tried to quit. A marriage had turned out badly and
she decided to "get away from it all," assume a new character
and inaugurate a new career. She left burlesque for a job as a
clerk in a book store in a small Midwest city. In some circuitous
way the "lady" book buyers, coming for the latest overdose of
printed sex, learned of her past and threw up their hands in
holy horror. When they refused to do business with an ex-
burlesque stripper the proprietor let her out. She returned to
the murky honky-tonks to hear the shouted exhortations, in
which it was unnecessary long to persist, "Take 'em off, Peach!
Take 'em off!" sadly convinced that only a chameleon may
successfully change colors. I have not seen Mildred Strange in
some time, though as recently as the last year of the war I read

that she was featured in the Old Howard in Boston. It was more than twenty years ago that I first knew her. Burlesque women are durable.

Infinitely more subtle and insinuating than Peaches, Miss Hinda Wassau, in my humble opinion, was the greatest of all burlesque women.

She was small and graceful, and her bodily arrangements were as finely balanced as a Swiss watch. Of Lithuanian parentage, she had the prominent cheek-bones of the Slavic race and her face had a sort of elliptic design that imparted a sense of the exotic and the mysterious; and this was in no way lessened by the fact that the platinum hue of her hair obviously had been obtained by incessant dye-pot washings. Her stage name, constricted from the yard-long combination of letters on her baptismal certificate, with many "s's" and "z's," was happily chosen.

Walter Winchell called her the highest-priced woman in burlesque. Reading this, I decided that she must have something extra special. When I presently heard that she was to appear in the Palace Theater in Buffalo I made a trip to that city especially to see her.

"The girl can't sing, whistle, dance, or act," an old-time showman remarked to me after the show, "but she certainly makes the rest of these grinders, bumpers, and strippers on this burlesque line look like cheese soufflé. I don't know what it is. Whatever it is, she's got it."

Upon my return home I wrote, not a review of the show, but a special story about its star. Later I was told that this article was photostated and used on the façades of Midwest burlesque houses in which Miss Wassau was appearing. I have no certain knowledge that this article was responsible for the step-up of her career, but shortly after it was printed, Billy Rose engaged Miss Wassau to share headline billing with Miss Gertrude Nissen, the singer; Miss Eleanor Powell, later a Hollywood dancer; and Jimmy Savo, in his new night club, the Café de Paree, where she remained six months.

Rose later billed her jointly with Miss Sally Rand, World's Fair fan dancer, in another club, the Casa Manana. Miss Rand was allowed to continue; the police stopped Hinda in two weeks. Disconsolately she drifted back to burlesque. After working for the carriage trade, she found no thrill in panicking the hip-booted, coatless, rag-tag-and-bobtail audiences of burlesque. She had lost something of her spark. For a time she had a vague notion of trying the legitimate drama. Knowing this, I arranged to have her play the lead in Somerset Maugham's *Rain* with a Rochester stock company. When the contracts were prepared, she reneged. "I can't do it," she said. "I haven't the nerve."

She married again and now lives in Washington, D.C., and on rare occasions accepts spot billing in the Gayety Theater in that city. I last heard about her when I read a long interview with her in a Washington paper, in which she said she had practically given up show business for the role of housewife.

The Corinthian was always a house of fun, and we had much fun there that was only obliquely related to the performances on the stage. Glennon and his impish assistant, Frank Smith, were forever contriving some dodge of extra-curricular entertainment.

During the Prohibition era we were all amused at the dual role being played by a soft-faced, saintly-looking man, a grocer by trade, who was one of the most ardent "drys" and active re-

formers in town. Each Monday afternoon, shortly after the
house lights dimmed out for the opening number of the Corinthian matinee, we would see this worthy sneak down the left-
hand wall aisle of the theater to a second-row seat. The collar of
his topcoat would be turned high up, and without removing
this outer garment, he would sit with his face as hidden as possible through the better-than-two-hour peformance. A few
minutes before the show ended, while the house lights were
still dim, he would slip out of his seat and disappear up the
darkened aisle like a fugitive.

"Let's fool him one day," I suggested to Glennon. "When
he's halfway down the aisle, have the man with the lights
accidentally catch him with the baby spot."

Glennon gleefully agreed. He felt that if you scratched a reformer he'd bleed like the rest of us. So the next Monday
afternoon, as the pure grocer was halfway down the aisle, anticipating his usual visual orgy, a spotlight danced across the
darkened house and pitilessly illuminated his saintly features.

"Company in the parlor, girls," the spot light man called
out, being something of a wit on his own.

The confusion and consternation of the holy grocer was
tragic to behold. He threw his forearm over his eyes in the
gesture trial-bound criminals often employ as protection
against the telltale lenses of news cameramen, and a low cry of
anguish escaped his lips. Then he turned and ran—he didn't
walk—to the nearest red-lighted exit. The door slammed after
him. It was a good joke, but Glennon lost a regular patron. For
the saintly one never returned, fearful, I suppose that if the
Rochester Chapter of the Holier-than-Thous learned of his
secret revels in the carnal temple of burlesque he would be
instantly excommunicated.

Major Charles L. Clifford, my regular companion at the Corinthian matinees, was a professional soldier of long standing, with a fine war record. He did not scare easily, and only when retreat was much the better part of valor would he agree to such a measure.

Once I saw him in ignominious flight, and I was running swiftly at his side.

We were witnessing a particularly dull and dispiriting performance, relieved only by the energetic and whole-souled efforts of a small, dark-haired member of the chorus. She had no unusual talents. But those that she did have she employed to the fullest. She was a lively and rather pretty little figure, much more alluring than the large, splay-footed females who danced with her in the chorus line.

Clifford thought something should be said about this willing and enthusiastic danseuse, and we asked Glennon her name, which was merely included among the "Ladies of the Ensemble." He inquired and told us that it was Sugar Shad.

In my "review" next day I told that a pretty, unidentified show girl, Miss Sugar Shad, made the large, lethargic spear carriers who cavorted in the chorus line with her look very bad indeed, and that without her presence in the cast the entire production would have been as flat and uninspired as a cold boiled potato. The day following this I had a note from Miss Shad saying how grateful she was for the mention; that it was the first time in six months in burlesque that her name had appeared in a newspaper, that she was sending the clipping to her mother, who she was sure would be very pleased and proud, and wouldn't I stop backstage and receive her thanks in person?

I showed the note to Clifford. "We'll have to go and see her," he decided promptly. "She's a cute little tyke."

At the close of the matinee that afternoon the two of us, hats in hand, waited backstage while the stage manager summoned Miss Shad. She was almost tearfully grateful for my small favor. As the three of us were talking in a darkened recess I became conscious of an ominous murmuring around us. I looked up. We were surrounded by four or five large, heavy-handed, huge-bosomed women, with gross thighs.

"So that's the guy who called us spear carriers, eh?" one of the lumbering vestals remarked, pointing a forefinger at me. "The Goddamned nerve of him."

They were closing in and they were very menacing. "T'weren't me who wrote it," I shouted defensively. "It was this guy," and I put a finger on Clifford, who never wore a uniform except on actual duty. Then I bolted.

A large hand grasped the Major's lapel. He shook himself free and raced behind me for the stage door. The thunder behind us was like a charge of cavalry. The door opened onto an iron stairway. Down this we clattered at breakneck speed, the outraged spear carriers gaining at every leap and spewing us with words of vituperation no true daughter of a good mother should employ. It was half a block from the theater to the Four Corners, Rochester's busiest intersection. There police aid would be available. Before we found it necessary for this we shook off our pursuers in the Main Street throng, and in another block slowed our precipitant flight to an apprehensive walk.

"W-whew," Clifford panted, daubing at his sweat-beaded brow with a handkerchief. "That's the closest shave I've had since Europe." He stopped and turned to me irritably. "Hey, what's the idea your telling them I called 'em spear carriers?"

"You're a soldier. You know the old maxim. All's fair in love and war. We'd have been at war in another minute."

# CHAPTER XIX

# THE SHOW GOES ON

O NE LATE August Sunday afternoon I started through the short alley leading from the *Herald* office to Main Street. Sunday afternoon was usually a dull time in the *Herald* city room, and the news this day was particularly uninspiring. It was too early to compile the week-end total of motor accidents, and little else of local interest was in immediate prospect. My own assignment left me cold and unenthusiastic. I had been sent to check the standings in an egg-laying contest at a poultry show.

The town seemed deserted. City dwellers who followed normal pursuits and made the Sabbath their day of leisure had migrated by the thousands to the lake shore and the adjacent countryside. The afternoon was too perfect for anyone to work. I was lamenting the hard lot of a morning newspaper worker and feeling sorry for myself. An alley cat snooped panther-like across my path and nuzzled its bewhiskered snoot in a tin can. I was thankful it wasn't black. My luck seemed poor enough already.

As I turned dispiritedly out of the alley, my dull eyes quickened at the sight of a handsome, dark-haired young woman hurrying along the Main Street sidewalk. Her name was Peggy Cusack. She was a member of the Lyceum Theater's summer stock company. "Hey," I called, my step lifting with my spirits, "where's the fire?"

She turned and waved without stopping. "I'm in a terrible rush. Got to get up to the theater."

I ran and came abreast of her, matching my stride with hers.

For years the Lyceum was noted for the excellence of its summer stock. The list of actors and actresses who have lent their talents to these productions is a long and distinguished one. It included such well-known names as Helen Hayes, Sylvia Sidney, Dorothy Gish, Louis Calhern, Miriam Hopkins, Glenn Hunter, Louis Wolheim, and Bette Davis. The stage manager was George Cukor, now a famous Hollywood director. Howard Rumsey was producer. His wife, Florence Eldridge (the present Mrs. Frederic March), was leading woman.

Miss Cusack had played "second leads" with the Lyceum company, but had never starred. She was comparatively new to the theater. She had been a model for the well-known painter and illustrator, Penrhyn Stanlaws, in New York, and her picture had graced the covers of numerous leading magazines. Attracted by the beauty of her face, a New York producer had advised her to get some stock experience as preparation for a Broadway career, and she had joined Rumsey's company in Rochester.

We had been friends for some time and occasionally dined together. Since the Lyceum Players ordinarily did not rehearse on Sunday afternoon, I asked her why she was hurrying to the theater.

Excitedly she told me. Her big chance had come. It had come about in this way:

The bill which had closed with Saturday night's performance, was a light comedy. Miss Eldridge had, of course, played the lead. She was a popular leading woman, petite, blonde, quite lovely to look upon, with considerable talent.

A few minutes before the curtain rose Saturday night, a

telegram was handed Miss Eldridge stating that her mother had
been taken critically ill in her New York home. Miss Eldridge,
Rumsey, and the stage manager held a quick consultation. The
message was urgent. But without Miss Eldridge, the show
could not go on. She decided to play through. The curtain
would fall around eleven o'clock. A train would leave Rochester
for New York at midnight. Miss Eldridge would board this and
be at her mother's bedside in the morning.

At two o'clock Sunday morning Miss Cusack, who resided in
the Hotel Rochester, several blocks west of the Lyceum, was
aroused from sleep by a telephone call from the stage manager.
He said that since Miss Eldridge would not be available for the
new play opening Monday night it had been decided to cast
Miss Cusack in the leading role. Would she accept? If she
would, she was to hustle right up to the theater for a reading of
the part.

Leaping from bed, she got into her clothes, and called a
taxi. For three hours she read the part for the stage manager.
Returning with the script to her own hotel, she studied until
after daybreak. She slept an hour or two, and by mid-morning
was back at the theater for another reading. Again she returned
to her hotel to work on her lines and, at four o'clock Sunday
afternoon, she was bound back to the theater for a full three-act
rehearsal.

"It's a lead I'm going to play," she told me exultantly. "The
leading role. It's the chance I've dreamed about and hoped for
ever since I've been in the theater."

It had been a grueling ordeal. Almost no sleep, snatched-at
meals, work, work, work; I wondered how she stood it and still
seemed so fresh and zestful. She was doing it on her nerve, she
said. She simply *had* to make good. A chance like this might
make her.

"This rehearsal should be over by seven o'clock," I said when we reached the theater. "You'll be hungry. Say I meet you in the Seneca for dinner."

The Hotel Seneca stood next door to the theater, and she agreed to my suggestion. I left her and went on to the poultry show. A pen of Buff Orpingtons was leading in the egg-laying contest. I obtained the official score, returned to the *Herald* office, and wrote a short account of the contest with a couple of added paragraphs on the poultry show itself. At seven o'clock I met Miss Cusack in the Seneca.

We had a pleasant, leisurely dinner. My companion was filled with talk about the leading role she would play the next night, and which, nervous though she was, she was sure she would fill with credit. The stage manager and even Rumsey had been complimentary at rehearsal. The new show was drama, rather than comedy, and she would have an opportunity really to emote. At nine o'clock she decided it was time to return home.

"I'm still shaky on some of those lines," she said. "I'll work on them all night. I want to be letter-perfect for the opening."

"You'll do it all right, Peg," I said confidently. "You'll knock 'em."

"If I don't, it won't be for lack of trying," she answered determinedly. "What a day this has been. Sunday, the day of rest! Hah! If the critics are only halfway nice tomorrow . . ."

I paid the check and we left the restaurant.

The schedule of the Lyceum players was an arduous one. Playing one piece six nights and two matinees a week, their daytime hours were mostly occupied with rehearsals for the new show they would open the following Monday night. To insure proper rest and quiet for his wife and leading woman,

Mr. Rumsey, the producer, had rented a pleasant cottage on Conesus Lake, thirty miles south of Rochester. At the close of each night's performance the couple were driven to the lake by Fred Towner, who had a taxi stand in front of the Hotel Seneca. In the morning Towner again drove to the lake and brought the couple back to town.

As Miss Cusack and I left the hotel we saw Towner, lounging against the hotel's façade, chewing a toothpick and languidly observing the sidewalk parade.

"Hello, Fred," Peg said to the driver. "Nice night. Did you get Miss Eldridge off on the midnight last night?"

Towner removed the toothpick from his lips. "Why no," he answered casually. "I took her up to the lake. She ain't leaving until tomorrow night."

Miss Cusack gasped. "O-oh," she cried. "Tomorrow night! Tomorrow night on the midnight!"

Towner nodded.

"But her mother—I thought her mother was critically ill?"

"Well, she's sick all right," Towner grinned. "But not sick enought to keep Miss Eldridge from doing the opening."

"Y-you know that, Fred?"

"She told me she'd play the show tomorrow. So did Rumsey."

I took Miss Cusack's arm and started with her along the sidewalk. Drawn taut as a bowstring with the rush of work, lack of rest, and the nervous tension of learning and rehearsing in less than twenty-four hours a long role that Miss Eldridge had been studying a full week, she now seemed to come apart emotionally, and a tremor ran over her body. Her face was tragic, and tears bubbled in her eyes.

"That's a rotten shame," I said angrily. "Florence'll get all the credit from the critics, after you've done all the donkey work. You'll play it the rest of the week without a line in the papers. What a business you're in."

Miss Cusack made a vigorous effort to control herself and daubed her eyes with a small handkerchief.

"It's the theater," she said. "It's the part I hate about the theater, for all my love for it. I can't blame Florence. She's the star. It is *her* role. She worked on it all week. B-but it was such a glorious chance for me. I'm silly and vain, I suppose. But I did want those opening-night notices. They might be seen by some New York producer." A sob jumped up in her throat. She stifled it and walked on resolutely.

"I'd quit before I'd let 'em job me around like this," I said. "I'd wait until Tuesday night, and Florence had gone, and tell 'em I was quitting."

She shook her head.

But I could see, as we continued on toward Miss Cusack's hotel, that she was deeply hurt and dreadfully disappointed. I knew what it meant to a young actress, given her first starring role, to be cheated out of the opening-night notices.

In a block or two Miss Cusack's poor effort to be heroic about a piece of business that seemed to me inexcusably shabby gave way to anger. She agreed thoroughly with what I had said about the "lousy business" in which she was engaged; she conceded that to get along in it one needed to be completely self-centered and utterly ruthless. She delivered a spirited philippic against leading ladies. But she still stopped short of agreeing to quit the company Tuesday night, which, with Miss Eldridge in New York, would mean cancellation of the performance.

Suddenly I had an inspiration.

"Peg," I said excitedly, "I'll bet I can fix this."

"Fix it," she cried. "No one can fix it. They've fixed me. They wouldn't give me even this little chance. It's rotten!" She bit her lips and fresh tears—this time of anger—filled her eyes.

We were at the alley that led up to the *Herald* office. "I'm going to try, just the same," I promised. "You wait and see. Keep your chin up—and study your lines."

Before she had an opportunity to question me about my plan, I darted from her and started up the alley. I was thoroughly excited now. I had a *story*.

The city editor glanced significantly at the clock as I bustled into the city room.

"Where in God's name you been?" he demanded.

"What's doing?"

His tone changed. "Oh, the usual Sunday tripe. A couple of motor accidents. A Guinea stabbing down in Oak Street, but no one killed. One rescue at a lakeside bathing beach, and a $50 fire. Got anything to fill with?"

"Maybe I can give you something," I said enigmatically. "Something special, for a nice two-column head."

"Go to it," he encouraged. "The way things are tonight I'd reprint the first chapter of Genesis."

I hung my jacket over the back of the chair, rolled a sheet of copy paper into the typewriter, and lighted a cigarette. I fumbled about for an opening line, and then wrote, "The show must go on." After that the words spun swiftly off my finger tips. I knew the way now; I was sure I was fixing it for Peggy.

The marquee lights were full up Monday night when I stepped into the Lyceum foyer. The crowd was already pushing past the ticket takers, and a long queue serpentined up to the box office. Howard Rumsey's company did very well. A Monday opening was something of a gala.

I was waiting until the crowd thinned out and I could get an okay at the box office when Will Corris, house manager, saw me. Corris was a dapper little man with gold-framed pince-nez and a dinner jacket. He had managed the Lyceum for many years and was an excellent showman.

"Hey, who committed that Gawdawful blunder on the *Herald* this morning?" he asked belligerently. "Rumsey's fit to be tied and he's threatened to sue that rag of yours. Florence Eldridge nearly tore the roof off the place. I've been tossed around all day like a bowling ball. As though I had anything to do with it."

"What d'you mean, Will?" I asked innocently. "What blunder? What you bellyaching about?"

He drew a *Herald* clipping from his pocket and thrust it into my hand.

"You've seen this already, I suppose. Read it again and then ask me what I'm bellyaching about. Some jackass of a reporter went off half-cocked and stirred up a pretty kettle of fish."

I glanced at the clipping. The two-column line across it read:

TRAGEDY IN HER HEART,

LEADING LADY PLAYS

COMEDY ROLE

Below, the story opened, "The show must go on. . . ."
I knew it by heart. I liked it. I felt that it did me proud.

In swift prose it told that ten minutes before Miss Florence Eldridge stepped on the stage, Saturday night, to play the starring role in a light comedy, a telegram advised her that her mother was critically ill in New York. Miss Eldridge's natural impulse was to drop everything and speed to her mother's bedside. Then the trouper's instinct prevailed. She had a show to do. The audience was waiting. No one else could be thrown into the part at this eleventh hour. Tears sliding over the grease paint on her face, she bravely donned the habiliments of comedy and played through three hilarious acts with the audience blissfully unaware of the heavy tragedy in her heart. When the curtain dropped she rushed for the midnight train.

I handed the clipping back to Corris.

"What's wrong with that, Will?" I asked. "It makes your leading lady a heroine."

"My God, that's just the trouble with it," Corris exploded. "Florence wasn't going until tonight, not night before last. She wanted those opening-night notices. They'd help if she decided to do the show in New York in the fall."

"Well, she's going to get 'em, isn't she?"

"Get 'em! You don't think she'd dare walk out on that stage after that thing had been printed. They'd laugh her into the wings. Say the story was a publicity gag. Fred Towner brought her and Rumsey down from the lake this afternoon. She was all set to go on tonight, and lam it out of town for the rest of the week. Then she read that thing, and I want to tell you that in all my experience with leading women, and I go back to Mrs. Leslie Carter, I never saw a dame blow her top like she did. Boy—" Corris mopped his forehead with a silk handkerchief. "She couldn't stay here after that. She caught the Empire this afternoon, and she's probably in New York this minute."

"Who's playing the lead?"

"Why, Peggy Cusack. That pretty, dark-haired girl. We began to get her ready for it early yesterday morning. She wasn't to have gone on till Tuesday night."

"Well, she ought to get along okay. Give me a seat, Will, will you?"

"I shouldn't," he protested. "After what that paper of yours did to us." But he scrawled a note on a slip of paper, and I passed into the theater.

Miss Cusack played the role splendidly. I spoke to our critic and those from the other papers, confessing my little artifice on their promise of secrecy, and they treated Miss Cusack very well in their reviews.

I gloated immodestly over what I had done, driving a leading lady out of town, to save the day for her substitute. Miss Cusack was grateful. She quit the stage after that season, and married Edward Schlegel, of Rochester. She still lives there. Whenever we meet we still laugh over the incident, which meant a great deal to both of us at the time, and gave me perhaps an exaggerated notion of the power—of which I was wont to boast—of the press, and of my own prowess as a pressman.

~~~~~~~~~~~~~~~~~~~~~~~~~~~~~~~~~~~~~~~~~~~~~~~~~~~~~~

# CHAPTER XX

# OATMEAL LIKE THE REST OF THEM

I WAS never the regular police reporter for the *Democrat and Chronicle,* but during the four years that I worked for the *Rochester Herald* I covered many important crime stories and wrote a daily column of police court news. It was work that I liked immensely, and I had numerous fine and solid friends among the members of the force. Joseph M. Quigley was Police Chief at the time, and the Detective Bureau was headed by a wonderful character, the late Captain John D. (better known as "Jackie") McDonald.

In person McDonald was a stocky, bandy-legged, pot-bellied man of medium stature with a face the color of a ripe lemon. He had been reared in a tough neighborhood on the West Side and was well known in his youth as an amateur wrestler, boxer, and baseball player. Gloves and mitts were little used at the time of Jackie's devotion to the national pastime, and when he pulled and twisted his fracture-stiffened fingers, as he did during moments of grave deliberation, they cracked like breaking sticks.

McDonald had been appointed to the force in early manhood, and the business of the policeman was the only one he knew, had an interest in, or had ever practiced. His formal education had ended with the third year in grade school. He was scarcely literate, and his malapropisms were a legend and a source of constant amusement to his professional associates, the lay public, and the members of the legal profession with whom he was in frequent consultation. He had slight respect for modern, technical methods of criminology but depended upon an intuition sharpened by long experience with lawbreakers.

I suppose he was an adept at the despised technic of the "third degree." But he never boasted of his success with this practice and rarely revealed it even to the hardened eyes of police reporters; and though he was a violent and hard-handed man with the enemies of law and order, he was deeply sentimental, a good churchman, and a husband who stood in mortal fear of his wife.

All felons with the exception of those who perpetrated crimes of violence he listed under the category of thieves, and thieves were anathema to him. He hated them lustily and fought them with all the resources at his command. His respect for private property amounted to a passion and he found no excuse for anyone who committed depredations against it.

Once during the Christmas shopping rush two of his men picked up a woman of good family for shoplifting. The store management had no desire to book her on criminal charges and she was escorted by the detectives to the store office. There the merchandise she had taken was gently removed from her person and her husband tactfully advised of what had happened. It was then revealed that she was suffering a slight mental derangement, and the family lawyer called upon McDonald to explain her condition.

"Mrs. So-and-so is a sick woman," the lawyer said. "Her mental disorder has made her a kleptomaniac."

McDonald snapped his crooked baseball fingers and sputtered angrily. "Kleptomaniac, hell! That's just a fancy name for thief. The woman stole three bottles of perfume and a pair

of silk stockings. I told the boys to bring her in and I'll kleptomaniac her with thirty days in the workhouse. That'll learn her
to keep her mind on God and her hands off of store counters."

But nothing came of the matter. The store management
would make no formal complaint and the woman was given
over to the custody of her family. McDonald refused to be rec-
onciled to this humane procedure. He said it was a shame and
a crime that a large mercantile establishment be permitted to
use the members of his department to play games with thieves
rather than bring them into court for trial.

In his dealings with suspects McDonald's subtlety and cun-
ning often astonished even those who knew him best. But he
was most effective when his methods were direct and forthright,
as the following incident may illustrate:

One day during my early association with McDonald I was
in his office when report was made that a number of suits of
clothing had been stolen from the stockroom of a wholesale
clothing house, and I accompanied him when he called upon
the president of the company, a Mr. Cohen.

The president was confident that the clothing had been taken
by one of half a dozen stockroom employees, and after listen-
ing to his story McDonald agreed that the theft had all the
earmarks of an inside job.

"Bring those fellows in here one at a time," he told the
president, "and I'll turn up the thief that's been doing this
dirty business."

Mr. Cohen ordered the first of the stockroom employees to
step into his office. As the young man crossed the threshold the
Captain leaped from his chair, grasped the suspect by the throat,
banged his head resoundingly against the wall, and cried out in
a fierce, threatening voice, "God damn you, you low-lived thief,

tell me what you done with them twenty suits of clothes."

Shaken and terrified by the violence of McDonald's actions and words, the young man pleaded tragically that he knew nothing about the theft except what he had heard. McDonald released him, scoured him with a withering glance, and dismissed him. A similar routine was followed with three other employees. When the last of these had left the room, Mr. Cohen, who had witnessed Jackie's demonstration with growing unease, interjected a nervous protest.

"All of these young men can't be guilty, Captain," he said. "Don't you—er—think you might be a little easier on them?"

"You been reading them Shylock Holmes stories," McDonald replied irritably, wagging a crooked forefinger in Mr. Cohen's face. "That's book writing. This is a thief we're trying to catch and I'll catch the sonofabitch if you'll leave me alone. Fetch in the next one."

The next one was a large, surly, defiant young man, who for several seconds successfully repulsed McDonald's efforts to grasp his throat. There was a brief struggle. But the doughty detective captain soon got a fierce hold on his victim's windpipe and squeezed so hard that the latter's tongue shot out like a red signal of distress. "Now you tell me, you thieving bastard," McDonald cried, "what you done with them twenty suits of clothes."

His tongue out and his breath cut off by the pressure of Jackie's hands on his throat, the young man was unable to answer. His face flushed and then seemed to purple, and for a moment I had the sickening feeling that I was witnessing a homicide. Suddenly the Captain stepped back from the suspect. The young man straightened his buckling knees, rubbed his bruised throat with a shaking hand, and blurted out, "It wasn't twenty— it was eighteen suits of clothes!"

A benign smile spread over McDonald's lemon-colored face and he nodded to Mr. Cohen. "There's your thief for you," he said triumphantly. "It was *eighteen*, not twenty suits, that was stolen?"

"It was," Mr. Cohen agreed.

Jackie brushed off his hands. "Get your hat and fix your necktie, punk," he told the young man. "We're going for a ride."

In court the defendant's attorney moved for dismissal of the charge on the grounds that a confession had been wrung from his client by violence. The motion was denied and Mr. Cohen's stockroom employee was tried and found guilty. The penitentiary sentence given him by the court was suspended when the clothing he had stolen was turned up in his uncle's barn.

Brutal though he may have been at times, McDonald's intuition occasionally worked to the advantage of the suspect, and I recall one example of this in connection with the theft of $75 in cash from the register of a music shop.

The finger of guilt pointed sharply to a clerk who was in charge of the register, and the proprietor of the store was positive that he had committed the theft. He was a thin, nervous, weak-chinned youth who had had some difficulty with his father, a local businessman, that had resulted in his being temporarily turned out of his home. When the proprietor accused him of the theft he hysterically protested his innocence, but his pleas only strengthened his employer's belief in his guilt. McDonald dismissed him after a five-minute interview.

"He's no thief," the Captain said. "Bring in that other one, that big good-looking one out there. I want to talk to *him*."

"But Captain, I know you're mistaken," the proprietor insisted. "That fellow you let out was the only person who could possibly have had access to the register. I've been suspicious of him right along. Since his father cut him off he's been in need of money. I know he's guilty."

"He's no thief," McDonald repeated doggedly.

"But how do you know?"

"He just ain't the type. I can tell. Bring in the other one."

So the other one, the large handsome young man, a favorite of the proprietor, was sent for.

McDonald looked him over slowly, from head to toe. Suddenly he rose and peered intently into the young man's eyes.

"How strong are you, punk?" he demanded, employing the underworld argot for doing time.

The clerk's eyes wavered, his lips trembled, and before he knew what he was saying, the words were out, "I—I only did a year in Auburn," he whimpered. "It was a mistake. I was innocent, I swear to God."

"Don't swear a lie to God and put your soul in Hell," McDonald said sternly. "Now tell us about that money."

And while his incredulous employer, who hadn't the remotest notion that he had hired an ex-convict, sat with mouth agape, McDonald forced from the handsome clerk the admission that he had taken the $75 from the register and cunningly attempted to place the blame on the clerk that Jackie insisted was innocent.

Ray F. Fowler, former District Attorney for Monroe County, of which Rochester is the county seat, claimed that McDonald had a sixth sense in his dealings with criminals that made him one of the best police officers Fowler had ever known. But there were times when threats, cajolery, and intuition failed him; and sitting in the press room in Police Headquarters, a few doors down the corridor from McDonald's office, I often heard the thump of fists intermingled with Jackie's blasphemous harangue as he attempted to beat a confession from some police-wise and stubborn prisoner after more gentle methods had failed.

During his tenure in office one of McDonald's most celebrated cases concerned the alleged embezzlement of $140,000 from Mrs. Harriet J. Brewster, a socially prominent East Avenue matron, by a glass-smooth character known as "Captain" George D. Ball.

Mrs. Brewster first met the "Captain" in a Midwestern city and was at once charmed by his social grace and fascinated by the stories he told of his successful operations in the stock market. During the course of a friendship that appeared to be swiftly progressing to romance, the "Captain" let it be known that he and several of his friends were planning a stock pool that promised to net the participants huge profits.

Mrs. Brewster was immediately interested. But the hitch was, Ball explained, that while he appreciated her good faith, his partners did not know her and would insist on some guarantee of financial responsibility. This Mrs. Brewster agreed to furnish, turning over to Ball $45,000 in cash and nearly $100,000 in securities. Shortly after the transfer of this sizable fortune the "Captain" mysteriously disappeared.

A nationwide search was vigorously prosecuted for months. It ended when the Rochester police were notified that Ball was under arrest in Paris. The sum involved and the prominence of the complainant inspired the local authorities to send McDonald to the French capital. He was accompanied on this safari by his wife; the late John Doyle, a private detective; and Sheriff Albert H. Baker.

Mrs. Brewster and her daughter Gwendolyn preceded the police party to France. Arriving in Paris late at night, McDonald decided to wait until the following day to interview the Brewsters. He overslept and met the other members of his party in the restaurant for lunch. This was his first real meal in France, and his first question to the waiter was, "What you got to eat?"

The waiter replied in French. Jackie looked at him questioningly. "No spake Deutsch?"

Apparently the waiter didn't.

"What's he trying to sell us?" Jackie demanded of Doyle. "Toasted snails?"

An American at the next table interposed. "He says he has very nice onion soup."

"Well, that's my dish," Jackie said, instantly in good humor. "Tell him to bring a big plate of it."

The waiter responded. The onion soup delighted Jackie's palate. He told about it later. "I ordered some of that onion soup," he related rapturously. "The waiter brought it. I smelled it. I tasted it. It was the most delicious delicatessen I ever had."

"Captain" Ball's gallant fight against extradition delayed his return to the States by three months. During this period the McDonalds and Doyle made a tour of Europe, visiting Switzerland, England, Ireland, and Italy. In the last-named country McDonald vividly recalled only one great memorial besides the Vatican. He described this as the "biggest smokestack he had ever seen." This baffled all who listened to his description until they realized that he was referring to the Leaning Tower of Pisa.

When he finally brought his prisoner back to Rochester, someone asked him how he had managed with the French authorities. "Well," he said, "to tell the truth, I ain't so influential with the French language, but I made signs and them frogs understood I was no man to trivial with."

"Captain" Ball was tried three times in County Court. Twice

the jury disagreed. In the third trial the jury voted for acquittal. The decision supported the plea of the defense that Mrs. Brewster had entrusted her money and stock to Ball for investment and that he could not be held guilty of crime because the investments turned out badly.

Ball had an ingratiating personality and a razor-keen mind that prompted one of the prosecutors to remark that he was the "ablest, cleverest, and brightest defendant ever to face a bar of justice in Monroe County." McDonald, in a session with the prisoner in the Detective Captain's office before the first trial, realizing that nothing could be gained with a man of Ball's intelligence by threats or bullying, attempted to appeal to his better nature.

"Captain," he pleaded, "Mrs. Brewster is a good, God-fearing, Christian woman—now for Christ's sake tell me what you done with her money!"

Ball's eyes saddened and he moved his delicate hands in a weary gesture of resignation.

"Captain McDonald," he answered. "I myself have many times invoked the aid of the Supreme Deity in this matter, but apparently he has washed his hands of the Big Board. When stocks fall God turns his gaze the other way. I'm afraid he disfavors speculation. I can only tell you Mrs. Brewster's money went into a supposedly good thing that turned out to be a bloomer."

One day I was in McDonald's office when a young woman, under escort of a police matron, was being subjected to Jackie's interrogation. She was accused of the theft of $100 from a man who had accosted her in one of the leading hotels.

The complainant, a New York security salesman, inquiring of a speakeasy proprietor the location of a house of pleasure, was advised that none existed in Rochester, but was told that he might have some luck around the hotels. In his search he had come upon the young woman in question. She was sitting primly in a chair on the mezzanine with a ball of yarn in her lap from which she was knitting a sweater. Certain that a young woman engaged in such a virtuous pursuit would never accede to his desires, but greatly attracted by her appearance, the salesman made a desperate and winning pitch.

"I was surprised myself when she agreed to have dinner in my hotel room," he later told the police. "She baffled me. Not only was she knitting, but when she got up in the room I saw that she wore a small gold cross at her throat. I tried then to treat her like a lady, but finally forgot myself. When I awakened in the morning she was gone. She had been through my pants pockets and lightened me up to the tune of $100, every cent I had with me."

In McDonald's interview with her the young woman proved exceedingly difficult, and after a wasted half hour of trying to win from her an admission of guilt, he ordered the matron to take her away. "Lock her up," he shouted. "Put her down there in solitary. Maybe by morning her sins'll choke her soul and she'll tell the truth like a good Christian whore."

The girl rose from her chair and moved slowly across the room with a little waggle of her hips. At the threshold she turned and blew her nose delicately on a small lace handkerchief, which she had used frequently for this purpose during the interview. "Captain," she said, with an imperious tilt of her head, "I'll need some Kleenex in the morning."

McDonald, whose temper when dealing with recalcitrant suspects was often short, dismissed the suggestion with a sharp movement of his hand. "T'hell you will," he answered angrily. "You'll eat oatmeal like the rest of 'em."

# CHAPTER XXI

# A CHAMPION AND A CHALLENGER

IN THE days before criminology became a recognized science, and all sorts of new-fangled gadgets and apparatus were introduced into station houses, and police cars with two-way radios prowled the city streets, applicants for the Rochester Detective Bureau were chosen more for their physical prowess than for their skill in the detection of crime, and several of the local gumshoe artists were men of considerable athletic reputation. One of these was Detective John Spillings, who for several years before his appointment had traveled with an athletic troupe headed by the late William (Iron Duke) Muldoon, one time trainer of John L. Sullivan, later proprietor of a famous health farm at White Plains, N.Y., and chairman of the New York State Boxing Commission.

Spillings' stunt with the Muldoon show was to meet all comers in a three-round boxing match, the agreement being that any challenger who was on his feet at the clang of the final bell would receive a cash prize of $25. The troupe traveled extensively, and in these impromptu matches, in which he generally managed to save his employer's money, Spillings acquired a distinguished pair of cauliflower ears, a flattened nose, and numerous other mementos of his hard trade.

He was still a rugged specimen of manhood when he joined the force, and for a time his duties as police officer were supplemented by those of physical instructor for the department. He was no boxing Fancy Dan but a rough, tough, hard-hitting fighter, and a terror to the hooligans on his beat.

Shortly after Spillings' appointment James J. Corbett, who some years before had lost the world's heavyweight championship to Robert Fitzsimmons, made his first visit to Rochester as a member of a theatrical company, and the police chief invited Corbett to meet Spillings in a three-round exhibition before a hand-picked audience of political dignitaries and top-drawer city officials in the police gym.

On the day of the scheduled exhibition Spillings was stricken with a severe cold. The police chief, determined not to disappoint the illustrious company he had invited to see Corbett in action, asked Patrolman William F. McGuire, who later became a detective sergeant, to substitute for Spillings.

McGuire was a large and powerful young fellow and the cleverest boxer in town. But he had never boxed professionally, despite many offers to do so. He was a man of intelligence and integrity who saw no future in the sport and despised the chicanery and shabby practices of the prize ring. He was the only avowed Democrat on the police force in a "black" Republican city, and he had no desire to make a Roman holiday for a group of political bigwigs whose hostility he had provoked by his refusal to follow the party line. But the Chief's request was tantamount to an order, and he reluctantly consented to be the foil for Corbett's demonstration of the manly art.

"Corbett's a wily, tricky fellow," he told a friend before the exhibition. "If he starts to make a monkey out of me I'll kick him in the belly, right in front of those big dogs with their brass collars, and t'hell with 'em."

Knowing McGuire as I did (and in time he was to become the best friend I had in the Detective Bureau), I have no doubt that he would have done exactly as he said, and damn the consequences, if he felt that such an act was warranted. He was a man of sensitive nature, proud, fearless, and uncompromising when he felt that injustice was being done; and he had heard rumors that the politicians had conspired with Corbett to have the former champion "show him up" as punishment for his political heresy.

I do not believe this rumor was true, and certainly Corbett did nothing during the exhibition to give support to it. A lissome, graceful figure in full-length black tights, he attempted no murderous assault upon his amateur opponent, and throughout the first round the two men exchanged light, swift blows, ducked, blocked, weaved in and out of one another's defense, and thoroughly delighted the audience with their fine skill. The second round was a repetition of the first, and the third began in a similar manner.

But now the athletes were well warmed to their work. The tempo was quickened and there was considerably more force behind their blows than in the previous rounds. The spectators sensed this. In their growing excitement several rose to their feet and wildly exhorted Corbett to knock McGuire cold, to "put him away," to "finish him off," forgetting that what they had been invited to see was a boxing exhibition and not a fight.

The round was more than half over when the two men tangled in a clinch in the middle of the ring. As they broke away McGuire's right glove, with lightning swiftness, clipped Corbett solidly on the jaw, and an amazed gasp rose from the spectators as the man who had knocked out the immortal John L. Sullivan sprawled on his back. Instantly McGuire reached to assist his fallen rival to his feet. "Sorry, Jim" he remarked quickly, and stepped back, left fist extended, jaw tucked into his shoulder, anticipating—as did the spectators, who were now clamoring wildly for blood—that what had begun as a polite demonstration of the "sweet science" would end as an old-fashioned Donnybrook.

Corbett shook his head vigorously, as though to dispel any fuzziness that had gathered on his brain, made a comic gesture, and resumed; and never, I believe, did he wear the appellation "Gentleman Jim" more gracefully than during the closing minute of that round, for he made no display of temper, seemed thoroughly to have forgotten the incident of the knockdown, and attempted no retaliatory mayhem.

At the close of the set-to the participants were given a rousing ovation, and McGuire had become the hero of the police department. For years afterwards his professional associates, telling and retelling and re-retelling of the time he knocked down the great Corbett, created a legend—which still has some currency—that Corbett was not only down, but out, and that McGuire's charity alone carried him through the final stages of the round.

McGuire was always at pains not only to deny that he had knocked Corbett out, but that he had knocked him off his feet, claiming that the latter tripped as he was breaking from the clinch. This, I think, is no more true than the legend of the knock-out, for it is difficult to imagine a man of Corbett's grace and sure-footedness floundering around like a stumblebum. I saw the knockdown, and I still believe it was cleanly scored. But it was the last thing McGuire desired or anticipated.

Possessed of the best police brains on the local force, McGuire's political convictions prevented him from rising beyond the grade of detective sergeant. When he presently retired he ran for sheriff on the Democratic ticket. He made a formidable candidate and might have achieved the phenomenon of victory except that he was compelled to accept the support of Clinton N. Howard, professional reformer and Prohibitionist, who

alienated voters who normally would have followed the Democratic banner. McGuire is dead now. But my memory of this
fine and gallant police officer, who once knocked James J.
Corbett kicking, is still vivid. He was a handsome, upstanding,
honest public servant who should have closed his career as chief
of the Rochester Police force.

Freddie Kane was a steam fitter by trade, with a dream of
lush living, diamonds, and a blonde baby done up in sin-and-
go-to-hell finery. Freddie thought the prize-ring offered vast
rewards. He was a broth of a lad, shouldered out like a behe-
moth, the muscles of his back and biceps coiling and squirming
under the clear white skin like nests of baby snakes. In a large,
open-faced Irish way, he was not a bad-looking kid, and he
wanted very much to be a pugilist.

I never served as sports editor, but sports were simple for
me to write and I occasionally helped out with football, baseball, track and field, and boxing. I wouldn't want the job for
steady diet, though it has its compensations. A sports editor is
pretty much his own boss, and sometimes his is the most lucrative post in the editorial department. His salary may be no
larger than that of other sub-editors. But the open-handed
sports promoters with whom he deals often "cut him in" on
their promotional ventures and secrete substantial gifts in the
folds of their publicity copy. Some publishers frown upon the
acceptance by their sports editors of these perquisites; others
apparently consider them "legitimate" graft. It is not my intention to discuss the ethics of this common practice. I merely
mention it in passing.

Though my professional duties only occasionally required
that I have contact with people from the so-called world of
sports, many of these characters were friends of mine, and I had

known Freddie Kane for some time. In his off hours he hung around the Eggleston Hotel, the meeting place of fighters and fight managers, horse-trot men, card cheats, professional wrestlers, and such, and it was there that I first met him. He was courting a fight manager at the time. The fight manager had a couple of good boys, who were doing nicely for him, and he was disinclined to take on an untried amateur. He brushed Freddie off. When Freddie came to me with a bleeding heart and an eloquent jeremiad I thought I saw a chance for fame and fortune. Why not take him on myself? The world needed a new heavyweight champion. Perhaps I had him in my lap.

We drew no contractual papers. I merely promised to try to get him a match. In the meantime Freddie went into training. He ran on the roads before he went to work and after work boxed in the Union Hall of the ironworkers, to which he had access. He looked good to me. His defense was negligible; he was as wide open as a corner saloon. But he had a swooping, powerful right hand which, if it landed, was like a roof falling in, and it was this upon which we counted.

"I don't fiddle around," Freddie said. "I don't tango and one-step. I just hit 'em with my right, and leave 'em lay."

I was sufficiently impressed to invest in a bath sponge and a dressing gown for Freddie. The dressing gown was a lovely thing of deep, rich purple. For a time we talked of having "Freddie Kane" embroidered in gold letters across its back, but decided to wait for this until after our first triumph.

The first, and incidentally the last, match I made for Freddie was a six-round preliminary bout at Danny Deegan's club in Geneva, a lovely little city hard by Seneca Lake, and the seat of Hobart College. I packed a bag with a bottle of rubbing lotion, Freddie's trunks and boxing shoes, the bath sponge, and the purple dressing gown. We left for Geneva in high spirits.

In the dressing room, before we went up to the hall, Freddie was very confident. "I'll knock this bum kicking," he assured me. "I'll make him look awful bad."

"We'll murder him," I said, already having adopted the managerial "we." "He'll never have a chance. He can't hurt us."

A fat man, with a chewed cigar in his mouth, rapped on the dressing-room door. "You're next, Kane," he called. "Hurry up, Kane."

"We're ready," I told him.

I had rubbed Freddie carefully. I was a good masseur. He was nice and smooth and limber, and I had covered his face with a thin coating of vaseline, to make the blows slip. I helped him on with his purple dressing gown, put the bath sponge in the second's bucket, and up we went to the ring.

Freddie had had no experience except as a club fighter, boxing raw kids off of laundry wagons, rugged bus boys, and the like, who were striving for a reputation around the smokers, and with a momentary qualm I saw that the formalities of a professional fight club were having their affect upon him. The hall was packed and noisy. It was dark except for the pitiless white lights that flooded down upon the raised ring. He turned to me with a slightly greenish grin.

"Jeez," he said, and a sort of shudder ran over his huge body, "a guy's got to have his nerve, to get up there under them lights without no pants or shirt."

"That won't bother us," I said firmly. "It's just like fighting in the clubs, Freddie, except for the lights."

"Y-yeah," he said, but without his old assurance.

We stood in the center of the ring, my arm over his purple shoulders as the referee instructed the fighters. "Our" opponent was a squat, stocky, scar-faced veteran pro who had once enjoyed a fair reputation in rings in Central and Western New

York. Now he was definitely over the hill, an old battered and
tired trial horse for fresh young aspirants like Freddie Kane. He
seemed slow and sluggish and unimpressed with the importance
of his lines. The first hint of middle-age obesity showed in the
belt of fat around his waist. I began to feel sorry for him. My
God, I thought, if Freddie's good right ever sloughs into that
blubbery belly, a block and tackle will be needed to get it out.
His attitude baffled me. He was so very insouciant under this
threat of slaughter.

"All right, boys," the referee said, concluding his instructions.
"Go to your corners, and come out fighting."

I snatched the purple dressing gown from Freddie's shoulders,
patted him on the naked back, and started for the ring steps.
"Take your time, Freddie," I called cheerily. "Remember the
ol' right."

The bell rang before I made my descent. With my back to
the ring I busied myself a moment with the equipment in my
charge, the bucket and bath sponge, the ring stool, and purple
dressing gown. Then I looked to see how Freddie was doing.
He was doing badly. He was flat on the floor, the referee
crouched over him, one arm upraised. Through the thunderous
chorus of that blood-lusty throng I heard the first toll of doom.
"O-n-e," the referee shouted. Freddie never moved. He was
stiff and chilled as an icicle.

Even after the count had run clean out, he was still immobile.
I thought we would need to stick pins under his fingernails to
see if he was actually alive. He certainly didn't look it. But somehow, aided by the old-timer's manager and the referee, I got
him up and out of the ring. Another bout was coming up and
the ring was needed. Stumblingly, my arm lent in support,
Freddie proceeded along the aisle of the hall, and down to the

catacomb dressing room below. I helped him onto the rubbing table, where he lay face upward.

"Freddie," I asked. "Freddie, what happened?"

He moved his head painfully, gazing at me with eyes that had not yet lost their glaze, and rubbed a shaky hand over his jaw, upon which the scar-faced veteran had scored a bull's-eye.

"Th-the lousy bastard," he said. "H-he fooled me. He said, 'Your tights are falling off.' I reached to grab 'em, thinking how I'd look under them white lights if they fell off. Then—something happened."

Our return home was funereal in its gloom. I said good-by to Freddie and turned over to him the bag in which were contained the new bath sponge and the lovely purple dressing gown. I saw him only once after that. He came to see me just before he moved to Utica. He had a fine job in Utica, he said, with a contractor who needed a good steam fitter.

# CHAPTER XXII

# THE DECLINE OF THE THIRD WARD

D URING my first week as a "sub" reporter for the *Democrat and Chronicle,* one of my contemporaries went to considerable pains to explain to me that a man working for a morning newspaper could hardly pursue the gay career of a cotillion leader.

I do not know why he thought it necessary to make this explanation, unless he assumed that because my father held membership in the Genesee Valley Club I had definite social leanings.

Actually my interests were not at all along these lines. And I was so thrilled to be known as a newspaper reporter and so fascinated by the work I was doing, despite its lack of material rewards, that I was rarely envious of the few socially eligible young men I knew whose evenings were free to dance with, dine, and court the attractive girls who each holiday season made the official transition from the gangling adolescence of finishing schools to young womanhood in elaborate coming-out parties.

My own social activities and those of my younger newspaper associates were more or less confined to rowdy goings-on in the old Bristol Hotel, hard by the New York Central Railroad tracks, where were staged what we called the Tuesday Musicals, which consisted of singing, dancing, and copious beer drinking with the ladies who each week comprised the chorus of the traveling burlesque troupes.

Yet sometimes it became my professional duty to observe the fetes and festivities of orthodox society, and for years one of my pet assignments was the Rochester Horse Show. This both before World War I and for several years after it was one of the most celebrated horse shows in the country. It began each year on Labor Day, attracted most of the leading exhibitors of show horses in this country and Canada, and made a week-long gala that had something of the combined aspects of a New Orleans Mardi Gras and opening night at the Met.

As a result of the contacts I made as a Horse Show reporter, and the knowledge that it was assumed I had acquired of Rochester society, I was later engaged to edit for the year of its abortive career a local society weekly; and still later I was given temporary custody of the society department of the *Democrat and Chronicle*, until the inexperienced young woman who was being groomed for the job was thought ready to take over.

But long before this, learning a great deal about my home city as a consequence of my constant peregrinations through all quarters of it, I had become acutely aware of the rigid lines of demarcation that separated the socially elect from the mavericks with new wealth, zestful ambitions, and reasonably good manners, who still had no more chance of penetrating the jealously guarded citadel of the town's fashionable circle than a bindle stiff with a pack on his back.

Rochester was very earnest about its social life in the first three decades of this century, as it had been for several decades before 1900. Up until the mid-eighties of the last century the Third Ward was the town's Belgravia. It was a close and tightly locked community, very jealous, very proud, and very high-toned. Its residents were mostly descendants of the city's founding fathers, and the ivory tower of their confraternity was as cold, as aloof, as inaccessible as the peak of the Matterhorn. A Third Warder, as one of the Ward's own historians remarked, became such "only by birth, marriage or immemorial usage," and his chief and highest end "was to glorify the Ward and enjoy it forever."

But the lower reaches of the Ward extended almost to the heart of Rochester's business section, and as the city continued to grow the threat that the grimy fingers of trade would soon reach into this previously inviolate territory gave real cause for alarm. When this actually happened the wealthier members of the "ruffled shirt" ward began a slow but steady movement across town to East Avenue to build great solid-walled houses, deep set in beautifully landscaped lawns, along a thoroughfare that only a short time before had been flanked by farm lands and uncut wood lots.

At the height of its glory East Avenue was one of the most imposing residential streets in America, a long boulevard of impressive grandeur and cloistered aristocracy. Its broad pavement was untrammeled by such bourgeois conveyances as trolley cars, and above it, during the summer months, the intertwined branches of enormous elms that stood like palace guards along each curb formed an arched canopy of living greenery. From it at right angles ran numerous shorter streets, the fine if less pretentious houses of which were occupied by persons of authentic social status, though sometimes lacking the magnificent opulence of their East Avenue neighbors; and the whole district was looked upon as sacred territory by the reverent and awesome outlanders from other parts of town.

The *Post Express*, one of the three evening newspapers in Rochester when I began my newspaper career, was a daily "must" for members of the city's social hierarchy. Decorous to

the point of dullness, it was a fussy little lady of high Tory
family, which observed the local scene through a gold-handled
lorgnette. Its news was scant and its circulation small. But it
had once enjoyed a certain distinction because of the fine
writings on its editorial page of the late Joseph O'Connor.

Mr. O'Connor was a man of scholarly attainments and an
Addisonian prose style that had gained him some fame outside
of his native bailiwick; and it was his contributions and a policy
of handling news that was supposed to be dictated, and perhaps
was, by decency and good taste, and the Saturday society
column conducted by Miss Emily Munn, that made the *Post
Express* infinitely more attractive to the town's gentlefolk than
its noisier and newsier rivals.

The paper was published and edited by Francis B. Mitchell,
part of whose fortune had come from the William S. Kimball
Company, at that time the manufacturer of several popular
brands of cigarettes, later absorbed by the American Tobacco
Company.

Mr. Mitchell was a professional newspaper man and member of one of the city's first families to boot. He was a learned
and capable gentleman. But the *Post Express* was more a whim
than a business enterprise, and upon it he imposed such rigid
editorial restrictions that it had little chance—if, indeed, Mr.
Mitchell desired it to have—of wide circulation, and its annual
statement usually showed a loss.

Reporters had to familiarize themselves with an extensive
list of editorial taboos. One of these prohibited any direct or
hinted defamation of the cigarette, the use of which professional blue-noses were crying down as only a degree less vicious
than the habit of opium.

Miss Munn kept her Saturday society column chaste, aloof,
and unalloyed by the intrusion of any names whose owners

were not at least eligible for membership in the two ultra-
exclusive clubs, the downtown Genesee Valley, and the Rochester Country Club. She wrote simple, unadorned paragraphs
reporting that Mr. and Mrs. So-and-so were visiting at Bar
Harbor, Newport, or the Waldorf-Astoria; that this or that
member of the elite (although the word was never employed
by her) was entertaining at dinner, a dance, or a tea; together
with restrained descriptions of fashionable weddings, debutante
parties, and the grand holiday fetes at the Genesee Valley Club.

Miss Munn was a lady of culture and breeding. She herself
was a member of society's deepest inner circle. But her family
had suffered reverses that made it necessary for her to earn a
livelihood. She was in no sense a snob. But she closely subscribed to the recognized and accepted standards of what was
called society, and she treated the people she wrote about—
many of whom were her personal friends—with dignity and
respect.

When Mr. Mitchell sold the *Post Express* to William Ran-
dolph Hearst, in a gesture that in the minds of many made him
an apostate to his class, and Hearst added the words *Post
Express* to his recently launched *Rochester Evening Journal*,
for a brief time Miss Munn served as society editor for the
*Democrat and Chronicle*.

The paper at that time was being published by Jerome D.
Barnum, who had been brought from Syracuse to Rochester
for this purpose. Understanding nothing of Rochester's caste
system, Barnum insisted that Miss Munn broaden the scope
of her department to include in it the social activities of the
general public.

Miss Munn made no attempt to defend her own way of
doing things. She simply drew her weekly pay envelope and
quietly walked out of the office. She had agreed to go to the

*Democrat and Chronicle* as society editor, the functions of which office (at least as they applied to Rochester society) she rightly presumed she understood better than her new employers, and not as a reporter of the shenanigans and high-jinks of the ladies' auxiliary of the Hard-a-Lee Social and Athletic Club.

Miss Munn's exit from the newspaper scene and the end of the city's only "social register" society column were probably more fortunately timed than she realized. For the depression of the late 20's was only a few years away, and with that catastrophe Rochester's tight little social hierarchy began to come apart at the seams.

The wealth of many old families disappeared, together with the savings of small shopkeepers, ribbon clerks, greengrocers, streetcar conductors, and all sorts and classes of men and women who had believed that the tip of the spiraling market would reach at least to the moon.

Clubs that had been the exclusive domain of the city's most exclusive people found themselves in difficult straits. Their bars had been closed by prohibition. Their bulletin boards were studded with the names of highly respected members who had been posted for non-payment of dues. There was a threat that they might have to close their doors.

All but washed away by the waters of Lethe, the waiting lists of the two exclusive clubs for years had carried the names of persons who were considered definitely ineligible for membership. In desperation membership committees brought these lists out for review. Upon them were found the names of several forgotten applicants who had survived the depression in full solvency, and who now seemed much less objectionable than they had previously been thought. Happily, their long-held hopes at last realized, men who would once have been unable to gain entrance to the Genesee Valley or Country Club with a set of burglar's tools, were "tapped" for membership, and the first wedge in the once impenetrable walls of these organizations soon widened to a sizable aperture.

Under the corrosion of the depression the grandeur of East Avenue at first became shabby and then definitely decadent. Many of the great solid-walled houses were razed when owners were unable to meet tax bills. Others were converted into rooming houses. And a city ordinance was passed that permitted the building of apartment houses on this once holy thoroughfare.

Old families drove in old cars, shiny and well cared for, but close inspection often revealed that the tires had been worn to the white canvas. Debutantes who had "come out" in the booming twenties, in the deflated thirties found it prudent to obtain genteel employment in stores and offices. New wealth was springing up from the most surprising sources to find its way into the hands of the most astonishing people.

Some were blatant, and ostentatious, and crude in their use of it. Their taste and their deportment were sometimes outrageous, or such was the idea of society. They knew little of the swiftly disappearing art of gracious living. But these people were strong, and vital, and quick with life, and without them Rochester might have been in a very bad way indeed.

They were unimpressed by the "blue-blooded" families whose sons and daughters were much less capable than themselves, and in a way they took over the town. Today their dominance is quite secure. Their own issue, educated in the best schools, freely intermingle with the children of the third and fourth generations of Rochester's aristocracy, scarcely conscious of the privileges accorded them.

~~~~~~~~~~~~~~~~~~~~~~~~~~~~~~~~~~~~~~~~~~~~~~~~~~~~

# CHAPTER XXIII

# EASTMAN AND THE ARTS

---

FOR A few years after the opening of the Eastman School of Music, and during the time when the Eastman Theater, part of the property of the University of Rochester, was often favored with performances by the members of the music and ballet schools, Eastman was frequently in the company of visiting musicians and members of the Music and Ballet School's faculty.

Eastman thoroughly enjoyed his association with these people, the appeal being that of novelty rather than tempermental compatibility. He frequently entertained them at his own home and in turn occasionally accepted invitations to the mad goings-on of the "musical crowd" that had the authoritative unrestraint of true Bohemianism. Mrs. Mulligan had died by this time, and the members of a gray-haired dynasty of Rochester *grandes dames* were fiercely competing among themselves for the place in his social life and the position in his home left vacant by her passing; and these zealous and jealous ladies were not a little outraged at the easy familiarity that was growing between their skull-capped glamour boy and svelte ballerinas, sideburned cellists, operatic directors, and sopranos sometimes with more sex appeal than voice.

For once in his life Eastman had left the tight grooves of long habit and rigid practice, and while he never broke out in a rash of indiscretion, for a time he derived keen enjoyment from the company of these mimes and minstrels.

But Eastman was aging and his fling in Rochester's new Bohemia soon ended. The policies of the Eastman School of Music and the Eastman Theater were changing and becoming more conservative. Once called the most beautiful motion picture palace in America, the Eastman Theater was briefly given to the operation of a theatrical syndicate, lost prestige, lost patronage, and presently was laid back in the lap of the University of Rochester. It was closed as a picture theater and is now used only as a concert hall in which the Rochester Philharmonic and Civic orchestras, together with visiting orchestras and artists, perform at regular intervals during the winter season. Little was heard any longer of the ballet school. This long had been a University department disfavored by the late Dr. Rush Rhees, a Baptist clergyman and president of the University of Rochester. It was facetiously referred to as the BBB—Better Baptist Ballet. But the spectacle of barefooted young women in diaphanous draperies making gazelle leaps across the stage, or grouping in curious poses and interpretative attitudes while fond parents and devoted aunts and uncles applauded decorously, without quite knowing what the performance was all about, generally disappeared from the Eastman stage.

Although Eastman seemed to be tiring, his home was constantly the temporary abode of distinguished authors, painters, musicians, lecturers, industrialists, scientists, and even soldiers who visited Rochester for one purpose or another.

One day a contingent of Swedish royalty descended upon the town. It was headed by Prince Gustav Adolf and his younger brother, Prince Sigvard, sons of the Crown Prince, and included an assortment of counts, countesses, barons, and baronesses, who had come to this country specifically to attend the wedding of Count Folke Bernadotte to Miss Estelle Manville at Pleasantville, N.Y.

With the wedding over, the royal party decided on a grand tour of the United States, and Rochester was one of the first stops on its itinerary. A dinner for the royal guests, to which the current local debutantes were asked, was given in Eastman House, and next day plans were made to permit Prince Gustaf and several other members of the party to enjoy a fox hunt with the Genesee Valley hounds.

On a cold, drizzly December morning I was sent to the home in Geneseo of James Samuel Wadsworth, one of the great characters of the Genesee Valley, and a first cousin of former United States Senator James W. Wadsworth. Jim Sam that year served with Ernest L. Woodward, multimillionaire sportsman from LeRoy, as joint master of fox hounds.

A Harvard man, a member of the exclusive Porcellian Club, known in his younger days as a polo player, owner of race horses, and a backer of musical comedy, Jim Sam had long since run through a sizable Wadsworth patrimony, and at that time resided in a small country house on the Avon-Geneseo Road. Lacking money, he still had great charm, bonhomie, and wit; and once I heard his senatorial cousin remark, "Jim, we've got all the money, but you've had all the fun."

Suffering from a persistent attack of gout, throughout the early hunting season he had ridden as master of fox hounds in a pair of shabby carpet slippers. But this would hardly do for the hunt to which the royal Swedish family was invited; and when I reached his home Jim Sam was already splendidly accoutered in the "pinks" of his office, and with considerable blasphemy was attempting to pull a shiny hunting boot over his swollen and aching toe.

The ritual of fox hunting permits only the most unusual guests to ride in front with the master—or, in this case, masters —and this privilege had been conceded to Prince Gustaf. As

Jim Sam, with a violent jerk and a great oath, pulled his boot over his gouty toe, I said, "Jim, you'll have to be careful of your royal charges this morning. How are you going to distinguish them from other riders?"

"We're going to put numbers on the bastards like football players," he answered tersely. "Jesus, how that toe hurts."

The hunt ended with an elaborate midday breakfast at one of the fine upper Valley homes, after which the royal party was hurried back to Rochester, where Eastman was to entertain the women at a performance in the Eastman Theater. Though every dollar of the several millions spent in the erection of the building was Eastman's gift, he was extremely punctilious about turning in tickets when he and his guests passed through the doors of the theater. This day he had neglected to bring them with him.

Since it was my assignment to remain all day with the visiting Swedes, I arrived at the theater shortly after the party had been shown to seats in the mezzanine. The manager told me that Eastman had left his tickets at his home, that a messenger who had been dispatched for them had just arrived, and asked me if I would hand them to Eastman.

The performance had already begun as I crept up to the mezzanine. In the gloom of the half-darkened theater I located the party. Eastman sat in an aisle seat, next to a rather brilliant Countess. He wore the small black skull cap he had affected since he had become bald, his chin was deep sunk on his chest, and he was sound asleep and snoring gently. Diffidently I shook his arm. He did not awaken. I repeated this act more vigorously and he looked up sharply. "Oh," he said, "I'd like an apple."

I knew the significance of this remark. Each night before he retired his Negro butler placed a Jonathan apple on his bed-side stand. He had fallen asleep this time without his apple, and awakening suddenly—presumably under the illusion that he was home in his own bed—he desired it. I quickly explained my mission and handed him the tickets, which he later would turn over to the ticket taker in the foyer. He thrust them into a pocket of his waistcoat and favored me with a rare grin. "Clune, was I asleep—next to a Countess?" he whispered.

I admitted that he appeared to have dozed off, and I moved farther back in the house to await the end of the performance.

As Eastman moved from the second to the final act of his life he was far from the ruthless, uncompromising fighter of his early years. Sometimes he seemed almost wistfully eager for human companionship. His fabulous fortune was giving him serious concern. He had no heirs. His closest associates had profited greatly through the industry he had created and were in no need of legacies from his estate. He was determined that it should not descend to individuals to make "wastrels, race-track touts, and whoremongers of their sons or gilded parasites of their daughters," and in the end the bulk of his fortune went to the University of Rochester and the Medical School that is part of this institution.

I saw Eastman often in his declining years, and think particularly of one of my last meetings with him.

I had been assigned to interrogate him upon some matter that perhaps was important at the moment, but the nature of which I have long since forgotten. I was admitted to the house after the usual altercation with his sincere but over-vigilant house-keeper and found Eastman lying on a divan before a slow open fire in one of the smaller lower-floor rooms.

He greeted me with his usual courtesy and his usual lack of warmth. My business quickly ended, I was preparing to depart, when he rose for the first time to a sitting position.

"You interested in guns?" he asked suddenly.

I had no interest in guns and knew nothing about them. But my reply was as rote-like as that of one of his domestic or industrial subordinates. "Yes, Mr. Eastman," I said.

Slowly he got up from the divan, and slowly led me to an elevator in the rear of the house, in which we ascended to the third floor. Eastman had once pursued the Midian sport of big-game hunting in Alaska and Africa and derived some pride from his skill with a rifle. The small room into which he showed me was furnished with glass cases reaching from floor to ceiling that contained an astonishing assortment of sporting guns, some of them large enough for the destruction of an elephant.

He seemed quite feeble. His hands shook so violently with the first palsy of senility as he lifted the guns from the cases that some of their mechanism spilled to the floor. Yet for more than an hour he instructed me in the use and purposes of these fire-arms and described in elaborate detail his exploits in the field. I was conscious of having consumed too much of the great man's time and was again on the point of leaving when he surprisingly suggested, "Let's see some pictures."

I agreed, of course. We went next to a small studio, where we sat for more than an hour while a variety of motion pictures, of the sort amateurs make with a Ciné Kodak, were run off, one following the other with slight interruption. Several of these were taken in his own elaborate gardens and showed small children romping over the beautiful lawn.

I expressed some surprise at these. "It's curious, Mr. East-man," I said, "that a bachelor like yourself should be so inter-ested in the play of children."

"Humph," he grunted. "They're a lot more graceful than those damn dancers we have down at the Theater."

I had been with him nearly three hours. He looked tired and drawn. His speech and movements had become more halting than ever when we descended in the elevator to the main floor and I left him.

I was curious all the way back to the office as to why he had spent so much time with a newspaper reporter with whom, in the past, his relations had been brief and directly to the point; and decided that he was rather a lonesome little old man hungry for the informal companionship of even the most casual acquaintance who had no ulterior designs; who was neither soliciting for some philanthropic agency nor seeking the moral support of the Eastman name to some cause.

It was much earlier in this mellowing period of his life that Eastman met, and for a time was beguiled by the charms of Miss Mary Garden, the beautiful diva of the Metropolitan Opera Company.

He had been introduced by a music critic for a Rochester newspaper, who had been one of Eastman's advisers when he was planning to establish the Eastman School of Music as one of the departments of the University of Rochester. After this first meeting, Eastman persuaded Miss Garden to return to Rochester to sing the leading role of a famous opera with a supporting cast of music-school singers.

This performance was followed by a supper party in Eastman House with the famed singer, who was dressed to the nines in an evening gown that left her magnificent shoulders free even of supporting straps.

During the course of the meal Eastman's cold eyes, now warmed by the delightful vision next to him, swooped caressingly over the softly curved shoulders of the singer and stopped abruptly at the low-cut line of her *décolletage*.

"I can't understand, Miss Garden," he said perplexedly, "what it is that holds up that dress."

The diva turned upon him one of her most devastating smiles.

"Only your age, Mr. Eastman," she answered, tapping her host lightly on the hand. "Only your age."

Eastman failed to blush. But his comment was stammered and incomprehensive. He picked up a fish fork and was instantly and deeply engrossed in the business of separating the bones from the finny carcass on his plate.

# CHAPTER XXIV

# THE ROMANCE OF THE OX

THE CITY fathers have long prided themselves on the orderliness of Rochester and have made loud claims that it is the "best-governed city." But no qualifying phrase follows this slogan. It is never specifically boasted that Rochester is the "best-governed city" in the United States or even in the State of New York. Perhaps the city fathers mean that it is the "best-governed city" in Monroe County, an indisputable fact. Rochester is the only city in Monroe County.

But it isn't a seething caldron of purple vice. There is very little open prostitution and that little closely confined to a disreputable neighborhood in close proximity to the New York Central Railroad tracks. The city courts are conducted with fair competence. Its police department is neither better nor worse than the average city of its size. Each year, like every other city in the country, it rolls up an appalling toll of traffic fatalities that annually inspire the convocation of Safety Committees and briefly provoke much frou-frou and head wagging, while little that is constructive is done. For the only practical solution of these wholesale homicides, which make a national tragedy comparable to war, and to which the citizens of every American community appear to be case-hardened, is rigid and honest enforcement of traffic laws, which a city government depending for survival upon patronage and preferment would not dare employ.

But Rochester does not even make the gesture of a traffic

court, and traffic cases in which persons are horribly maimed or killed outright are heard between the pleas of inveterate drunks, common pickpockets, milk-bottle thieves, youthful vandals, and other lesser misdemeanants in magistrate's court.

The main and vastly the most profitable illegal industry in Rochester is gambling, which appears to have the complete approval of the city fathers and their subordinates in the police department, and which for years has made the town a paradise for followers of the Goddess of Chance.

Several of the operators of these innumerable horse rooms, dice parlors, and black-jack salons enjoy a quasi-respectability, and their business places, known to the trade as "stores," make no more pretense to disguise than a small shabby outer room, uniformly equipped with a cracked and dusty case of weedy-looking cigars, sometimes presided over by an amiable retired police officer. Behind this the business of the establishment is conducted and patrons stream in and out with no more hindrance than they would experience in entering a corner drugstore for a package of aspirin.

The operators of these resorts are selected men who have been given the tacit approval of someone in authority. And though over the telephone wires of one unmolested gambling establishment more than $100,000 in horse bets is negotiated daily, let the unsanctioned owner of a neighborhood cigar store run a penny ante poker game in his storeroom, and the police will descend upon him like vultures and hard-handedly hale him into court, the judge in wrathful indignation will mete out fines to the proprietor and the players, and much ado will be made in the press about a gambling raid.

I do not pretend to understand the philosophy of all of this. But I do know that allowing established local gamblers to operate in open defiance of the law has tended to prevent the intrusion of outside mobs and nationally known gambling syndicates. The professional gamblers in Rochester are of varied sorts, and some of the better known of these are gradually assuming the aspect of solid citizens. Several I know are devoted churchgoers. Others pride themselves on their abstinence from drink and tobacco. Still others, following the example of bankers, professional men, merchants, and industrialists, have acquired elaborate country places and crested station wagons; their children are instructed in the genteel pastimes of tennis, golf, and riding, and their wives are gradually insinuating themselves into the middle class of suburban society.

Though gambling rooms are much more numerous than ever before, with scarcely a downtown block without one, they are much less imposing in their physical aspects than formerly.

Shortly before the adoption of the city manager form of government, with its gloomy promise that its honest and non-partisan organization would eliminate such illegal practices as gambling (which, for a brief time, it more or less successfully did), there were three elaborate downtown places of such repute and appeal that players from all sections of the state constantly converged upon them. Nightly, and throughout all hours of the night, one might court Lady Luck at any one of the variety of games that included faro, crap dice, poker, roulette, chuck-a-luck, and even so exotic a pastime as *chemin de fer*. The stakes were high, the places were choked with patrons, and the proprietors were feverishly determined to reap one last golden harvest before the forces of purity and justice took over.

Directly inside the entrance of one of these places the proprietor had erected a steel cage, dotted with peep- and gunholes, in which a lookout with a tommygun presided during

the hours of play. The novelty of this added to the reputation
of the resort besides giving the patrons a sense of security. But
the cage and the armed guard were soon removed under police
orders.

"Hell," a police captain, who had given this order, explained
to me, "one of my men went in there the other night to sel! a
batch of tickets to the policemen's ball, and that monkey in the
cage menaced him with his gun. First thing you know, if we
didn't get that guy out of there, he'd be shooting a policeman
by mistake."

It was during this gambling boom that the Ox, as co-
proprietor of one of the large downtown places, was in his glory.
The Ox was a professional gambler of long standing. He was
then in his mid-forties and it was his boast that he had never
sullied his hands with legitimate toil since he was a kid in knee-
pants. I knew him well and delighted in his company, for
besides his gambling skill he had rare talents as a raconteur.
Some of his stories were supported by fact. Others were woven
widely out of fancy. But his telling of them was masterly, and
in their style and spirit they reminded me of those Bret Harte
wrote of Poker Flat.

Indeed, in some ways the Ox might have been the prototype
of Harte's gentleman gambler, John Oakhurst. He was tall,
lean, immaculately groomed, handsomely dressed, courtly of
manner, a lover of fine wines, expensive food, fast horses, and
beautiful women. Beautiful women were his avocation; and if
sometimes they were not quite beautiful the Ox conceded a
point and still loved them. He prided himself on his taste, his
delicate discrimination, his familiarity with what he called
"class."

One night as he was moving from table to table, overseeing

the play, consoling losers and congratulating winners, an employee touched his sleeve and advised him that a woman desired to see him.

Devoted though he was to the gentler sex, the Ox made a rigid rule to exclude the lighter pleasures from his working night, and he impatiently ordered his employee to send the lady on her way.

"But I've tried," the man said helplessly. "She won't go. She's stubborn. She says she'll wait all night to see you."

"Young? Old? What sort of a woman is she?"

"She's young and a kind of pretty woman. She's in the little downstairs office. I didn't want to get in a jam, shoving her into the street."

Furrows creased the smooth, pale brow of the Ox and he took decision. "I'll see her, Hogan. You shouldn't have let a woman into the office. We don't want women around this place."

He left the busy game room and followed Hogan downstairs. His visitor sat in the single extra chair in the tiny office. She was young and she was more than "kind of pretty." As the Ox's keen eyes took her in from head to toe he realized that she was uncommonly handsome. She was slim and dark with fine features and faultless skin. There was an expensive simplicity about her attire that his finer instincts instantly commended. He bowed slightly from the waist.

"Good evening, madam. You asked to see me. I am sorry— you have the advantage—"

She tossed her graceful hands in a little gesture of despair and her voice quavered when she spoke. "My name—I'm Mrs. Harrington. Mrs. Francis Harrington."

The Ox's eyes narrowed slightly and he remembered.

A few nights before he had taken a check signed by Francis

Harrington for $5,000 when Harrington, a newcomer to the resort, had lost that amount in four hours' play.

"You know my husband?"

"He was here the other night."

After a moment's pause the woman said impulsively, "This is a great confidence, but I implore your help, Mr.—. That $5,000 my husband lost was our entire fortune. It's put even our home in jeopardy. I am pleading with you never to mention this conversation to him. If he knew I had come to you our domestic life would be ruined. But please—please don't let him gamble here again."

The Ox's keen eyes had never left his visitor. He prided himself that he needed no one to point out "class" when it was visible to his eye, and "class" this charming lady had in abundance.

"You say that money was your entire fortune?" he asked quietly.

"Yes." There was a shine like tears in her eyes. "We can somehow overcome this loss. But I'm afraid he'll borrow and try to recoup. That would be the end."

In his mid-forties romance was still an important factor in the Ox's life. The springs of gallantry in him bubbled to the surface. In years he had met no woman with the appeal of Mrs. Harrington, the charm, the quiet elegance.

"Please pardon me a moment."

He left her and stepped out of the room. In a few minutes he returned. Taking her slim hand in his he pressed a bundle of bills against her palm.

"O-oh, no—no—"

His raised hands checked the impulsive movement she made toward him. "I'll bid you good night, Mrs. Harrington," he said, and bowed her out of the office.

At midnight three nights later the Ox stopped at a roulette table and stared at the profile of a young man whose chips had just been raked in by the croupier.

"Mr. Harrington," he said quietly.

The young man turned sharply. "Yes," he said. "What do you want?"

"May I see you a minute?"

"I can't beat your damn wheel," Harrington said sullenly. "I might as well talk to you."

The Ox faced his patron in a quiet corner. "Mr. Harrington, you lost a good deal of money the last time. Five thousand dollars—"

A flush spread over Harrington's features. "My check was good. What are you kicking about?"

"Yes, your check was good," the Ox agreed. "I still think you're playing over your head."

"Well, you've got a hell of a nerve," Harrington exclaimed angrily. "What business is it of yours how much I lose?"

The Ox's temper was becoming edgy. A confidence was a confidence but this man was proving insuperably difficult.

"I'm violating a confidence in telling you about this, but your wife—"

Harrington's angry expression turned to surprise.

"My wife! Good God, man, I've never been married."

The Ox had the gambler's knack for dissembling his true feeling, but to do so in this instance required considerable effort.

"It's all a mistake," he said calmly. "Excuse me. Go bet your head off."

Slowly he turned and left the room. But once out of sight of his patrons he plunged down the stairs, stormed into the small office, slammed and locked the door, and put his head in his hands.

"Well, I'll be God damned," he moaned. "And she was such a classy-looking broad."

During this same period an out-of-town gambler named Jack Cotter, whose practices in the past had often involved him with the police and who, I believe, had served more than one penitentiary sentence, had become a partner of a man we all knew— and still know, for he is doing business at the same old stand— as Uncle Luke. Uncle Luke was then and still is the high-shot gambler of the town. He is known from coast to coast as a "dead square guy" and the reputation is merited. Uncle Luke and Cotter made a very fast team, and it was their resort that accepted the highest bets and attracted the top-drawer trade.

Once a man of few scruples, Cotter had reformed before he came to Rochester. The main proof I have of this is that Uncle Luke accepted him as a partner. The combination lasted until the city manager government came in and gambling temporarily went out. Then Cotter left Rochester to die of natural causes in another city.

In Rochester he was once very close to death from a cause that is not natural—i.e., gunfire.

During his residence in the city he made his home in the fashionable Sagamore Hotel in the business end of East Avenue, which is separated on the north side from the large building of the Rochester Gas and Electric Corporation by a narrow alleyway, suitable only for pedestrian traffic.

One night after making a notable "score," as the gamblers call it, at crap dice, Cotter left the resort for his hotel with many thousands of dollars packed into a shabby handbag. It was very late, and since no cab was in sight he elected to walk the short distance from the gambling room to his hotel.

The streets were deserted, but as he passed the light company and was within a few steps of the entrance to the hotel three men leaped at him from the shadows of the building. Cotter clung to his moneybag and, somehow fending off his assailants, retreated into the alleyway. Outraged at the escape of their quarry, the trio whipped out guns and fired into the unlighted alleyway, the bullets missing the gambler by inches.

Cotter might have continued and escaped into a back street at the far end of the alleyway. Instead of doing so, he drew his own gun and returned the fire. No hits were scored either by the assaulting party or the gambler. But the mobsters apparently realized that the noise of gunplay would attract the police. Pocketing their pistols they leaped into a car that had been standing at the curb and sped out East Avenue before anyone attracted by the fracas was able to make a note of the license number.

Guests and employees of the hotel were aroused and police prowl cars were quickly on the scene. Desiring no notoriety, Cotter did not report the attempted robbery and was trying to hide away in the hotel when the police collared him. He was taken to the station house, questioned, and released, and next day a report of the incident was published in the papers. In this report Cotter's name was printed, but the address he gave was a number far out East Avenue that was not listed in the street directory.

Andrew J. Kavanaugh was Police Chief at the time. He had considerable ability as a police officer, and he was a reformer at heart. But he knew that the place operated by Uncle Luke and Cotter enjoyed the approval of the politicians and that it would be a policy of little wisdom to hold Cotter on charges.

I was on the police run, and on the afternoon following the attempted hold-up I stopped at the Chief's office to ask for more details about the affair.

"Where does Cotter live?"

"He gave his address as —— East Avenue."

"There's no house there, Chief," I insisted. "It's a fake number. Cotter's been registered at the Sagamore for weeks."

"Well, I suppose a man can be mistaken in a street number," Kavanaugh replied irritably. "After all, there's no charge against Cotter. He's merely the complaining witness."

"Why should a complaining witness try to disguise his residence?"

"I don't know anything about that. Why don't you ask Cotter?"

"I should think *you're* the one to ask Cotter. Why wasn't he arrested?"

The Chief looked as though he were surprised at the question.

"Arrested? Why should he be arrested? He was only defending himself against stick-up men."

"Wasn't he violating the Sullivan law by having that gun on his person?"

I knew very well Cotter possessed no license to carry the revolver he had used during the gun fight, and I am sure the Chief was also aware of this fact. All that I could get out of him was that he would look into the matter.

I returned to the office and wrote a story explaining that Cotter had faked his street address and that he had violated the Sullivan law by carrying a revolver without a permit. It never got into print. The political leaders had considerable influence with the publisher for whom I was working, and the matter of the attempted hold-up was quickly dropped with no arrests being made. Cotter continued his partnership with Uncle Luke for some time and continued also to live at the Sagamore.

If left to his own devices I feel sure that Kavanaugh would have arrested Cotter, and had he done so the lid would have been blown off the gambling racket in Rochester. This time he apparently compromised with the politicians. His later failure to continue to do so brought him into bad repute and he ultimately resigned under pressure, taking with him a lifetime pension. This now supplements an excellent salary he receives from the city of Wilmington, Del., which he serves as Commissioner of Public Safety.

# CHAPTER XXV

# CRIME WAVE

A S A boy in my early teens I made my first contact with the law through my father's friendship with a justice of the Supreme Court, a distinguished jurist and an outstanding citizen. He was a man of great dignity and impeccable manners. He had a deep, resonant voice, a noble brow, and a fine, manly, upright carriage. He carried a walking stick and wore a high silk hat on Sundays. He made a deep impression upon me, and I felt that he perfectly represented the majesty of the law and typified all members of the legal profession.

As a young reporter I found quickly that not all members of the legal profession were cast in the mold of my father's friend; and during the years that I covered the magistrate's court (we called it police court) for the *Herald*, my illusions were further shattered by my constant association with a group of rather shabby practitioners who haunted this minor tribunal like vultures.

I liked many of these police-court lawyers, and two or three of them were good friends of mine. They were pleasant and amusing fellows, popular at political clambakes, Elks' stag parties, and other similar entertainments. Their clients for the most part were petty thieves, drunks, wife-beaters, bartenders arrested under the Mullan-Gage Act, and husbands arrested for non-support. Their work was necessary and the rewards from it were not lucrative. But their professional practices were often questionable and their ethics sometimes negligible. I learned that a number of them were more skillful as out-of-court fixers than as trial lawyers before a judge and jury.

The crime wave, if this term has any meaning, that swept the country at the close of World War I, and which was aggravated by widespread disregard for the Eighteenth Amendment, had not escaped Rochester. The *Herald* opposed Prohibition. But Antisdale was justifiably aroused by the increasing number of crimes of violence in the city, and he was convinced that in some measure this was due to political fenagling in the district attorney's office.

I did not wholly share this belief. The district attorney was a capable lawyer who later was elevated to the Supreme Court bench, where he has made a splendid record. But Antisdale was unsparing in his criticism of the administration of his office. Moreover, the district attorney was a Republican, whereas Antisdale was a Democrat, and one who was ever alert to make political capital out of real or fancied derelictions on the part of Republican officeholders.

One day after a particularly vicious outbreak of hooliganism had made a sensational news story, Antisdale called me into his office and told me that henceforth my chief duty would be to keep a vigilant eye on the district attorney's office.

"This city is becoming a gangsters' paradise," he said angrily. "There's a mob of hooligans here who seem to operate with utter impunity. Time after time these same fellows are arrested without ever being punished. I'm suspicious of the way they continually escape conviction. I've compiled a list of the names of repeated offenders. The next time one of these thugs is arrested I want you to follow his case from the moment of his first arraignment. If I find there is any fixing in the district attorney's office I'll raise a cry that will be heard all the way to the capital in Albany."

I did not relish the assignment. The district attorney was a friend of mine. A few days after Antisdale had given me my instructions one of the offenders on his list was arrested and I went to the district attorney to obtain his past record. The D.A. knew what was up. He told me in an aggrieved tone that he thought I was a friend of his. I answered that I also considered him a friend of mine, but that I was only acting on the instructions of my editor. For some time there was a definite coolness between us. But I never turned up anything that proved very damaging to his office, which, I am sure, was a grievous disappointment to Uncle Louie.

It was some time before another of the thugs on Antisdale's list was re-arrested. But to make sure that I would not miss the arraignment of one of these fellows, I made a daily visit to police court. The place interested me immensely. The comedies and tragedies of city life, it seemed to me, were played each morning on this small stage, and I found the court a rich mine of human-interest stories. If no well-known culprit was brought to the bar, rather than leaving empty-handed, I usually found two or three cases on the docket that could be played up dramatically. Antisdale liked the style and character of these pieces. They brought what previously had been a rather obscure court into considerable prominence, and the *Herald*'s readers appeared to find them readable and entertaining. Antisdale in time more or less forgot the original purpose of my assignment, and kept me in court to write a column that became a popular feature of the *Herald*.

I learned a lot about criminal law during this time and something about the extralegal tricks of its practitioners. Besides the legal small fry who appeared daily in police court, sometimes merely in the hope of catching a client on the wing, the court was frequently honored by the presence of well-known criminal lawyers who appeared only in the most important cases. There were no William J. Fallons practicing at the Rochester bar. But the Great Mouthpiece had several eloquent, breast-beating imitators who defended wrongdoers able to pay large fees and divided this practice with the even more profitable one of acting for the plaintiff in negligence actions in which huge sums sometimes were collected for very suspicious damages. They cultivated newspaper men, for publicity was part of their stock in trade, and though they were often—and perhaps unjustly— discredited as ambulance chasers, they were usually the most colorful and sometimes the most brilliant trial lawyers in town.

It was Joey, a criminal lawyer of some prominence, whose secretary one day called me on the telephone and invited me to lunch with her employer. Joey was only a casual acquaintance of mine, and I was surprised at this unexpected display of hospitality. I met him at the appointed hour in a downtown restaurant. Over an excellent lunch we discussed a number of general topics, none of which pertained to the law. Shortly before our meal was finished Joey leaned across the table and favored me with his best courtroom smile.

"You remember Dr. So-and-so I defended on an abortion charge some time ago?"

"Oh, yes," I said. "You got him acquitted on some legal technicality."

"*Some* technicality, is right," Joey said, and smiled again. "He was guilty as hell. He left town for a time. He's back now and back in business. At a new address."

"Back in the same business?"

Joey shrugged. "Abortion's a nasty thing in theory. But you can't control the biological urge. And you can't populate the place with little bastards."

He reached into a pocket and brought forth a sealed envelope addressed to me. "Open this when you're back in your office," he said. He paid the check, I thanked him for lunch, and we parted.

In the office I slit the envelope and took from it a type-written note that read:

Dear Mr. Clune:
   I wonder if you would insert this notice, exactly as it is written, in the paper?
   "Mrs. So-and-so this week is holding an exhibition of several paintings she did on a recent trip to Mexico. Mrs. So-and-so is the wife of Dr. So-and-so, who some time ago was arrested, tried, and acquitted of a charge of performing a criminal operation. The couple have now returned to Rochester after a several month's absence, and are living at No. 178 —— Street, where Dr. So-and-so has resumed practice."
                                             Appreciatively,
                                                Dr. ——

Ten new $10 bills were attached to the note by a paper clip.

This was "hot" money, and my fingers burned as I riffled through the crisp bills. In fifteen minutes I was in Joey's office.

"Did you know what was in this envelope?" I asked, as I tossed it on his desk.

Joey grinned. "Sure. They're not counterfeit. What's the matter with 'em?"

"In the first place," I said, trying to sound indignantly right-eous, "I'm not in this sort of business. In the second place, if Antisdale knew I had even *touched* this money, I wouldn't last half a second in the *Herald* office. Just hand it back to your client with my compliments."

"I told him I didn't think you'd take it," Joey said placidly. "He thought it was worth a try, anyway."

"One thing I can't understand," I said. "If he wanted to pay me for putting a squib in the paper about his wife's art work, why in the world did he add that damaging information that he had been arrested as an abortionist? That's the screwiest thing I ever heard."

This time Joey didn't smile or grin. He threw back his head and roared with laughter. "And they say you newspaper birds are wise guys," he said, when he was able to control himself. "Cripes, you're innocent as a babe in arms. Doc's wife can't paint for peanuts. That art exhibition is just a blind. Doc was an abortionist. He's still an abortionist. But a lot of people who need his services think he's out of business. If you'd get that paragraph printed in the paper, people who need him will know that he's back in business and know where to find him. A hundred dollars is a cheap price for that kind of advertising. If you want to reconsider—"

I didn't want to reconsider. But I left Joey's office a wiser young man than when I entered.

On Antisdale's list of hooligans who had experienced repeated arrests without suffering legal punishment was an underworld character known as Handsome Slats. He was tall, lean, carefully dressed, with a quick tongue, a good right hand, and more nerve than Blondin, the man who crossed Niagara on a tightrope.

He had a swart, handsome, deadpan, sinister, movie-gangster's face. He was a member of a small mob of independent taxi drivers who operated from the New York Central Station and who were suspected of everything from rum-running to rape; from assault with brass knucks to robbery with a gun. They were a bad gang. The police were hard put to it to break them up, for they hid much that they did behind the pseudo-respectability of their taxi trade and all seemed to have strong political connections.

Slats had a talent for leadership that raised him quickly to command of the taxi fleet. But his soaring ambitions could not be confined to a taxicab. He knew there was big money to be had from large and daring operations, and he was determined to get his. He left his cab and enlisted in the services of an established syndicate that was moving bottled goods from Canada across the waters of Lake Ontario in large, swift power boats. Soon Slats was captain of the fleet. In time he was boss of the syndicate.

His business took him to many places in the East. To Boston and New York and Montreal where consignments of French wines and liqueurs and English whiskies were constantly arriving as "super cargo" in the secret holds of transatlantic freighters. He was a skillful trader with colossal nerve. He was no small-time operator but a fellow who commanded the respect of the infamous Purple Gang of Detroit, with whom he frequently dealt. He was riding high, wide, and handsome. He had money and women and enormous cars and suits that cost $225 apiece. He was frequently in court, but he always beat the rap.

I knew Slats and, with reservations, liked him. He was a unique personality. He was amusing. He made good copy. He was unmoral rather than immoral. I was sure there were few desperate acts he would hesitate to commit if he found himself in a sticky corner. He had been involved in numerous hijacking feuds in which violence had been done. One day he slugged a fellow with the butt of a pistol, and the victim of the assault proved unexpectedly persistent. He had barely escaped a fractured skull, and thug though he was himself, he was willing to have his own nefarious past exposed to obtain redress in court.

Slats appealed to his political pals. This time it was thumbs down.

"Your jams are becoming too much of a habit," he was told. "If you fix this one, you'll have to fix it without our help. Go hire—" and they named the then leading criminal lawyer in town.

Slats habitually carried a roll large enough to plug a dangerous hole in a dyke. He was so burdened when he presented himself to the lawyer. For the first time in his life he was really worried. The lawyer listened to his story and said calmly, "This will cost you $5,000."

"Christ," Slats exploded, "I ain't got that kind of money. I've got exactly two thousand."

Without a word the lawyer opened a desk drawer and took from it an automatic pistol. He laid it on the desk.

"Take that," he said, "and go get the other three thousand. Then we'll have *two* good cases."

Slats reached and got up the full amount of the fee.

The case presently went to trial. Slats' lawyer was brilliant and resourceful, but the evidence against the defendant seemed irrefutable. It was common talk around the courthouse that this time Slats was going for a ride.

The jury was out five hours. It returned in disagreement, one juror stubbornly holding out for acquittal. The judge made no disguise of his displeasure and ordered a new trial immediately. But a week before the second trial was scheduled, the complaining witness mysteriously disappeared. It was said that he had gone to Mexico for a "vacation," and perhaps he had. To my knowledge he never returned. Slats was soon back in circulation. His operations expanded and he became fat with bootleg gains. But violence was one thing he eschewed.

"It's only them mugs," he used to say scornfully, "that get mixed up in sluggings and shootings. Hell, I'm a *businessman*."

# CHAPTER XXVI

# THE SOUL OF A CRUSADER

WILLIAM L. CLAY has for years been one of the stormy petrels of the Rochester bar—perhaps the stormiest. He is no shrinking violet when it comes to publicity, and he makes no claim of modesty. Some people, familiar to all newspaper reporters, if asked for a photograph of themselves hedge and say, "Oh, I don't want my picture in the paper," and then reach eagerly into the desk drawer. "But this is the best one I have, if you must have one." But not Clay.

He has done many sensational things both in and out of the Rochester courts. Once he was suspended from practice for six months by a ruling, charging professional misconduct, of the Appellate Division of the Supreme Court. Clay promptly obtained a stay of execution, carried his case to the State Court of Appeals, and won a reversal of the suspension. Another time he used his fists to fight his way into the District Attorney's office, where a client of his was being questioned behind locked doors. Still later he unsuccessfully ran as Democratic candidate for the office of district attorney. He has made loud-voiced charges of irregularities in the district attorney's office. Recently he stirred a smelly kettle of political stew when he appeared as counsel for Joe Sargent, charged with maintaining a room in which bets were taken on racehorses.

Sargent was formerly a big-league ball player. He played shortstop for the Detroit Tigers. He was then, and still is, a kindly, happy, hail-fellow-well-met person, and as irresponsible as a monkey in a drawing room.

Sargent was a green rookie with Detroit when the club stopped off at Buffalo for an exhibition game with the International League team of that city. Joe's parents went over from Rochester to see their pride and joy in action.

Joe got to first base, his first time up, on the scratchiest sort of hit. He saw his parents in the stands. He waved his cap in the air and took a long lead off the bag, dancing and prancing like crazy. "Hi, Mom! Hi, Pop!" he shouted. The Buffalo pitcher, not interested in a family reunion, was playing a ball game. With a quick shift he plunked the ball soundly into the baseman's mitt, and Joe was out.

Ty Cobb was manager of Detroit at the time. Though this was an exhibition game, Mr. Cobb saw no reason why the filial devotion of one of his players should jeopardize the chances of victory. Mr. Cobb wanted to win ball games whether they were for money or marbles. He wanted to win this one. What he said to Sargent when Joe walked blithely back to the bench, resounded over all that section of Buffalo.

In this same game Cobb was having trouble with a Buffalo left-hander, who got him out twice in the early innings. He was starting to the plate for the third time when the irrepressible Sargent touched him on the arm. "Mr. Cobb," he suggested eagerly, "if you can't hit this fellow, I think I can. Want me to take your cut for you?" The wonder of it was that Joe got out of the ball park with his skull intact.

When Sargent was knocked off as a horse-room proprietor, Clay appeared in court with his client. Before he asked for adjournment and a jury trial, he brought from his pocket a typewritten list of perhaps half a hundred gambling establishments that were being operated with no molestation from the police. Clay demanded to be told why Sargent had been arrested and the keepers of these resorts were granted full immunity. It wasn't the magistrate's duty to answer this question. The red-faced and embarrassed police made no attempt to answer it. "It is very strange why my client should be subjected to this sort of persecution—for it obviously isn't honest prosecution—and I'll give this matter a real airing when the case comes to trial."

It was a threat that was never carried out. A night or two after Sargent had appeared in court, Joe was "consulted with" in the Elks Club by a committee of horse-room proprietors who reputedly talked to him like a Dutch uncle. Joe had a change of heart. Then he changed attorneys. He advised Mr. Clay that it was expedient for him to engage another attorney, one of the inner sanctum boys of the Republican Party, to represent him in court on the adjourned date. The new counsel entered a plea of guilty for his client, who was fined $50. Joe left court with his sins absolved. He promptly returned to his horse room, opened the door, and resumed business. He was still doing nicely at it when last I saw him.

Clay was philosophical about the matter. "Joe hasn't the soul of a crusader," he said. "He found it more profitable to conform. We had a bully case if he'd fought it before a jury. A real story, with big, black-letter headlines!"

Many of Clay's cases have made "big, black-letter headlines." One of these was the trial of Frank Nentarz, charged with first-degree murder for shooting Deputy Sheriff Frank C. Sova.

Nentarz was a native of Oswego, N.Y. He was a graduate of a state reform school, a road kid who had traveled clear across the continent in various pursuits that were never too clearly explained in court, and a skillful small-time burglar who for weeks had committed almost nightly depredations against householders in the fashionable suburb of Brighton. He was twenty-eight years old at the time of his arrest. In court Clay constantly referred to him as "this boy."

The case against Nentarz looked perfectly open and shut. In the opinion of the police and court-house habitués he had no more than one chance in a hundred to escape the chair. His record was all against him. He had made a statement to the district attorney on the morning of the fatal shooting that he was guilty and expected to pay dearly for his act. The shooting had taken place in the immediate presence of Cyril Pemberton, Brighton constable, who had leaped upon Nentarz and overpowered him while Sova, with a bullet in his abdomen, was writhing in mortal agony a few feet away. The defendant had no means to pay for his defense. Clay took the case, relishing a fight with the district attorney's office and the police, and the publicity that was certain to result.

Nentarz was a curious, psychopathic character, a weak sister, the product of a broken home, and definitely underprivileged. He had been in numerous scrapes both before and after his sentence to reform school. After several Brighton houses had been entered, the sheriff directed that the township be closely patroled. Each night, officers on foot and deputies in prowl cars moved frequently about the neighborhood in which the burglaries were being committed. The weather was warm, and Nentarz hid among the upper branches of a high tree in the neighborhood and watched the sheriff's men make their rounds. When they departed, he slid down from his leafy perch, used an ice pick on a screen door, entered a house, and usually emerged with the house owner's trousers.

"I never entered a house unless I was sure the man of the house was at home," Nentarz said. "I knew the man of the house would have the money and that he would keep it in his pants pocket. If I got hold of his pants, I almost always had a haul."

He maintained a room in the Hotel Seneca, in Rochester, but rarely went there. He slept during the daytime hours in the woods in Brighton and at night sat in trees in the residential section and watched the prowl cars go by until the moment seemed right to begin his night's work.

Deputy Sheriff Sova and Constable Pemberton were two of the officers detailed to police the Brighton streets. Early one morning their attention was attracted by a small moving light pricking at the dark around a house in one of the better streets of the suburb. They stopped their car and got out. The light was extinguished. Soon they saw a figure running through the back yard of the house. They gave chase, firing pistols in the air. After a short sprint, they captured a young man, later identified as Nentarz. Pemberton superficially searched the prisoner, and found nothing but the ice pick he used as a jimmy. He was handcuffed and led back to the police car. While Sova was holding him, Pemberton moved around to the other side of the car to get in behind the driver's wheel. He heard a shot, a cry from Sova, "Oh, my God! He's got me in the belt!" Pemberton flew around to the other side of the car, and knocked Nentarz down with blows on the head with the butt of his gun. It was assumed that Nentarz, in a brief struggle with the deputy, had managed to get a handcuffed hand into a pocket that held a revolver Pemberton had overlooked in his search. Sova died the following day.

Engaged as defense lawyer, Clay's first act was to make a motion in the Supreme Court for a change of venue on the grounds that a fair trial for his client was impossible in a section where so many people had formed a prejudicial attitude toward the alleged slayer of a popular and respected deputy. The day the motion was to be argued, Clay was—he later stated to the court—confined in bed with a heavy cold. The judge was impatient and sent a court officer to Clay's home in East Rochester. Clay called down to the officer who rang the bell that he was too ill to leave his room.

"The judge wants you in court and you'd better be there," the officer told him. "He won't stand any more monkey business."

Clay slammed down the window. Two minutes later he emerged from the front door. He was clad only in pajamas, bathrobe and slippers. In this costume he entered the court chamber and faced the robed figure on the bench.

The judge was patently annoyed at this affront to his dignity and that of the Supreme Court of the great State of New York.

"But Your Honor, you insisted that I come down here," Clay told him blandly, as he toyed with the tassel of his bathrobe cord. "What could I do? I explained to your officer that I was ill in bed."

Clay's appearance in this unorthodox costume again put him in the headlines. But the motion for change of venue was denied, and the trial was held in the Rochester Court House. It lasted two weeks. The only defense Clay could make for his client seemed as flimsy as gossamer. It was predicated on one of two suppositions. The first was that the bullet that had caused Sova's death had been accidentally discharged during the struggle between the defendant and the deputy. The second was that it had been fired by Pemberton, whose intention was to shoot Nentarz, but the constable's erring aim instead had sent the slug into the body of his fellow-officer. Neither of these explanations was considered adequate, and a quick verdict of "guilty as charged" was expected.

All in the courtroom except Clay were surprised when, after a long period of deliberation, the foreman reported, "Not guilty," and Nentarz was granted full freedom.

"I accepted for one juror a large, good-natured, Dublin-born Irishman, with a brogue as thick as loose cement," Clay explained later. "From the start I was sure he was okay. I said to myself, 'That man wouldn't hang anyone except an English landlord,' and I think I was right."

As the jurors filed out of the box to begin their deliberations, the Dublin-born Irisher dropped a great wink in Clay's direction. The lawyer then had his first qualm of apprehension. If the judge had seen the wink, there might have been trouble. But His Honor's head was turned the other way.

When the jury returned with its verdict, and the judge dismissed its members with the customary word of thanks for their services, Clay stepped forward and shook each man by the hand. When he faced the Irishman, the latter said: "Well, are ye satisfied?"

"I should say I am," the lawyer answered. "It was a just verdict."

The juror grinned. "We had some trouble coming to it," he said. "Oi had to knock a couple of thim stubborn ones down before they saw the light. But couldn't Oi see that the judge was all against that poor lad? Couldn't Oi see that the district attorney was all against him? Couldn't Oi see that all thim officers was against him? Someone had to be for him, so Oi thought it was up to me."

# CHAPTER XXVII

# THE GREAT PYTHON SENSATION

IN THE days when newspaper salaries were a deep cut below those of a plumber's helper or an apprentice bricklayer, reporters often found it necessary to take a job on the side to keep their families in shoes and groceries. This practice still persists. I know some city-room workers who devote themselves quite as faithfully to their "outside rackets," as they are commonly called, as they do to their regular newspaper jobs. But the pure economic necessity of this has been obviated by the all-along-the-line-increase in reportorial wages.

Years ago I had my share of this sort of work. At various times I acted as press agent for a hotel, a movie theater, a dog show, a National Guard company, and an amusement park. Once I wrote a series of advertisements for a savings bank in which I described precisely how a man on a modest salary might put away a little money each week, but lamentably failed to benefit from my own formula.

The job for the amusement park was the most fun and the one for the hotel the simplest and best-paying. The hotel's business had fallen off so badly that the directors decided a new managerial deal was necessary, and they brought in a man who had previously been associated with several rather gaudy Broadway hostelries. His advent instantly ended the conservative policy the hotel had followed in the past. He had few personal or professional inhibitions. He was about as modest as a dog in love. He said that he was the best blankety-blank hotel man in

America, and that to prove this he needed only a free hand and a publicity man to help him keep the name of the hotel in circulation. A publicity man was a new dodge in the hotel business in Rochester, but the directors let the manager have his way, and I was engaged for the job.

"This place is about as lively as a home for the aged," he told me disgustedly, the first day I reported to him. "I want our rooms filled, and I don't care how many doubles go to 'Mr. and Mrs. John Smith,' so long as they don't break the furniture, squirt White Rock siphons at the walls, and make bawdyhouse whoopee. I can't be bothered inquiring about marriage licenses. There's no life in the lobby. Lobby leeches don't spend a dime, but they give the place a busy look, and I want 'em in here. I like my lobby looking like a Union depot at train time. I'm going to have a jazz orchestra with fortissimo brasses in the café, and a blonde singer to bait—and date, for all I care—weary bagmen who come back after a hard day with the trade. The main dining room'll be for quiet talk and snookie-ookie stuff. We'll have soft music and low lights and waiters who won't snitch on a cheater. I know how to run a hotel for money, and that's the way I'm going to run this one."

The new manager was an inveterate joiner. His billfold bulged with a sheaf of cards attesting his affiliation with a wide variety of clubs, lodges, fire, police, merchants' and hotel associations, and soon he managed to have his name included on many prominent civic committees. He was a gusty, back-slapping, Welcome Brother Elk sort of fellow, who always wanted to be among those present. It was with some difficulty that I dissuaded him from attempting to gain membership in a newly organized Theosophical Society, the name of which he had come across in the daily press, on the grounds that he would find the symposiums of the members of little interest, and their fellowship somewhat less than his own lusty notion of what constituted social entertainment.

"But, Harvey"—he always addressed me as "Harvey," why I never knew, nor had the temerity to ask—"Harvey, it's such a swell-sounding order—Theosophical Society. It's got the stamp of class."

A month after he arrived he was three-cheering the town as though he were a fourth-generation native and proposing new names for downtown streets. He was a lavish entertainer; and quickly I realized why he granted such extreme license to couples of dubious marital status, since he frequently booked into the hotel young and unattended ladies with whom he seemed on exceedingly friendly terms and whose bills were often discounted by a managerial frank.

The hotel prospered under his management. The cuisine in the café and dining room appreciably improved, he induced many of the organizations to which he belonged to transfer their luncheon or dinner meetings from wherever they had previously been held to his hotel, he flushed up banquets and conventions like a good bird dog in partridge cover, and soon the place was in constant hubbub and bustle each day from shortly before noon until well after midnight.

Much of this activity made news of a sort, for even a meeting of the most obscure luncheon club merited a paragraph in the paper, if someone took the trouble to write it, and it was partly for this that I was being paid a handsome salary. Each day I clipped from the newspapers every item that mentioned the name of the hotel, and at the end of each month I presented an imposing bundle of these notices as evidence of my energy and enterprise. "Harvey," my employer would say, as he swiftly fingered through the packet of clippings, on each of which the name of the hotel was ringed with a red pencil, "keep up the good work. We want to let the public know we're doing business at the old stand."

But the manager's tenure was short-lived and his job and mine ended approximately at the same time. Although he had instructed his staff not to snoop on the guests, an aged house detective with a rigid code of morals one night apprehended a telephone call between a well-known musical comedy tenor and a pretty red-headed waitress in a restaurant across the street. The talk was in the dulcet tones of love. Sometime later Old Eagle-Eye saw a pretty, red-headed young woman enter one of the hotel's elevators. It was after one A.M., she was unescorted, and her manner was suspiciously furtive. When the sleuth learned from the elevator operator that the young woman had alighted at the floor upon which the tenor was luxuriating in an $18 suite, his suspicions were confirmed and he decided to cleanse the house of sin.

With malice prepense he waited until a bellhop had delivered to the tenor's suite two bottles of bootleg champagne, still delayed until the corks had a chance to pop, and then rapped authoritatively upon the door. It was opened merely wide enough to permit a hand wielding one of the bottles to reach through and crash down upon the meddling dome of the house dick, and then slammed tightly shut.

The detective crumpled to the floor, where he lay in a comatose state until descried by a passing room-service waiter. A holy din was raised. Unfortunately the manager, skillful in smoothing out contretemps of this nature, was out of town, and an alarmed assistant imprudently summoned the police The door to the suite was opened with a passkey, and the tenor and his red-headed charmer were removed to police headquarters in the Black Maria. The tenor was booked on a charge of assault, second degree; the lady benevolently released.

I was covering the police court at the time, and the tenor was the first person called to the bar the next morning. He was sobered, chastened, and disheveled after a night in jail and bore little resemblance to the handsome and romantic Prince Charming of his light-opera role. He readily admitted to his impulsive act and was humbly apologetic. But the rap upon his door had come at a most inopportune time, and he was sure the judge would understand. The judge didn't. He sternly ordered the defendant held for the grand jury.

The case never went to trial. Later that day the tenor visited the bedside of his victim and eased his aching head with a very substantial honorarium. The complaint was withdrawn and the tenor left town, but not in the gay and lilting manner in which he had arrived.

Since my newspaper had first claim on my services, I had printed all of this, when as publicity man for the hotel I should have attempted to suppress it. The directors thought my loyalties uequally divided, and I was out of the press agent's job. They also thought the manager's broad-minded policies had encouraged an incident that brought a good deal of unfavorable publicity to the hotel, and he soon resigned.

Years before I was installed as press agent at Sea Breeze Park, an amusement resort on the shore of Lake Ontario given over to the more blatant forms of entertainment, the job had been held by a sports editor for the *Rochester Herald* who had made a good thing out of it for several seasons, and through it incidentally acquired a wife. Subsequently he also acquired a family of formidable proportions—fifteen children, in all—the whole company of whom in later years was trucked to the resort on occasions of large fraternal picnics, where invariably they

won a hands-down victory in the competition for the largest
family on the grounds.

The story of the romance goes this way:

One summer one of the leading attractions at the Park was
*The Great Tenement-House Fire*. The tenement was a flimsy,
two-storied structure, sheeted I presume with asbestos, inside
of which a sudden and engulfing flame was kindled, which
roared high into the air, sent the lower-floor occupants scurrying and tumbling through doors and windows, and brought fire
apparatus clanging to the scene. The final act of this colorful
and dramatic spectacle was performed by a young woman,
trapped on the upper floor, who leaped shrieking from a
window to land in a safety net spread by buskined firemen
below.

*The Great Tenement-House Fire* had been a sensational
success for many weeks when the star of the piece was taken
suddenly ill, and the management was forced to make an
eleventh-hour substitution, who went on that night without
the opportunity of a rehearsal. At the proper moment, seconds
before it seemed that the entire structure would be consumed
by the savage flames, the figure of a young woman, whose
agonized screams chilled the spectators to the marrow,
appeared at a window. With a last desperate wail, she flung up
her arms tragically, and leaped through the red curtain of flame.
She had miscued. The safety net was held below a window on
the far side of the house, and the new star landed on the hard
ground in a crumpled heap, suffering a fractured pelvis, a
broken arm, and a couple of bashed-in ribs.

His compassion aroused by this tragedy, the press agent faithfully attended the lady during her days of hospitalization, fell
in love with her, gained her hand in marriage, and years later,
with his better than a dozen issue, and his leap-of-death partner,

returned many times to the scene of his romance, to win acclaim and more substantial rewards for his phenomenal parenthood.

I succeeded myself several times as press agent at Sea Breeze, but my achievements there were undistinguished, though I was still in office when the most remarkable story the resort has ever known splashed the name of the park on the front pages of the newspapers, and kept it there for some time. It was known as the Great Python Sensation, and appropriately burgeoned forth during the summer of 1929, the climactic months of the Era of Wonderful Nonsense.

Unlike many another sensation, the episode of the python required no buildup, no slowly accelerating momentum, but sprang in the Athenian manner full-panoplied to life. The data in the case were simple:

The proprietor of a combination freak show and menagerie doing business at the park one morning discovered, so the police were told, that his prize exhibit, a python variously estimated to measure from fourteen to twenty-five feet, had escaped from its cage.

The press, with Mr. Hearst's short-lived *Journal* setting a brash, swift pace for the older and more conservative papers to follow, grabbed at the story with the avidity later shown for atomic fission, and Page One headlines warned all western New York that the monster was at large.

Police posses combed the Sea Breeze countryside and even grappled through the near-shore waters of the lake, and official warnings cautioned all persons of the peril. Featured writers, turned herpetologists overnight, elaborately discussed the habitat, hereditary inclinations, and general mode of life of the python.

In no time Sea Breeze was given a wide berth by all of its potential patrons, and the wistful appeals I made through reading notices and display ads for the return of the faithful were as ineffectual as peas shot through a tin tube at the Fortress of Gilbraltar. No family group or Sunday-school class or fraternal order was going to congregate with a basket lunch in the picnic grove when any moment an enormous serpent might leap among the pleasure seekers from the grass.

Official statements were issued daily. The snake had been seen here, twelve miles from Sea Breeze, or there, a full thirty miles away; and both city folk and residents of the rural areas were becoming afraid to enter their darkened cellars, and retired at night only after apprehensive glances under their beds. Like a will-o'-the-wisp the python seemed to flit about the countryside, with quaking possemen winding their safaris on its serpentine trail.

The fears of the citizenry were mingled with indignation, and demands that the authorities end their futile scurrying about and stop the mad career of the python were constant. Political reverberations were freely predicted.

Into this atmosphere of unease, dissension, and jittery vigilance, the story of deliverance burst one day like the announcement "Mafeking Relieved" or "Armistice Signed." But this headline read, "Python Found and Shot."

Monroe County breathed easily after a strained fortnight.

Those who read past the joyful headlines learned that a python had been found under the wood floor of a fortune teller's tent at Sea Breeze, a few hundred yards from its place of escape, and dispatched, unostentatiously and without a yoicks or a tally-ho, by an unidentified man who had shot it three times with a revolver. The killing had been almost as undramatic as the shooting of a rat burrowing under a porch.

But the snake was very dead, and that—the police announced emphatically—ended the matter.

Persistently one over-zealous reporter pointed out that the dead snake measured only twelve feet, two to thirteen feet shorter than the length credited to the reptile that had caused all the stir and commotion, but his objections were generally disregarded. There was a vast will to believe that this was the authentic python; and to the few remaining skeptics the police offered the speculation that the snake, long in captivity, had lost its talent to forage for itself, and more fearful of its pursuers than they were of it, had coiled disconsolately under the tent floor, where lack of substance and sunlight had reduced its weight and shrunken its length. And so, as suddenly as it had begun, the Great Python Sensation ended.

It was half a dozen years before I again heard mention of the snake, and learned that the published climax of *l'affaire Python* was not its true denouement.

Though I served as official press agent for Sea Breeze Park, the owner of the freak show and menagerie had engaged a former newspaper man, one Bartley Brown, to plump for his individual attraction, and it was Bartley, a bibulous character, in a bout of indiscretion, who supplied me with the un-embroidered version of the incident.

Bartley said that the original python, according to his latest information, was starring in a tent show in the Middle West, and that he had played its part in the Sea Breeze story vicariously.

Like almost everyone else in those days, the snake's owner was armpit deep in numerous Big Board securities, one of which had taken a sudden dive. The snake man needed money to protect his margin and needed it badly. His python was his most valuable negotiable property. Frantically he telephoned a carnival show, then playing in a town in Northern Pennsylvania, offering the snake for sale. When the offer was accepted the python was spirited from its cage under the dark of night and the manager saved his stock but lost his stellar attraction.

Brown alone shared the manager's confidence, and with the snake gone he knew that the freak show would lose much of its appeal. Without consulting his employer he decided to advise the public that the snake had escaped its cage during the night, in the belief that this would stimulate fresh interest in the show, and thus the story of the Great Python Sensation was born.

It proved to be a boomerang. The public avoided Sea Breeze Park as though it were a lepers' colony. Under threat of libel the angry snake owner demanded that Brown purchase with his own funds another snake, place it under the fortune teller's tent, and there "discover" and shoot it.

"That was the reason why I bought such a *short* snake," Bartley explained. "You probably don't know," he added, "that snakes come by the foot. It's a fact. When you buy a python they charge you so much for the first ten feet, and the price increases in geometric ratio. If you get a big one, like we had at first, it costs a small fortune. Even the one I bought nearly broke me."

He was silent a moment, fingering an empty whisky glass. "I suppose, at that, the manager was right in wanting me to shoot the thing, rather than put it on display. The public had had enough of snakes. The Park management was threatening to throw us off the grounds for the way we'd ruined business." He paused again and his eyes lighted with pride. "But what a story, eh? Why, I got that guy I worked for $1,000,000 worth of publicity, with his name on the front page every day, and he never appreciated it. I was too good for his lousy little show—I'd oughta been with Ringling!"

~~~~~~~~~~~~~~~~~~~~~~~~~~~~~~~~~~~~~~~~~~~~~~~~~

# CHAPTER XXVIII

# BACK WHERE I STARTED FROM

---

UNTIL the epidemic of newspaper strikes that followed the second World War, one of which closed
the *Democrat and Chronicle* for three months, it
always seemed to me that a newspaper—and a morning newspaper in particular—was one of the most enduring things that
men could put together. As a young man I was deeply in-
culcated in the tradition of its constancy and dependability. It
came out as surely as the sun rose each morning, three hundred
and sixty-five days a year, three hundred and sixty-six on leap
year. Other human enterprises might be stopped by such fortui-
tous happenings as war, pestilence, and high water, but somehow the newspaper had to be printed and got out on the street.

It was my youthful conceit that the men who wrote the news
and who set the news in type and manned the whirring presses
were not ordinary men, but creatures apart whose first duty was
to their newspaper; and it was not until the death of Louis M.
Antisdale, of the *Herald*, that I was even slightly disabused of
this notion. Mr. Antisdale seemed to me a newspaper man in
the truest tradition. He was an extreme individualist, and his
paper reflected his character and personality to a high degree. It
was difficult to conceive of the *Herald* without Antisdale and
equally difficult to imagine anything of a serious nature happening to a man of his vigor and vitality. Yet one day we were told
that he was gravely ill, and shortly after this we were shocked by
the announcement of his death.

We were all in a great dilemma. A relative with no more than a counting-room understanding of the operation of a newspaper was given charge of the *Herald*. It was quickly evident that he was incapable of fulfilling the trust heritage had imposed upon him. The *Herald* was in need of money. In the past the problem this not unusual circumstance made had always successfully been solved by the loyalty several men of means felt that they owed to Antisdale. These loyalties were not owed to his successor. The *Herald*'s spark died out with the death of its editor-publisher. Its spirit and the *esprit de corps* of its workers disappeared. It was a weak and inept thing with no strong hand to guide it and no inspiring force to give it motivation. I saw the handwriting on the wall and resolved to abandon ship at the first opportunity.

Yet I lingered on for several months before succumbing to the beguilements of two young men with a few gobbets of gold and nagging literary aspirations who were determined to launch a local weekly. Their scheme seemed to me fantastic. It was not a weekly of general topic they desired to publish, but one limited to the goings-on and high-jinks of what they understood as "society."

They pleaded long and earnestly that I take on its editorship. With equal earnestness I attempted to persuade them that the appeal of such a specialized publication would be disastrously limited in a city the size of Rochester. When they presently showed me the color of their money I resigned from the *Herald* and started their gloss-paper little book, which was exclusively devoted to the chi-chi and tea-table chit-chit of the so-called smart set and issued under the not inspired title of *Five O'Clock*.

A brief flurry of interest was excited by the novelty of a new

Rochester publication on the newsstands. Baited into a purchase of *Five O'Clock* by the cover picture of a lovely debutante, ordinary newsstand patrons discarded the magazine in disgust when they found that it was written in close imitation of the lavender prose of Lucius Beebe, and our next issue went begging.

For a few weeks my employers persisted in their determination to keep their publication very high cake. Realizing in time that something more than a description of a Junior League soiree was needed to sell a weekly on the stands, they reluctantly permitted me to change its tone and character. Inside of six months we made the book into a rather interesting little publication, departmentalized similarly to the present *The New Yorker*, and I managed to dig up several talented contributors. One of these was Marjorie Kinnan Rawlings, later author of the Pulitzer prize-winning novel, *The Yearling*, and other fine works, who had moved to Rochester at the time of her marriage to Charles Rawlings, then a local reporter. I assigned Mrs. Rawlings to cover the burlesque shows, the gym training of professional pugilists, and other raffish, non-social activities, which she wrote in a highly amusing manner under the *nom de plume* of Lady Alicia Thwaite.

My employers were eager and enthusiastic young men who possessed some talents. What they woefully lacked was business acumen. Determined to boom the circulation of *Five O'Clock*, they inaugurated a subscription campaign and announced that the winner's prize would be a trip to Bermuda. When a popular traffic policeman on the East Avenue beat, who during the period of the campaign appeared to have forgotten that such a thing as a code of traffic laws existed, turned up with the winning number of subscriptions he was offered a *one-way* steamship ticket to Bermuda. Having no desire permanently to settle on that halcyon isle, he demanded that the sponsors of the campaign provide him with a round-trip passage.

The issue was warmly contested. When the policeman threatened court action, a cash settlement that seemed more satisfactory to him than the promised boat trip was made. But by now the weekly's expenses had mounted alarmingly, and one payday, after eleven months of my editorship, I was handed a check that bounced from the teller's cage like a hard-hit squash ball coming off a wall. The check ultimately was made good. But by then I had resigned.

Out of a job, I promptly returned to my old bailiwick, the *Democrat and Chronicle*. I had not worked there in seven years and many changes had taken place during my absence. Colonel Pond, the old Republican fire-eater, Civil War veteran and partner, with W. Henry Matthews, in the paper's management, had died in bed several years before at the ripe age of eighty-nine. Matthews retired a few months after Pond's death. He too was an ancient, with eighty-three years behind him, more than half of which had been devoted to the newspaper. But his grip had weakened during his last few years in office and, like the old gray mare of the song, the *Democrat and Chronicle* wasn't what "she used to be."

Frank E. Gannett, editor and publisher of the *Rochester Times-Union*, had become the city's leading publisher. The competition furnished him by Hearst's *Journal*, spirited in the matter of news coverage, was negligible in the matter of advertising. The *Democrat and Chronicle* was the morning rival of the two afternoon papers.

For many years the *Democrat and Chronicle* had held undisputed leadership in Rochester and the adjacent rural areas.

Now this supremacy was being wrested from it by the *Times-Union*, and one of the two spinsters who controlled the largest holdings in the first-named paper is supposed to have appealed to George Eastman for advice as to how her property might be saved.

It was Eastman's interest to preserve the *Democrat and Chronicle* as a prosperous and influential Republican organ. In those days Gannett was a comparative newcomer to Rochester and there was no certainty that he would adhere rigidly to the Grand Old Party line. Hearst's *Journal* frequently baited the Big Interests and clamored constantly for a lower tariff, which must have made Eastman see red. Eastman is supposed to have recommended that Herbert J. Winn, one of the city's leading industrialists, be installed as president of the Rochester Printing Company, which published the *Democrat and Chronicle*. I cannot vouch for the truth of this. But the fact is that even before Matthews' retirement, Winn was elected an officer of the company. When Matthews left he became president and treasurer and assumed full control of the newspaper.

President of the hugely successful Taylor Instrument Companies, a bachelor, and a kindly and earnest man, Winn was nothing if not conscientious and whole-souled in his devotion to a business that was as unfamiliar to him as Hegelianism. His first move was to select an assistant, who would give full time to the management of the paper. His choice was a man who had been reasonably successful in the manufacture of women's shoes but who was as unfamiliar with the newspaper business as himself.

Next, with his assistant in tow, he made a survey of the newspaper property. His own plant was as modern as that of any industrial establishment in the city, bright, cheerful, and finely arranged for the convenience and comfort of his employees.

When he ascended to the long, narrow, rat-infested city room
of the *Democrat and Chronicle,* his outraged nostrils sniffed
the fetid air and he announced that it was little wonder that the
paper was slipping when editors and reporters were required to
work in such cramped and squalid quarters. Long habituated
to these conditions, the editors and reporters were as incapable
of envisioning themselves working in a large, bright, sanitary
office as an East Side tenement child of fancying himself re-
established in the country seat of a Westchester millionaire.

Mr. Winn was not a man to delay action when the need for
action was clear. In no time a host of workmen descended upon
the *Democrat and Chronicle* building. They remodeled the
façade of the ancient structure and graved upon it a noble line
from Byron, *Without or with offense to friends or foes I sketch
the world exactly as it goes.* The workmen rose to the city room
and knocked it apart like a bowling ball splitting a set of ten
pins. The space occupied by the old city room was considered
inadequate, and the department was moved forward in the
building, greatly expanded, and modernly furnished and
lighted. It was made beautifully antiseptic with carefully
polished floors and spotless white walls, upon one of which
Winn caused to be displayed in large gold letters the creed of
that Sir Galahad of newspaperdom and politics, Warren
Gamaliel Harding. The thing was done with the expeditious-
ness of a man who got action when he demanded it. In a surprisingly short time the new city room was ready for occupancy.
Winn brushed off his hands, smiled benignly, and said that
now his people were prepared to produce a newspaper that
*would* be a newspaper.

But in the confusion of all this physical reorganization he
had permitted the cogwheel of the city room to roll clean away
from it. Morris Adams, for many years the paper's city editor,

and in my humble judgment the best the city has ever known, had been lured to the *Journal* by a promised increase in wage that Winn apparently made no attempt to match.

I suspect that Winn found Adams a curious subordinate. A singularly courteous man, he was given to no light talk, never fawned upon or bowed and scraped before his superiors, and when spoken to by Winn he answered directly and briefly and went on with his work. He did not say "yes, sir" with the deference Winn expected from his employees. In fact it is quite possible that he may not always have said "yes," but sometimes "no." If this were true, Winn must have thought it egregiously outside of precedent. In any event, Adams was allowed to go.

With the big, bright, beautiful city room ready for occupancy, the newspaper that *would* be a newspaper didn't quite come off. I have been told, and I half believe, that Winn did make certain beneficial changes in the newspaper, and he may have saved it from utter collapse. Whatever these were and however the paper was saved, I am sure the credit could not be attributed to his knowledge of a newspaper's chief function, the dispensation of news. He tried hard. He was painfully honest and persistent in his determination to do the right thing. But his first training had been in the manufacture of thermometers and other instruments requiring precise technical workmanship, and he had little sense of news values and viewed with an unsympathetic eye the comedy of manners that each day was being exhibited on the broad stage of the city's life.

The paper was chaste but dull. It was definitely prejudiced against crime news, personal scandal, and unsavory litigations. It became a house organ for big business, and its local pages were crowded with statistical reports from the executive offices of large local industries and banks, which were printed in full with scarcely the change of a comma. A handout from the publicity department of the Eastman Kodak Company was "must" copy, and the headlines under which it was displayed outmatched in size and black lettering anything the copy desk dared create for the most luscious love-nest murder. Winn had a pet reporter who was above and beyond the jurisdiction of the city desk and who was really no more than a public relations officer for the large interests whose reports he turned in for spot news and which were accepted as such. The reporter in time became so intimate with many high-bracket executives that he followed them into the stock market and collapsed with them— on the day of the market crash—to the tune of many thousands of dollars.

It was Winn to whom I applied for a job on my old paper and it was he who gave it to me.

The Winn regime continued for several years. But the paper made little progress. The *Times-Union* and the *Journal* outmatched it every day in news, and the former led it in daily circulation. Winn presently realized that the task of managing two businesses, one of which was still considerably of an enigma to him, was beyond his capacities. Still maintaining his office of president and treasurer of the publishing company, he engaged Jerome D. Barnum, publisher of the *Syracuse Post-Standard*, to take over the active management of the *Democrat and Chronicle*.

Barnum did not abandon his Syracuse paper for the new post in Rochester, but commuted between the two cities, a distance of ninety miles. He swept into our midst like a high, piercing wind of almost cyclonic velocity and immediately began to blow us apart. We were archaic, slow, dull, dead on our feet. He'd show us how he did things in Syracuse, a city—incidentally—more than a third smaller than Rochester. The first thing he did was call a "pep" meeting. None of us had ever attended a "pep" meeting before, and the experience was not lacking in novelty.

"My God," remarked one cynical old timer, when he heard of this innovation. "A pep meeting! I didn't suppose there were such things outside of Sinclair Lewis' novels." And the next pay day he was gone.

Barnum did not walk through the city room, but skipped on the tips of his toes. He wore beautiful clothes, Kollege Kut, for he was a Cornell grad of the deepest dye. His neckties were brilliantly striped and he had the exuberance and zest of a college sophomore suddenly and unexpectedly elevated to the post of cheer leader. Every minute we expected him to demand a long "rah" for the team. Sometimes we wondered if his purpose was to get out a newspaper or organize a daisy chain.

Knowing little about Rochester, and less about the tastes of the city's newspaper-reading audience, he attempted to refashion the *Democrat and Chronicle* in the pattern of the much smaller *Syracuse Post-Standard*. Features that had become a habit with local readers were summarily discarded. He detailed me to engage, not a professional newspaper worker, but a young matron of solid social status to assist on the society desk. I managed this to his satisfaction. The young woman worked mornings and devoted her afternoons to her normal social activities. One day she invited her employer to a cocktail party at her home. The following week she found a substantial increase in her pay envelope.

"I can't understand it," she told me perplexedly. "Is this a thank-you gesture for a few martinis and a plate of canapes? I can't believe I merit a raise in the few weeks I have been working."

During the gay festivities of Horse Show Week, Admiral Richard E. Byrd favored Rochester with a visit. A friend of the explorer's, Barnum made elaborate arrangements for his reception and public display, and for days preceding the Admiral's arrival the paper was filled with reports of his exploits. Assigned by Barnum to "cover" the Admiral, I was instructed to remain with him from the time he alighted from the train in the morning until he repaired to his hotel late in the afternoon to prepare for a dinner dance that was to conclude his visit.

The chief photographer for the *Democrat and Chronicle* at the time was the late Al (Stony) Stone, oldest in point of service and the most expert news cameraman in town. He was not told to accompany me on the Byrd assignment. Instead, Barnum sent for a photographer from his Syracuse paper, who presumably knew exactly what was expected of him, for few pictures were taken of "Dickie"—as the publisher persistently addressed his friend—in which Barnum was not posed in juxtaposition with the illustrious visitor. Barnum later explained that Stony was not up to such an important assignment.

Despite Barnum's enthusiastic efforts, the paper seemed to make no more progress than it had under the active administration of Winn, and real fears for its future were expressed by many of its old-time employees. Then one day announcement was made that it had been purchased by Frank E. Gannett. Gannett's newspaper experience had been confined to the afternoon field, and I do not believe he particularly wanted a morning paper. But the *Democrat and Chronicle* appeared to be going swiftly down hill and soon might go a-begging. It would have been wrong to let it lapse, and Gannett's purchase of it was heartily approved by the public. The city had not taken kindly to the *Journal*, owned and controlled by the Hearst syndicate. It was felt that under Gannett's ownership the *Democrat and Chronicle* would continue as an autonomous institution.

Gannett made no immediate sweeping changes in the paper's

policy. He seemed to be feeling his way and studying the public's reaction toward his new property. He did restore two or three of the features Barnum had discarded. He insisted on more thorough coverage of news. He added new services. But it was not until he installed as managing editor an ex-Hearst man, Lafayette R. Blanchard, now editorial director of all Gannett newspapers, that the quality of the paper appreciably improved.

Blanchard found it necessary to wield a heavy hand in effecting a much-needed reformation. The habits of subeditors and reporters had become careless and sloppy. These he corrected with some pain. He put speed and spirit into the paper and kept everyone on top of the news. He was complained about as a martinet, and in the early days of his regime workers in the city room suffered a bad case of jitters. But what he did was generally for the good of the paper and it was his efforts that were largely responsible for restoring it to its strong place in the community's life. Those of us who worked under him at least had the satisfaction of knowing that we were directed by a man who thoroughly understood his business.

# CHAPTER XXIX

# THE CONSERVATIVE CITY

ERVING a conservative city, Rochester's successful newspapers have been conservative newspapers. The *Journal*, the least conservative, had the shortest life; the *Herald*, which many times failed to conform, failed when its nonconformist editor and publisher died. The *Democrat and Chronicle* and the *Times-Union*, both highly conservative, have survived and profited. They have never renounced the proprieties to attempt the bizarre, the eccentric, or the sensational.

There are limits to conservatism, however, and when these are exceeded propriety sometimes becomes ludicrous, as the incident of what came to be known in our city room as the Fig Leaf Crisis indicates. The episode happened a number of years ago and concerned a great work of art, Raphael's "Alba Madonna," for which the late Andrew J. Mellon paid a record price of $1,080,000, thereby causing eyes to pop not only in art circles but in Wall Street and other less aesthetic precincts. A million dollars wasn't cigarette money in those days, as indeed it isn't today, and Mr. Mellon's Maecenean purchase was good for Page One headlines almost everywhere in America.

In the *Democrat and Chronicle* office, where a newly installed managing editor was engaged in the delicate task of attempting to improve the paper's content without violating its decorum, it created something approximating a seismic disturbance.

Like the paper's Sunday comic page, the rotogravure section

was printed some days in advance of publication, and once copy was closed and the deadline passed, the rotogravure editor waited in trepidation and hoped against any untoward circumstance that might make a nightmare out of his week's work.

The advanced printing of newspaper sections is often fraught with embarrassing and tragic possibilities. In our office we had heard only recently of the agony suffered by a Syracuse neighbor as the result of this perilous practice. After the paper had printed 75,000 copies of a special Sunday section describing the glitter and beauty of the city's crowning social event, it was constrained to announce on a local page that because of a blizzard of record proportions, the cotillion so brilliantly reported in another part of the paper had had to be canceled.

The *Democrat and Chronicle*, like most other American dailies, had given wide space to a report of Mellon's purchase of the "Alba Madonna," and several days later the Sunday gravure section went to press with a reproduction of the famous masterpiece smack-dab in the center of its front page.

Arriving late Saturday afternoon to begin the routine of getting out the Sunday paper, the new managing editor found upon his desk copies of the gravure and comic sections. Some 115,000 more copies, printed on presses in another city, had just been unloaded for distribution the next morning.

The editor's eyes ran appraisingly over the first page of the brown gravure sheets, and then stopped. He blinked and looked again. An expression as pained as though he had suddenly discovered that a tooth had fallen out of his mouth spread over his face. Then he picked up the page and headed for the art department, where he agitatedly spread it before the gravure editor and pointed in horror at the "Alba Madonna."

The gravure editor stared uncomprehendingly. No, the picture wasn't upside down, a possibility which editors cannot wholly dismiss. He hastily read the caption; it seemed unexceptionable. Still the accusing finger pointed. The gravure editor then realized that it was aimed specifically at the figure of the Christ child. He gaped and turned incredulously to the new executive. Could it be true? But true it indubitably was.

The managing editor's extreme agitation had been caused by the failure of the gravure editor—and, incidentally, Raphael—to equip the Infant Saviour with a fig leaf.

Some 115,000 homes faced moral contamination because of this revelation of male anatomy. The *Democrat and Chronicle's* cherished reputation as a palladium of respectability hung in the balance. Reminders that hundreds of other newspapers had printed the reproduction and that millions of persons had seen the "Alba Madonna" without conspicuous detriment to public morals were like pop guns against a Sherman tank. Something had to be done.

What could be done was limited by the ineluctable facts: one hundred and fifteen thousand copies of the gravure section were waiting to be distributed next morning. A replate and rerun were impossible.

The managing editor proved equal to the formidable implications of the crisis.

In a twinkling he had the circulation department on the telephone. It was Saturday, the day the *Democrat and Chronicle's* carrier boys were calling at the office to make their financial returns. In less than an hour several squads of these boys, armed with brown grease pencils, were racing through the 115,000 gravure sections, retouching Raphael's so that any evidence of the sex of the Infant held in the Madonna's arms was expunged.

By late afternoon the situation was well in hand. By nightfall it was saved. One circulation department worker, delightedly sniggering over the crisis in a corner saloon, reported that several thousand copies had escaped the mass bowdlerization, but this was never confirmed. As is usual in cases when staff members sweat out some emergency, the impact of their efforts upon the readers of the newspaper was negative. It seemed ungracious that no one wrote in to thank us for saving so many thousands from moral leprosy.

There were likewise no overt reverberations in the city room. None of us was witless enough to bring up the matter before the new boss. The sudden accession of a morality which would make Cotton Mather seem like a libertine was put down to some opaque Freudian vagary beyond our common frame of reference. The golden mean of keeping our newspaper clean but newsy, so eagerly striven for by the managing editor, had been heroically achieved.

A man living as long as I have in the same city, and that city populated by less than 400,000 inhabitants, might become so accustomed to its face and physical aspects that he would fail to look farther and learn something about the character of the community. I hope I have not fallen into this indifferent attitude, and I do not believe that I have. Curiosity is one of the prime requisites for a reporter, and without this he would poorly serve his profession and his paper.

Rochester is not a particularly exciting city. But neither is it humdrum nor dull. It rides on an even keel, without deep lists one way or another. Its citizenry is singularly contented and happy. In proportion to its population it has as many interesting people as the average American city, and many of them are engaged in fine and interesting works. I know the city and its people. I like them both immensely. Rochester is my home, and I have no desire to leave it. I am aware of many of its faults, but like the faults of an old and dear friend, I find them easy to condone.

One noon as I was lunching alone in the diner of a Rochester-bound train a man I know took the opposite chair, fixed me with an intense gaze, and without a preliminary word flung what sounded like an indictment into my teeth.

"Clune," said he, "I can't understand you. You're the only person I know who doesn't seem envious of anyone."

Surprised at the forthrightness of his remark my reply must have seemed very naive. "But whom should I envy?" I asked. "And why?"

"Why—why?" he cried, his voice querulous and impatient, "My God!" Still holding me with his keen gaze, as though trying to decide whether my questions were sincere, he went on. "Look at the people you're always writing about who have done big things in Rochester or have left town to do them. You know most of them. They're your contemporaries. They started with you from scratch and ran clean away from you. They've got big jobs, and fortunes, and some of them national fame. You seem content just to amble up and down Main Street, writing your little pieces for the paper. Why shouldn't you be envious of them?"

I was a little discomfited by the intense manner of my interrogator and the severity of his inquiry. I tried hard to think of someone of whom I was envious and at the moment was unable to do so. Half shamefully I admitted this to the man across the table. He made me feel that I was lacking in some quality most normal persons possessed, and I wondered if this deficiency was caused by lack of pride.

It was simple for me to list in my mind numerous people whose talents I greatly admired. To envy the possessors of these talents was another matter. It seemed to me that if I were to envy anyone I must be willing completely to change places with him. This would mean full acceptance of his undesirable along with his desirable qualities. If I acquired his assets, I must also assume his liabilities, and should he suffer a serious liver complaint, a drunken daughter, or a nagging wife, these too would be my burden. I must subscribe to the tastes of the man I envied, which might be entirely contrary to my own; cultivate his friends, whom I might heartily dislike; and hold to his political and religious persuasions, distasteful though they might be to me. This I decided would make a very doubtful bargain—or no bargain at all. In each instance I decided that I would be unwilling to go through with it. My luncheon companion was right. I envied no man.

To tell this may sound smug, but I do not believe I am guilty of smugness. Certainly I am far from satisfied with all aspects of my life, and given the opportunity to relive it I assuredly would straighten out many of the tortuous courses it has followed. On the other hand, I have had experiences that I would not exchange for those of any man.

It is a long way back to the days when I started as a "sub" reporter and was thrilled by the sight of the first paragraph I had written impressed upon a page of newsprint. As my eyes conned those simple sentences I felt that they marked the beginning of a career that would culminate in a golden burst of literary glory. I knew that many of the contemporary literary greats of America had mastered the fundamentals of their trade in the slatternly city rooms of newspaper shops, and my program for success would follow this common design.

Handicapped by sketchy academic training I learned slowly. I had become a competent journeyman reporter at the time the first World War interrupted my newspaper career. At the close of the war I was confident that with the new experience I had gained from it and with increased maturity I was ready for the success I had so long anticipated.

But the short stories I wrote were undistinguished and the novels I published made no great stir and were soon lost in the dark pit of obscurity into which most novels quickly fall. Yet all this time I was improving in the newspaper craft. The work fascinated me, and through it I gained a local distinction and occasional notice beyond the city in which I worked.

It made a good life. It brought me into contact with all sorts of people whom in some more ordinary or prosaic occupation I would never have met. It was always interesting and often exciting. I was disappointed at my failure to become a notable writer, but pleased and gratified at the newspaper success I enjoyed and the local prestige it had given me.

Limited though the area of my observations has been, I have seen a good deal of life. I have rarely felt confined in my home city and have never been bored with it. I know a great number of its people and its physical aspects are familiar to me. This has not staled my interest or dulled my enthusiasm. In a city of more than three hundred thousand people, a continuous comedy of manners is being enacted upon its stage, and a newspaper reporter who believes he may exhaust in a single lifetime the materials it offers for his typewriter is unworthy of his wage.

Walking the familiar streets of my home city, I never turn a corner without anticipating an unusual happening, or meeting some person who may tell me an unusual story, and what I anticipate not infrequently occurs. I am insatiably curious about my fellow-men and the motives that inspire their hates, their loves, their charities, their evil actions, their ambitions. Homo sapiens to me is the most interesting phenomenon on earth and infinitely more complicated than the atomic energy he has recently developed and soon stupidly may employ for his own destruction.

I have lived and worked as a newspaper reporter through what I am sure is one of the most interesting, exciting, and mutable periods of history. It is the time of all times I should prefer to live. It has been the best time for a newspaper reporter.

Hemingway, Maugham, Marquand, Sinclair Lewis (in the days of *Babbitt* and *Arrowsmith*), have been my latter-day heroes, and for the talent, and fame, and fortune of any one of them I would give something handsome. But Main Street, not the area of the giants, has been my ground. I still walk it eagerly, confident that in the next block it will reward me with grist for my mill. It has been my beat for many years and helped me to a full and satisfying life. I like it and there hope to remain.